Vision and Wisdom of Sanatan Dharma

"Truth reveals its true nature, no matter from which side one looks at it."
Shantilal Goradia

Vision and Wisdom of Sanatan Dharma

The Union of Quantum Physics, Cosmic Spirituality and Universal Morality

Sudipta Kumar De

KALPAZ

ISBN: 978-93-5324-956-4

First Published, 2022

Published by

Kalpaz Publications
C-30, Satyawati Nagar,
Delhi – 110052
Ph.: 011-47034999, 9811692060
www.kalpazpublications.com
E-mail: kalpaz@hotmail.com

Printed at: Gyan Press, Delhi.

Contents

Introduction

"Sanatan Dharma is like a river which has shallows that a child may play in and depths which the strongest diver cannot fathom."

Annie Besant (1847-1933)

Sanatan Dharma is the actual name of what is now popularly called Hinduism or Hindu Dharma. The terms Hindu and Hinduism are more recent developments while the more accurate term is Sanatan Dharma (original Sanskrit words – Sanatan means no beginning and no end, and Dharma means path of righteousness). Thus, the term Sanatan Dharma can be roughly translated to mean 'the natural, ancient and eternal way of Truth'.

All actions done adhering to Dharma are Dharmic (righteous actions). The person who follows the direction of Dharma is also called Dharmic (righteous person). Dharmic also means sacredness e.g., Dharmic scriptures. The ultimate goal of a Dharmic is freedom from 'Samsara' (the causative world, transmigration world), i.e., Moksha – the end of the reincarnation cycle achieved by self-realisation and elimination of material desires and attachments.

One should not confuse the term Sanatan Dharma with Hinduism. In fact, the term 'Hindu' is a secular word, not a religious word. But what the majority of the people of India believes in is called Hinduism by people of other faiths. The word 'Hindu' is not a Sanskrit word; it came into existence because of mispronunciation of a Sanskrit word by the ancient Persians some 3,000 to 4,000 years ago who supposedly shared some common ancestry with the ancient Indians. Those Persians used to refer to the Indus River as Sindhu, a major river that still flows in the north-western region of the Indian subcontinent, partly in India and partly in Pakistan. However, due to linguistic barriers they could not pronounce the letter 'S' correctly in their native tongue and mispronounced it as 'H'. Thus, for the Persians the word 'Sindhu' became 'Hindu' and the people of the Indian subcontinent became Hindus. The ancient Greeks, Armenians and the early Arabs followed the same pronunciation and gradually the name stuck. Megasthenes' 'Indica' epitomises the name for India and Indians around 310 BC. The British continued the practice and later they began using the word more as a religious term. The term 'ism' (means, a distinctive practice, system, or philosophy) was added to Hindu in the early part of the nineteenth century by the English writers. Soon the foreign word 'Hinduism' was adopted by the Indians themselves as a term that included their national, social and cultural identity.

The fundamental unity of India is emphasised by the name Bharata-Varsha (The land of Prince Bharata – Rajrishi Bharata is the name of an ancient prince, and Varsha means land).

> "*uttharam yathsamudrasaya himaadreyshaiva dakshinam*
> *varsham tad Bhāratam nāma bhārathī santhathihi*"
> (Vishnu Purana: 2.3.1).
> [The country that lies north of the ocean and south of the snowy mountains is called 'Bhāratam'; there dwell the descendants of Bharata.]

Ancient Indians, long before the beginning of Christianity, Islam, or other organised religions, believed in the concept of Dharma. Indian Dharmic Philosophy began about 5,000 years before Christ, and it has a continuity of more than 7,000 years. In the Indian tradition, philosophy is termed 'Darsana' (Sanskrit word means, 'seeing' or 'experiencing'). The aim of philosophy in India is direct experience of the Ultimate Reality and not mere intellectual speculation as in Western Philosophy. This concept refers to the principles that uphold the Universe and therefore apply to everyone regardless of religion or faith, and they exist whether we have discovered them or not. The ultimate principles are called Sanatan or eternal because they will exist forever, even if we forget them. Sanatan Dharma is so diverse in its underlying premises and practical manifestations that it has been called a living encyclopedia of the religions. This diversity is a strength rather than a weakness, and places it far above more restricted belief systems. Beliefs are like addictions and do not surrender their grip easily. In fact, there is no word in Sanskrit equivalent to religion. The term 'Dharma' is the closest but not exactly the same. Every event in the life of a true Dharmic offers glimpses of spirituality. While most of the original Sanskrit scriptures use the term Sanatan Dharma, some alternatively refer to the term as Sanatan Shastra, Sasvata Vidhi, Sasvata Dharma, or Sasvatam Vrttam to name a few.

In Dharmic scriptures, the words Shloka, Mantra, Stotra and Sutra are widely used. Shloka is a poetic form used in Sanskrit. It is the verse-form used in the Bhagavad Gita, the epics and the other sacred scriptures.

Stotra is a hymn to praise the God which is designed to be melodically sung. Mantra is a sacred chant, a syllable or group of words believed to have psychological and spiritual powers. Some Mantras have a syntactic structure and literal meaning, while others do not. The most powerful and widely used Mantra is the sacred syllable OM. Mantras can be a sound, a small text or a long composition, whereas Shlokas are verses only. Chanting of both Mantras and Shlokas brings inner calm and peace. Sutra is a code that expresses the essence of all knowledge in a minimum of words, as example, Patanjali's Yoga Sutras. A Sutra must be universally applicable and faultless in its linguistic presentation.

True humanness is represented by purity in thoughts, words and deeds – 'Trikarana Suddhi'. Without this, man is only human in form and not his true nature. If Sanatan Dharma is changed, humanity will cease to be human.

> "*dharma eva hato hanti dharmo rakṣati rakṣitaḥ*
> *tasmād dharmo na hantavyo mā no dharmo hato 'vadhīt*"
> (Manusmriti: 8.15).
> [If one will protect Dharma, Dharma will protect in return. If one will destroy Dharma, Dharma will destroy in return.]

Dharma expects us to look at others in totality and not as the other person. The practice of Dharma in this sense is more than ritual or ceremony because morality is superior to external rituals. A violation of this principle is 'Adharma' (unrighteousness – the Sanskrit antonym of Dharma). If Dharma is health, Adharma is the disease.

In religions we have a Prophet or savior and a holy book which alone is the way of liberation, whereas Sanatan Dharma does not bind God with a limitation. There are many ways and all the ways lead to the same God. All world religions, such as Christianity, Islam and Judaism have founders but Sanatan Dharma does not. The reason is, human soul (Atman) is eternal and Sanatan Dharma is the sacred, pure and original way of life of the eternal soul, and therefore it cannot be limited by any earthly boundaries. The way we cannot take out liquidity from water, or heat from the fire, similar way an eternal way of life (devoid of sectarian leanings or ideological divisions) cannot be taken out from an eternal soul. Therefore, any soul which has taken a human form on earth by incarnation, deep down belongs to Sanatan Dharma – a quest for Cosmic Truth. For this reason, Sanatan Dharma does not have a founder of earthly limitations, rather this is connected more with Cosmic Spirituality, unwritten laws of the Universe and Eternal Truth than it is with any historical person, revelation or community. The names of a host of sages are of course associated with Sanatan Dharma, but none can claim to be its founder, though each of them could claim prophethood because of their unique superconscious experiences and spiritual realisations. Each of them had played a part in their own specific ways, and a part only. The harmony consists in the sum total and not in one note. The Rig Veda sums up this limitless open mindedness in one all-encompassing richness.

"*āno bhadrāḥ kratavo yantu viśvato*" (Rig Veda: 1.89.1).
[Let noble thoughts come to me from all directions.]

Throughout the ages, organised religions had created an 'divide and rule concept' in the human society like political parties during election season, but Sanatan Dharma leads towards unity by promoting a value system that has spiritual freedom as its core which are inherent in the very nature and design of the Universe ('*Vasudhaiv Kutumbakam*' – the world is a single family). Hence, Sanatan Dharma is the business of all the people of the world, or even for all the living entities of the Universe.

"*ahimsa satya asteya brahmacharya aparigraha yama
jati desha kala samaya anavachchhinnah sarva-bhaumah maha-vratam*" (Patanjali's Yoga Sutras: 2.30-31).
[Ahimsa (nonviolence), Satya (truthfulness), Asteya (abstention from stealing), Brahmacharya (continence), and Aparigraha (non-possessiveness) are the five codes of self-regulations.
These codes are unbroken by time, place, purpose, and caste, and these are universal great vows.]

Thus, wherever the Universal Truth is manifest, there is Sanatan Dharma, whether it is in a field of art or science, or in the ordinary life of a person in a society. The ancient sages were mystics whose revelations disclosed a Cosmos in which all beings exist in interlaced dependence. **The whole is contained in the part, and the part in the whole.** They realised such great truth in their hearts that they ascribed to the infinite universal power, and not to themselves. Based on this wisdom, they taught a philosophy of non-difference of self and other, asserting that in the final analysis we are neither separate from the world and its manifest forms nor from the Divine which shines forth in all things and all people. From this understanding of oneness arose the philosophical basis for the practice of 'Ahimsa' (abstaining from causing hurt or harm) and strict adherence to it. In Sanskrit 'himsa' is doing harm or causing injury. The 'a' placed before the word negates it.

"*yo 'hiṃsakāni bhūtāni hinastyātmasukhaicchayā
sa jīvāṃśca mṛtaścaiva na kva cit sukhamedhate*

yo bandhanavadhakleśān prāṇināṃ na cikīrṣati
sa sarvasya hitaprepsuḥ sukhamatyantamaśnute"
(Manusmriti: 5.45-46).
[He, who kills harmless creatures for the sake of his own pleasure, never attains happiness, living or dead.
He, who does not seek to inflict sufferings of capture and death on living beings, is the well-wisher of all and obtains perfect happiness.]

Today "Holy" wars (actually wars of aggression) are waged with a claimed missionary purpose at the command of a given divinity while billion plus people are living under extreme poverty and oppression. This is the time we need to see an attitude of extreme tolerance and acceptance towards others for the intrinsic sacredness within all things.

Sanatan Dharma is best understood when compared to a fruit tree with its roots represented by the Vedas, the Upanishads and other ancient scriptures. The large trunk of the tree is comparable to the spiritual experiences of numerous sages whose insights grow out of these texts, and they are honoured as much as those of the sacred texts. The branches are analogous to the religious traditions that sprout from these roots and its trunk. These traditions together, are called Hinduism. Smaller branches symbolise various sects and subsects found in India.

Then, what are the fruits? The topmost fruit is liberation which begins with release from strict materialism and culminates in love of God. Other fruits of this tree are the realisations one gets by practicing the various forms of Dharma. The Atman is superior to the physical body, and it strives for 'Moksha' (liberation). All souls reincarnate due to their Karma and what they face in life is a result of their Karma. Once liberated, the 'Atman' is never reborn. Karma is a term about the cycle of cause and effect, means what happens to a person, happens because he caused it with his actions. Right conduct gives rise to happy life and wrong deed to misery. However, all may not be in the same birth but in various incarnations. This realisation helps us to build up a pious, dutiful, righteous, and well-balanced character.

Sanatan Dharma gives high importance to truth, knowledge, logic, reason and humbleness. Hence the reader will come across passages like these.

"*satyaṃ vada, dharmaṃ cara*..." (Taittiriya Upanishad: 1.11.1).
[Speak the truth, adhere to Dharma.]

"*andhaṃ bhuvanamandhasya prakāśaṃ tu sacakṣuṣaḥ.*
jagadekātmakaṃ jñasya mūrkhasyātīva duḥkhadam"
(Yoga-Vasistha: 6.11.33).

[The blind beholds the world all dark while the eye-sighted finds it fully bright and shining. So, the wise are blessed with the knowledge of the one soul of the whole while the ignorant are immerged in misery by their want of such knowledge.]

"yuktiyuktamupādeyaṃ vacanaṃ bālakādapi
anyattṛṇamiva tyājyamapyuktaṃ padmajanmanā"
(Yoga-Vasistha: 2.18.3).
[Words conformable with reason are to be received even if spoken by children, otherwise they are to be rejected as straws though pronounced by the lotus-born (The Supreme Lord).]

"yaḥ pumānadya tejasvī maṇḍalānyadhitiṣṭhati
sa bhasmakūṭatāṃ rājandivasairadhigacchati"
(Yoga-Vasistha: 1.28.6).
[The man who is very powerful today and presides over principalities, is reduced in a few days to a heap of ashes.]

The Sruthi and Smriti are the twin authentic sources and fundamental scriptures of Sanatan Dharma. The Veda-Mantras are spoken of as 'Sruthi' (that is heard or revealed). 'Smriti' (the things remembered or learned) lays down laws governing righteous conducts for individuals and for the society. The Vedas are the most ancient Dharmic texts. 'Veda' is a Sanskrit word from the root 'vid' (means, to know, to perceive, to regard etc.). Thus, Veda means knowledge or wisdom. The Vedas are meant to nourish our soul from deep within by invoking the cosmic element to endow us with real power, real courage and real commitments in life. They are considered to have no author; the texts were revealed to the ancient sages in their supernormal consciousness who passed them on orally for many years until they were written down on palm leaves around 3,000 BC. Indological scholars date some of the texts to about 7,000 BC according to internal astronomical evidence. The Vedas project the advancements, richness and infallible dignity of that era in the fields of science, medicine, art, music, literature, philosophy and obviously Dharma. There are four Vedas – Rig Veda (the oldest), Sama Veda, Yajur Veda and Atharva Veda. These expanded over time to include Brahmanas, Aranyakas and Upanishads. The uses of the Vedas are specified in Bhagavad Gita.

"yāvān artha udapāne sarvataḥ samplutodake
tāvānsarveṣhu vedeṣhu brāhmaṇasya vijānataḥ"
(Bhagavad Gita: 2.46).
[Whatever purpose is served by a small well of water is naturally served in all respects by a large lake. Similarly, one who realises the Absolute Truth also fulfills the purpose of all the Vedas.]

It means, the Vedas are certainly a useful way for achieving the goal by the aspirants who just started their spiritual journey and serve the purpose of the unenlightened. Only for a sage who has realised the Self or truth concerning Absolute Reality, the Veda Karma Kanda (the section of the Vedas that lists rituals, ceremonies and actions) are of no use because he is already in possession of the highest knowledge of the Self.

The Gayatri Mantra from the Rig Veda, also known as the Savitri Mantra, is considered as one of the most important and powerful Veda-Mantras.

"*OM bhūr bhuvaḥ svaḥ*
tat savitur vareṇyaṃ
bhargo devasya dhīmahi
dhiyo yo naḥ pracodayāt" (Rig Veda: 3.62.10).
[Let us meditate on that excellent glory of the divine vivifying Sun, may He enlighten our understandings.]

Upanishad is compilation of three Sanskrit words – Upa (near), Ni (down) and Sad (to sit), which means sitting near at the ground and learn from the Guru (spiritual teacher). There are 108 prominent Upanishads, thirteen of which are considered main such as, Brhadaranyaka, Chandogya, Taittiriya, Aitereya, Kausitaki, Kena, Katha, Isha, Svetasvatara, Mundaka, Prashna, Maitri and Mandukya Upanishad. Famous German Philosopher Arthur Schopenhauer was immediately impressed by the Upanishads, as he called them "*the production of the highest human wisdom and I consider them almost superhuman in conception*" (Sinha, 2013, p. 303). The Upanishads center on the doctrine of Brahmam (all-pervading God) and Atman (soul). They can hardly be surpassed as a document of spiritual philosophy.

We often hear the word 'Vedanta' in spiritual gatherings. In Sanskrit 'Veda' means complete knowledge and 'anta' means end. So, Vedanta means the culmination of Vedic wisdom. Its basic teaching is that our real nature is divine. God, the underlying reality, exists in every being. The Upanishads, the Bhagavad Gita and the Brahma Sutras constitute the basis of Vedanta providing reliable sources of knowledge.

The greatest teachings of Vedas and the Upanishads are about finding peace within ourself, and thereby finding peace with the world also. A focus on the ultimate goals of human life and the wisdom to achieve them forms the backbone of Vedas and Upanishads. These scriptures transcend time. Hence their ideas are most relevant today and deep insights on them are need of the hour. They are so mystic in their nature in many places that their real meaning is not grasped clearly by those scholars who do not care to go above worldly things.

The term 'Brahmam' is rather confusing for the English reader, as he is likely to confuse it with 'Brahmana', a member of the priestly class, commonly written in English as 'Brahmin'. The term 'Brahmin' is phonetically wrong, but I will use the term in this book because it has become an English word and is perhaps easier to distinguish from 'Brahmam'. The Upanishads point out that the Brahmam and Atman are the same. The Supreme has manifested Himself in every Atman. This idea provides the core of most of the Dharmic spiritual thought, and is developed later by Adi Shankaracharya (estimated 788 to 820 AD) into his doctrine Advaita Vedanta. This monistic doctrine (Advaita literally means 'non-duality') denies the existence of the world as separate from God. This doctrine adheres to the strict rules of logic and does not demand blind faith or unquestioning acceptance. The students are asked to examine and think for themselves with an open mind, a genuine desire to understand and an attitude of respect towards the scriptures before accepting the teachings of the Guru. The fundamental principle is that the final testimony of truth is actual spiritual experience. This makes it a very scientific system and therefore acceptable to present day intellectuals who swear by reason and the scientific method. In the subsequent chapters I will discuss more on this philosophy.

Atma Bodha (means, Knowledge of the Self, also known as Prakarana Grantha) is a supporting text attributed to Shankaracharya for understanding the main text of Vedanta. The text in sixty-eight Mantras describes the path to self-knowledge or the awareness of Atman.

The main systems of Indian Dharmic Philosophy are Samkhya, Yoga, Nyaya, Vaisesika, Purva Mimasa and Vedanta (also known as Uttara Mimamsa). Each of these six systems provides a particular insight into 'Reality'. They may be regarded as forming a six-tiered pyramid, the tiers providing higher and higher views of Reality with Vedanta as the topmost tier. Vedanta itself consists of several schools which may also be visualised as forming a pyramid with Advaita occupying its pinnacle. These systems had developed almost concurrently through mutual criticism and interaction. But the Samkhya system of Sage Kapila is the oldest school of Dharmic Philosophy, for it is the first attempt to harmonise the philosophy of the Vedas through reason. Other systems accept the basic assumptions of the Vedas and Upanishads though there are some individual differences amongst them. These philosophies are never in contradiction. Ultimately, all these philosophies believe in liberation or emancipation as the end goal of life. The basis of life is non-attachment, moral and virtuous life and spiritual superiority to worldly values.

Samkhya Philosophy holds a highly complex view of the nature of man as a spiritual and psycho-physical entity. It regards the ego as the center of both man and the Universe. Richard Garbe, a prominent Christian missionary, concluded in 1898 that in Samkhya, "*for the first time in the history of the world, the complete independence of the human mind, its full confidence in its own powers were exhibited*" (Durant, 1942, p. 536). Samkhya and Yoga are regarded as two aspects of the same discipline. The Samkhya-Yoga Philosophy had postulated the existence of two distinct and ultimate entities, Purusha (consciousness) and Prakriti (nature or matter, including subtle matter). Nyaya and Vaisesika take a simpler view than either Samkhya or Yoga. The aim of Purva Mimamsa is to give further details about the nature of 'Dharma'.

There are two great epics – Ramayan and Mahabharat. The popular epic Ramayan tells the life story of the noble prince named Ram who is believed to be an incarnation of the Divine. Ram and his wife Sita are generally seen as ideal examples of great manly heroism and wifely devotion.

The Ramayan is often appreciated for its sheer beauty, the poetry, settings and profound dialogues. The beauty also manifests in the sense of highest standards of morals and ethics found in its pages. Most of the inspirational personalities depicted in this epic are the highest peaks in the Ramayan's overwhelming beauty. Many Indians consult this scripture for guidance on everyday life. For a true Dharmic, the symbolic significance of Ramayan can be interpreted as this – Ram is his soul while Sita is his heart. Ravan is his mind that steals his heart from his soul. Brother Lakshman is his conscience, always with him and active on his behalf. Hanuman is his intuition and courage that help retrieve his heart to re-animate his soul. Homages to the Ramayan can be seen all around Southeast Asia through architecture and dramatic renderings of the epic.

The other one, Mahabharat (great tale of the Bharata Dynasty) is a historical epic with over 100,000 Shlokas. This is the longest poem the world has known – seven times of the combined length of Homer's Iliad and Odyssey. Based on an extended conflict between two branches of the Kaurava family, the Mahabharat is a trove of stories and dialogues on the practice of Dharma. The characters are complex and real, with depth of personality that is unmatched in any other story humanity has ever conceived. This book contains a great deal of philosophical and devotional material, such as the importance of truth, justice, self-sacrifice, and the ultimate futility of war.

> "*A striking feature of the Mahabharat is the unity of Indian culture it presents. The cultural traditions of different parts of this large country are described with sympathy and pride, and a gradually growing*

conception of a unified Indian culture is clearly revealed." (Sen, 1961, pp. 72-73).

Mahabharat contains an elaborate illustration of Dharma. On being asked by Yudhisthira to explain the meaning and scope of Dharma, Vishma, who has mastered the knowledge of Dharma, explains in Shanti Parva, 109. 9-11,

> "*It is most difficult to define Dharma. Dharma has been explained to be that which helps the upliftment of living beings. Therefore, that which ensures the welfare of living beings is surely Dharma. The learned sages have declared that what sustains this Universe is Dharma.*"

Though Ramayan lacks the immensity of the Mahabharat, this epic is a rich storehouse of material about Indian cultural traditions too.

These two epics are not mythology, rather they are parts of well-documented ancient history. The stories of Mahabharat have been verified by astronomical dating (the method of calculating the time of a particular astronomical reference with the position of stars and planets) which is an accurate way of dating historical events. The great mathematician Aryabhata acknowledged that Mahabharat was a real event and calculated that Mahabharat war happened around 3102 BC. Moreover, all places mentioned in Mahabharat are identified as real places scattered all around the undivided India (mainland India, Nepal, Afghanistan, Pakistan, Burma and Bangladesh). The ancient cave where Veda Vyasa composed Mahabharat still exists, and it is popularly known as 'Vyas Gufa'. Archaeologists have found the city of Dwarka, the birth place of Lord Krishna, under the sea close to Gujarat coast. The ruins they found have been verified to be of Harappan times or even earlier. Similarly, researchers have concluded that events in the Ramayan took place 6,000 years ago based on astronomical information such as position of constellations and time of eclipses available in scriptures. NASA satellite images confirm that the Ram Setu (Adam Bridge), the curvilinear chains of islands linking India with Sri Lanka, is a manmade bridge. The epic says that Lord Ram built this bridge to bring back his wife Sita from Sri Lanka who was a captive by King Ravan of Sri Lanka. The Sages Valmiki (the author of Ramayan) and Veda Vyasa (the author of Mahabharat) witnessed at least some of the important events of the story and had composed epics, not merely to share the story but to reveal how their central characters Ram and Krishna used Vedic wisdom to engage with society. Initially the methods of transmission of these two epics were drama, songs, recitation, story-telling etc., and later they were written down.

What was happening in the rest of the world at the same time when Mahabharat and Ramayan were taking place in India?

In connection to the great epic Ramayan there is a philosophical text attributed to Sage Valmiki called, Yoga-Vasistha (also known as, Vasistha Maha Ramayan). The complete text consists of six books containing over 29,000 Shlokas (not discussed in the traditional Ramayan). The short version of the text is called 'Laghu Yoga-Vasistha' and contains 6,000 Shlokas. The text is structured as a dialogue of Sage Vasistha to ten-years-old Prince Ram. The Yoga-Vasistha is throughout a philosophical work with extraordinary poetic beauty. Many scholars, such as Bhikhan Lal Arteya, Pandit Brindawana Saraswati, Walter Slaje, Wendy Doniger, Christopher Chapple, Bruno Lo Turco, Jurgen Hanneder, and Sthaneshwar Timalsina have done extensive research on this scripture. Indeed, this was once one of the most widely read books in India.

Sage Vasistha is a legendary figure who has been visioned and heard by mystics. The text is notable for expounding Maya, nature of consciousness, Brahmam, and the principles of non-duality. Christopher Chapple, a professor of Indic studies specialising in Yoga and Indian religions, summarises the Yoga-Vasistha Philosophy in one line, "*Human effort can be used for self-betterment and that there is no such thing as an external fate imposed by the gods.*" (Venkatesananda and Chapple, 2010, p. xi). This scripture also has many fascinating passages on extraterrestrial life on other planets (3.30.8 to 3.30.34), time, space, matter and cognition which have extraordinary parallels with recent speculations in physics.

These wisdoms do not stand in isolation. Similar ideas are to be found in the Vedic books in a tradition that is more than 6,000 years old. Those sages were actually highly advanced scientists of the ancient ages. What was most unusual about them was their ability to combine spirituality with science. Bhagavad Gita (2.55-57) adores them as 'men of steady wisdom' who are completely free from 'all the desires of the mind', and whether they face good or evil – their wisdom is firmly fixed.

Embedded in the Mahabharat is a text of special scriptural significance – the Bhagavad Gita (about 700 Shlokas from chapters 23 to 40 of Vishma Parva). Like the warriors of the 'Iliad', the leading personalities of the Mahabharat are aristocratic warriors fighting from chariots. One of the greatest of these chariot warriors is Arjun. As the great battle of Kurukshetra is about to begin Arjun despairs realising that he can be victorious in battle only by killing his Kaurava cousins. Even in victory, many of his friends and relatives will die in the fighting.

Unknown to Arjun, however, his charioteer Krishna is in reality the eighth incarnation of God Vishnu and hence is a reincarnation of

Lord Ram. Krishna suddenly reveals his true divine nature to Arjun explaining the cosmic 'plan of liberation' as understood by the ancient Indians. Krishna then encourages Arjun about his duty to fight. Krishna's teachings to Arjun, which takes the form of a highly philosophical and ethical discussion, is what has come to be known as the Bhagavad Gita (Song of the Lord Krishna). This book is often referred to as the 'Gitopanishad' because it follows the literary style and philosophical conclusions of the earlier Upanishads though the Upanishadic teaching had developed slightly different way.

Bhagavad Gita discusses man's duties in the world, claims indestructibility of the Atman, and strongly supports reincarnation and Karma. Also, selfless work is put forward as an ideal, and duties of every human being are emphasised. The timeless and universal message of the Bhagavad Gita is all-encompassing in its expression of truth.

All the Dharmic scriptures should not be viewed as competitive but rather as complementary. They never shirk from challenges. All are essential, like pieces of a big jig-saw puzzle, to conform the actual spiritual picture of Sanatan Dharma. We observe something similar in nature. Each species, no matter how we may feel about it or how small and insignificant it is, contributes something unique to the ecological balance of the physical world. Similarly, there have been many worthy spiritual guides in Sanatan Dharma, and there is no reason to worship one at the expense of another. Each knowledgeable individual has something unique to contribute through his speech and his writing. By expressing the primordial truths in his own way, each of them has afforded many people the chance to grow spiritually where this might not have been possible otherwise.

This book is heavy reading. I ask for readers' patience on this.

CHAPTER - 1

Quantum Consciousness and the concept of ATMAN (Soul)

"*Consciousness cannot be explained with a reductionist approach, because it does not belong to the realm of matter.*"

American philosopher David Chalmers

"*Nothing in science is as mysterious as quantum physics – except, perhaps, the mechanics of the mind. In fact, the two are intimately connected.*"

Sir Roger Penrose

The study of 'consciousness' has been of immense interest to scientists, philosophers, and laypeople alike for millennia. With different worldviews they have defined the term from various perspectives. The founders of modern physics, such as, Heisenberg, Schrödinger and Einstein pondered deeply on the nature of consciousness.

Sanatan Dharma put great emphasis to the idea of the consciousness from the very beginning, and teaches us that a balance is required between man's knowledge of the external world and his inner world. This 'inwardness' of Indian thought is what makes it distinguished from Western thought. Western philosophy began with the Greeks. It has laid much more stress on external phenomena than on the internal, and the study of the consciousness as a separate entity is a modern phenomenon. But in Sanatan Dharma, the 'I' or the 'Self' has been the topic right from the beginning – "*Some of the insights of modern Western psychology on the nature of the human self are truths which the thinkers of India had discovered in ancient times*" (Jacob, 1975, p. 5). The beginning of inward-looking search became the main feature of the Upanishads, and since then this philosophy had developed as chief characteristic of Indian thought. The entire philosophy of the cosmic laws is actually the exhibition of the consciousness which is enclosed in the physical body.

1.1: Consciousness and its quantum nature

Quantum physics is the study of matter and energy. The word quantum means 'a discrete quantity' such as a quantum of light (i.e., a photon). It is an isolated, indivisible amount of energy. When the physicists study matter at the subatomic level, they find that matter does not exist until it is observed by a conscious being. Conscious mind cannot be replaced with an inanimate device in its role of observer. It means, the effect of the observer on the physical system being observed must be understood as a part of that system.

The logic-defying double-slit experiment demonstrates that a conscious observer is required to collapse a probability wave into a particle. Basically, waves that pass through two narrow, parallel slits will form an interference pattern on a screen. This is true for all waves whether they are light waves, water waves, or sound waves. But light is not just a wave – it is also a particle called a photon. So, what happens if we shoot a single photon at the double slits? The experiment shows, even though there exists only one photon, yet it still can form an interference pattern, as if the photon travels through both slits simultaneously. If either path is monitored, a photon seemingly passes through one slit or the other, and no interference will be seen. Conversely, if neither is checked, a photon will appear to have passed through both slits simultaneously before interfering with itself, acting like a wave.

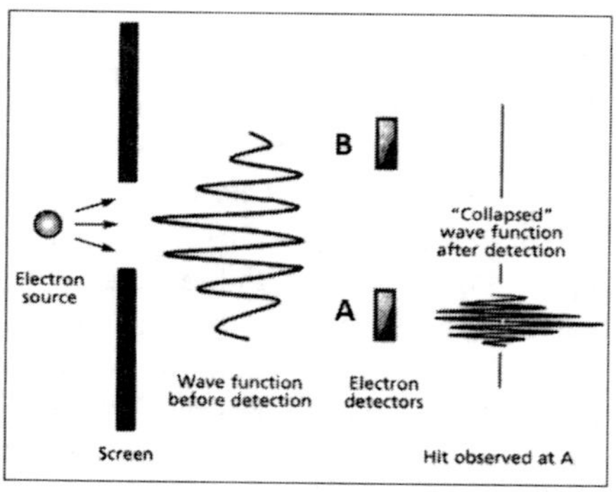

Wave function collapse in conventional quantum physics

In the above figure, an electron is localised by passing through an aperture. The probability that it will then be found at the particular position is determined by the wave function illustrated to the right of the aperture. When the electron is detected at A, the wave function instantly collapses so that it becomes zero at B. Also, this effect is dependent on the 'amount' of the observation – when the observer's capacity of detection increases, i.e., when the level of the observation goes up, the interference weakens. In contrast, when the detection capacity is reduced, i.e., when the observation slackens, the interference increases. Strange as it may sound, but humans have a psychic grip on subatomic particles.

Thus, consciousness is necessary first before matter can exist, and it is impossible for consciousness to have been produced by matter. Hence, the brain which is composed of matter cannot produce consciousness. Matter is only the medium through which consciousness manifests itself. Founders of quantum physics, including Nobel Prize winners in physics, such as Max Planck and Erwin Schrödinger have recognised this fact. Dr. Schiller, an eminent thinker of the West, commented,

> "*Matter is not that which produces consciousness, but that which limits it and confines its intensity within certain limits; material organisation does not construct consciousness out of arrangements of atoms, but contracts its manifestation within the sphere which it permits.*" (Schiller, 1891, p. 295).

In the 1970s, theoretical physicist Ennackal Sudarshan and his colleagues at the University of Texas in Austin showed in theory that "*a continuously observed quantum state cannot decay*", i.e., an atom in one energy state cannot change its energy as long as it is being observed (Runsheng, 2018, p. 52). Continuous observation of unstable radioactive isotopes can prevent them from disintegrating radioactively. Theoretically, if a nuclear bomb is watched intently enough, it cannot explode – this is the power of the consciousness.

It means, consciousness is an independent, causal factor in the real world, and we do not live in a pre-determined world. This truly radical discovery is not just a philosophical statement of the ancient sages; it is exactly what quantum physics tells us too. With this move the relationship between matter, life, and sentience can be approached in an entirely new light. The Vedic Seers knew the true nature of the consciousness and its relation to Eternal Consciousness. That is the reason, the central idea of the Upanishads is that the ultimate truth lies within man. Jahn (2001, p. 456) describes that, "*in studying consciousness, we are doing nothing less than studying our own vital essence: our minds; our spirits; our lives; and our eternal presence and purpose in the cosmic plan.*"

Though quantum physics falls under the category of post-modern science, it is fully at par with the ancient teachings of Dharma. Traditionally, physicists have treated consciousness as non-existent or beyond the scope of their discipline. For those who recognised its existence, the general premise within the discipline was that consciousness emerged from the physical, and fundamentally it was not any different from it.

Since observations can change the physical structure, materialism is impermanent and unreal while consciousness is permanent and real. In Vedanta nothing is more important than consciousness. That's why in Vedanta there is no dogmatic rule that affect the free will of consciousness or impose any restriction upon its choices. Hence, a student of Vedanta becomes an experimenter himself, instead of remaining a mere believer. Vedanta is independent of determinism or materialism but it absorbs the principle of them as the effects of Karma. The core understanding is that Absolute Consciousness permeates in its quantum nature throughout the whole Universe. Thus, Erwin Schrödinger stated on the nature of consciousness,

> "*Consciousness is a singular of which the plural is unknown; that there is only one thing and that, what seems to be a plurality, is merely a series of different aspects of this one thing, produced by a deception (the Indian Maya); the same illusion is produced in a gallery of mirrors, and in the same way Gaurisankar and Mt Everest turned out to be the same peak seen from different valleys.*" (Ranganathananda, 1997, p. 118).

Nobel Laureate Erwin Schrödinger, a pioneer of quantum physics, was impressed by ancient Dharmic scriptures, and according to his biographer Walter Moore, there is a clear continuity between Schrödinger's understanding of Vedanta Philosophy and his research. Soon, as a result of his studies in his search for truth, Schrödinger became a Vedantist, i.e., a Dharmic. He read books on Vedas, Yoga, and Samkhya Philosophy and he reworked them into his own words, and ultimately came to believe them. The Upanishads and the Bhagavad Gita were his favourite scriptures.

Proponents would argue that the findings within quantum physics are significant at the subatomic level. But are not we all existing at the subatomic level? When we observe ourselves and our physical environment at the smallest level, we are made up of atoms and subatomic particles. Quantum behaviour is not limited to the microscopic world. New experiments carried out in the laboratories with huge molecules called buckyballs show that quantum reality extends into the macroscopic world we live in. If our consciousness makes sense of the world, then what we perceive by five senses cannot be present without our consciousness.

1.2: Dharmic understanding of Quantum Consciousness

"*After these conversations [with Nobel Laureate Rabindra Nath Tagore] about Indian [Dharmic] philosophy, some of the ideas of Quantum Physics that had seemed so crazy suddenly made much more sense. That was a great help for me.*"

Werner Karl Heisenberg

The oldest answer to what consciousness is can be found in the great Upanishadic Sage Yajnavalkya's conversation with King Janaka. This discussion is a significant part of Brihadaranyaka Upanishad (Mantras 4.3.1-38). According to Sage Yajnavalkya, there is an inner light in every person which illuminates or reveals things so they can be known. The 'inner light' that Yajnavalkya talked about is what we would call 'consciousness'. The Mantra 4.3.36 is of particular importance.

"*sa yatrāyamaṇimānaṃ nyeti - jarayā vopatapatā vāṇimānaṃ nigacchatitadyathāmraṃ vodumbaraṃ vā pippalaṃ vā bandhanātpramucyate, evamevāyaṃ puruṣa ebhyo'ngebhyaḥ saṃpramucya punaḥ pratinyāyaṃ pratiyonyādravati prāṇāyaiva*"
[When this (body) becomes thin – is emaciated through old age or disease – then, as a mango, or a fig, or a fruit of the peepul tree is detached from its stalk, so does this infinite being, completely detaching himself from the parts of the body, again go, in the same way that he came, to particular bodies, for the unfoldment of his vital force.]

In short, what Sage Yajnavalkya spoke to King Janaka is that the consciousness is the pure awareness that shines as the light within the heart, surrounded by the senses. Another famous illustration of the nature of consciousness is found in the metaphor of the chariot.

"*ātmānaṁ rathinaṁ viddhi, śarīraṁ rathameva tu:*
buddhiṁ tu sārathiṁ viddhi, manaḥ pragraham eva ca
indriyāṇi hayān āhur viṣayāṁs teṣu gocarān,
ātmendriya-mano-yuktam bhoktety āhur manīṣiṇaḥ"
(Katha Upanishad: 1.3.3-4).
[Know the Atman as the lord of the chariot and the body as, truly, the chariot. Know the intellect as the charioteer and the mind as the reins. The senses, they say, are the horses; the objects of enjoyment the paths (they range over); (Atman) associated with the body; (comprised of) the senses and the mind – the enlightened ones declare – is the enjoyer.]

People used to think just few decades ago that only three states of consciousness existed – waking, sleeping (dream state) and deep sleep (dreamless state). However, brain imaging suggests there are more states of consciousness than these basic three. The Dharmic scriptures that have been in existence for thousands of years have clearly and repeatedly elaborated this fact. Many early founders of quantum physics, e.g., Bohr, Schrödinger, Heisenberg, have noticed various conceptual parallels between the philosophy of Sanatan Dharma and quantum theory. They were not only well-versed in but also heavily influenced by the sacred wisdom contained within the Upanishads. Schrödinger (1956, p. 219) famously quoted,

> "*The multiplicity is only apparent. This is the doctrine of the Upanishads. And not of the Upanishads only. The mystical experience of the union with God regularly leads to this view, unless strong prejudices stand in the way.*"

This notion of unity, interconnectedness, and wholeness among all the constituent parts of the Universe, is an integral part of the 7,000 years of spiritual, religious, philosophical, and social dimensions of Indian thought. About this cosmic unity and harmony, Olivelle (2008, p. iii) posits in his commentary of the Upanishads as this,

> "*The assumption then is that the Universe constitutes a web of relations, that things that appear to stand alone and apart are, in fact, connected in other things. A further assumption is that these real cosmic connections are usually hidden from the view of ordinary people; discovering them constitutes knowledge, **knowledge that is secret and is contained in the Upanishads**.*"

This 'secret knowledge' that to a great extent the Universe is based in consciousness is outlined in the Aitareya Upanishad (Mantra 3.1.3). The text concludes that everything is supported and guided by consciousness. The basis of the Universe is consciousness. Hence, consciousness is Brahmam (Prajnanam Brahma).

So, we can see, a person who had well studied the ancient Dharmic literatures are always at home in the Universe because he conceives of it "*as the product of his own inner most Spirit, the Atman, ... and all the gods were its products and he himself was created as the field of their activities and enjoyment*". (Radhakrishnan, 1960, p. 225). The findings of quantum physics are nothing new for them. Father Jacob (1975, p. 9) explains,

> "*The Upanishads draw a distinction between man's empirical self and his true Self or Atman. The empirical self is the existential self, subject to sorrow and suffering and subject to change. **The true Self is the unchanging Atman that observes the empirical phenomena but is unaffected and undying**.*

The Upanishads believe in the ultimate identity of the empirical self with the Supreme Self."

"*indriyebhyaḥ parā hyarthā arthebhyaśhcha paraṃ manaḥ manasastu parā buddhirbhuddherātmā mahān paraḥ*"
(Katha Upanishad: 1.3.10).
[Beyond the senses are the objects of the senses, subtler than the objects of the senses is the mind. Beyond the mind is the intellect, and subtler than the intellect is the Atman.]

"*aṇoraṇīyānmahato mahīyānātmāsya jantornihito guhāyāṃ tamakratuḥ paśyati vītaśoko dhātuḥ prasādānmahimānamātmanaḥ*"
(Katha Upanishad: 1.2.20).
[Subtler than the subtle, greater than the great, in the heart of each living being, the Atman reposes. One free from desire, with his mind and the senses composed, sees the glory of the Atman and becomes free from grief.]

The Brihadaranyaka Upanishad (4.4.25) states that the Atman is glorious, unborn, deathless, free from old age, immortal, and fearless – "*sa vā eṣha mahān aja ātmājaro 'maro 'mṛito 'bhayaḥ*". The subtlety of Atman is again elaborated in the following Mantras.

"*sa paryagāc chukram akāyam avraṇam asnāviraṃ śuddham apāpaviddham*
kavir manīṣī paribhūḥ syayambhūr yāthātathyator'thān
vyadadhāc chāśvatībhyaḥ samābhyaḥ" (Isa Upanishad: eighth Mantra).
[He (the self) is all pervading, bright, incorporeal, scatheless and veinless, pure, untouched by sin; a seer, all-knowing, superposed and self-begotten. (It is He that) has duly allotted to the eternal creators their (various) duties.]

"*vālāgraśatabhāgasya śatadhā kalpitasya ca.*
bhāgo jīvaḥ sa vijñeyaḥ sa cānantyāya kalpate
naiva strī na pumān eṣa na caivāyaṃ napuṃsakaḥ
yad yac charīram ādatte tena tena sa yujyate"
(Svetasvatara Upanishad: 5.9-10).
[Know the embodied Atman to be a part of the hundredth part of the point of a hair divided a hundred times; and yet it is infinite.
It is not female, it is not male, nor is it passive. Whatever body it takes, with that it becomes united.]

This identity of the Atman is illustrated in the Chandogya Upanishad (Mantras 6.1.2 to 6.16.3) through the lessons given by Uddalaka Aruni to his son Svetaketu. Uddalaka was one of the most exalted Vedic Rishis.

Mahabharat (Sabha Parva, Chapter 7.12) mentions his name as a great teacher.

When Svetaketu was twelve, his father sent him to a spiritual teacher where he studied the scriptures for twelve years. When he returned home very proud of his intellectual knowledge, his father said, "My son, you seem to have a high opinion of yourself; you are proud of your learning. But did you ask your teacher for the spiritual knowledge that enables you to hear the unheard, think the unthought and know the unknown?"

"What is that knowledge, Father?"

"By knowing a lump of clay, everything that is made of clay can be known because any differences are only words, and the essential reality is clay. Similarly, by knowing a piece of gold, all that is made of gold can be known because any differences are only words, and the reality is only gold".

"My teachers must not have known this or they would have taught it to me. Father, please teach me this knowledge."

"Some people claim that in the beginning there was nothing at all and that everything has come out of nothing. But how can this be true? In the beginning there was only one Being, and that Being thought, 'I want to be many so I will create'. Out of this creation came the entire Cosmos. Of everything that exists, this Being is the innermost Self. He is the truth, the Self Supreme. And you, Svetaketu, **Tat Tvam Asi** – You Are That!"

"Please teach me more about the Self, Father."

"Let's start with sleep. When a person is absorbed in dreamless sleep, he is one with the Self although he doesn't know it. We say he sleeps but we mean he sleeps in the Self. A chained bird grows tired from flying in every direction, finding no rest anywhere, and settles down at last on the very same perch on which it is chained. In the same way the mind, tired of wandering around here and there, settles down at last in the Self, its life and breath, to which it is bound. All creatures have their source in that Being. He is their home; He is their strength. When a man is dying, speech folds into mind, mind folds into life, life dissolves into light, and his light merges into that one Being. That Being is the seed, the truth, the Self, and you, Svetaketu, **Tat Tvam Asi** – You Are That!"

"Please tell me more, Father."

"My son, bees make honey by gathering nectar from many. So not one drop of honey can say that it came exactly from one specific flower. You can't identify the juice of one particular flower in the honey. And so it is with creatures like us who merge in that Being, whether in sleep or death.

And as the rivers that flow from the east to the west merge in the sea and become one with it, forgetting that they were ever separate rivers, so all creatures lose their separateness when they merge into pure Being. Whatever creature it may be – tiger, lion, wolf, boar, mosquito, worm – it only becomes aware of a particular life when it is born into it or is awake.

If you strike at the root of a tree, it bleeds but still lives. If you strike at the trunk, the sap oozes but the tree lives on. The Self is similar to the life that fills the tree and supports it, and the tree flourishes in happiness gathering food through its roots. If life departs from one branch, that branch dries up, and when life leaves the whole tree, the entire tree dries up. Remember my son, your body dies, but your Self does not."

Uddalaka told Svetaketu to bring him a piece of fruit from a nearby banyan tree and to break it open. Svetaketu did and said, "There are seeds inside, all very small."

"Now break one of the seeds and tell me what you see."

"Nothing, Father."

"My son, this great banyan tree has grown from a seed so small that you cannot see it. Believe me, an invisible and subtle essence is the Spirit of the whole Universe. Now, take this salt and put it in some water and bring it to me tomorrow morning."

The next morning Svetaketu looked for the salt but couldn't find it because it had dissolved. Uddalaka asked his son to taste the water. "Salty", he said, adding "the salt will always remain in the water".

"That's right. The salt permeates the water, just like the Self. Even though we cannot see it, the Self is within all things and there is nothing that doesn't come from Him. This invisible and subtle essence is the Spirit of the whole Universe. That is reality. That is truth. And you, Svetaketu, **Tat Tvam Asi** – You Are That!"

> "... *idaṃ sarvaṃ tatsatyaṃ sa ātmā*
> ***tat-tvam-asi śvetaketo*** *iti taddhāsya vijajñāviti vijajñāviti*"
> (Chandogya Upanishad: 6.16.3).
> ['That (Self) is the Self of all this. It is the Truth. It is the Self. ***You Are That***, Oh Svetaketu.' Svetaketu learnt this well from his father.]

In Taittiriya Upanishad, a distinction is drawn between man's body and his Atman – "*The Atman is the Supreme Being; man is the finite creature. But deep within man is the Atman which is man's true self*". (Jacob, 1975, p. 9). This philosophy appears absolutely realistic, devotional and logical.

> "*Whatever is taking place in my mind, whatever I may be thinking, believing, feeling or sensing, the one thing I cannot doubt is consciousness.* ***Consciousness is my only absolute, unquestionable truth. If the faculty of consciousness is God, then God is the truth.***" (Russel, 2003, p. 87).

Millennia ago, Sage Vasistha taught us that the whole Universe is really nothing but consciousness.

"*mano hi jagatāṃ kartṛ mano hi puruṣaḥ paraḥ*
manaḥkṛtaṃ kṛtaṃ loke na śarīrakṛtaṃ kṛtam"
(Yoga-Vasistha: 3.89.1).
[The mind alone is the creator of the world and mind alone is the supreme person. What is done by the mind is action, what is done by the body is not action.]

"*pratibhāsamupāyāti yadyadasya hi cetasaḥ*
tattatprakaṭatāmeti sthairyaṃ saphalatāmapi"
(Yoga-Vasistha: 3.91.17).
[Whatever appears in one's consciousness, that seems to come into being, gets established, and even bears fruit.]

One important element in the Upanishadic concept of the self is the ego which is called 'Ahamkara'. Please take a note, here I do not use the term 'ego' in the Freudian sense, but in the sense of a 'confused self'. The self believes in the absolute separation between itself and the other souls – this is the confusion. In deep sleep, the activity of the ego is suspended. It is active only in waking states. The distinction between the ego (Ahamkara) and the true Self (Atman) is of great significance. The psychic force of man resides not in the ego, but in his true Self. When the Upanishads say that the highest goal of man is to realise his true self, they are not proclaiming a doctrine of self-indulgence. To realise the true Self, one has to regulate the ego by ethical actions – actions according to 'Dharma'.

Both Jainism and Buddhism derive much from the original Dharmic thought. While rejecting the Upanishadic notion of a Supreme God (Brahmam), they still substantially adopted the Dharmic view of the world. According to Jainism, a soul is a conscious substance which may be theoretically arranged in a continuous series according to the degree of consciousness. All living beings have souls within them, but only the soul of a human being is most developed because consciousness in it is the most manifest. Also, it is potentially perfect and is capable of attaining infinite power, infinite knowledge, infinite faith and infinite bliss.

1.2.1: Understanding consciousness from Advaita Vedanta Philosophy

"*The unity and continuity of Vedanta are reflected in the unity and continuity of wave mechanics. This is entirely consistent with the Vedanta concept of All in One.*"

Erwin Schrödinger

> *"Quantum theory will not look ridiculous to people who have read Vedanta."*
>
> Werner Heisenberg

Adi Shankaracharya, the most important advocate of Advaita Vedanta Philosophy, did not start logical analysis from the observed world, but directly from the Absolute (Brahmam). 'Dvaita' means duality, and 'Advaita' means non-duality. Advaita Vedanta believes in non-duality of the Ultimate Reality. According to Advaita Vedanta, the Self alone is real and everything else enjoys only an apparent reality, having no independent existence of their own. This is similar to the waves in the ocean, having apparent reality only while the water alone is real. Individual Atman can be compared to the space in a jar and the Absolute Being to universal space. Freedom consists in realising the oneness of the individual with the Absolute. The Brahmam as Existence, Consciousness and Bliss (Sat-Chit-Ananda) is the Atman. All types of physical and mental appearances are changeable; the only unchangeable truth underlying them is Atman or Self.

The self cannot be known by means of thought. Shankaracharya does not deny the extra-mental objectivity but completely denies their ultimate reality. Atman is always one though the mental states may be two or more. The Reality is Pure Consciousness, and the rest is super-imposition due to Maya. We cannot think that 'I am not existent'. Atman cannot be doubted since it is 'the very essence of him who doubts it'. Vachaspati Misra (a ninth or tenth century scholar on Advaita Vedanta tradition), while talking about consciousness of the Self, says,

> *"No one doubts 'am I'? Or 'am not I'?' The self affirmation 'I am' comes before everything else, stands above and beyond all arguments. No proof can make it stronger, again no disproof found them on 'I am'"* (Besant, 1973, p. 4).

In other words, Atman is 'Svatah-siddha' (self-evident) which is the basis of all kinds of knowledge, pre-suppositions and proofs, and hence any external proof is superfluous. In fact, the very first principle of Shankaracharya's philosophy is that the existence of the self cannot be doubted. Even if we declare the whole world to be a mere void, this void presupposes an observer to witness the void. The Atman uses the body at the experimental level and the mind as instruments, and each function and faculty appears only on the basis of the Atman.

Here we can see the parallel western thought in the philosophical statement of René Descartes (a French philosopher, mathematician, and scientist, called the father of modern western philosophy) "**Cogito, ergo sum**" (I think, therefore I am). I cannot exist without being conscious of my own existence. Existence cannot be doubted, as it is immediately known.

According to Vachaspati, the fundamental nature of the Self is eternal, all-pervading and devoid of any empirical activity (Kriya). So, it must be self-revealed because it is impossible for an infinite entity to depend on anything for its revelation. (Hasurkar, 1958, p. 154). Light manifests itself without being manifested by another light; similarly, the Self manifests itself without being manifested by other. Vachaspati holds the view that it is through purified intellect the Self reveals its real nature, but due to the superimposition of the qualities of the not-Self, the pure Self becomes polluted and not-transparent. Shankaracharya stated in Atma Bodha,

> "*parichhinna ivdjnanattannase sati kevalah*
> *svayam prakasate hyatman meghapayensumaniva*"
> (Atma Bodha: Mantra no. 4).
> [The Atman appears to be finite because of ignorance. When ignorance is destroyed the Atman, which does not admit of any multiplicity, truly reveals itself by itself like the Sun when the clouds pass away.]

The bottom line of Advaita Vedanta Philosophy is that the sense organs and the neural processes of the body which are in space and time cannot produce consciousness. Human brain is "*just a collection of fat and protein made of eighty-five percent water squeezed into the dark enclosure of the skull*". (Hogan, 2008, p. 1). In medical science we have enough evidence for the suggestion that the mind and memory function perfectly well when half of the brain is removed or the brain doesn't develop fully. Atman is at once universal and infinite, and various attributes to the Atman are truth, independence and omnipresence. Other events, mental or physical, are all passing appearances.

1.2.2: Understanding consciousness from the Bhagavad Gita

In the two epics (Ramayan and Mahabharat), we have a more realistic survey of man in action than in the Vedas and the Upanishads. The Bhagavad Gita is a part of Mahabharat. The concept of the consciousness in the Bhagavad Gita is very similar to that of the Upanishads. Only difference is, this issue is powerfully dramatised, and the ethical values are prominent and straightforward.

The Bhagavad Gita provides a lot of insight into the nature of Atman and its liberation from the mortal world. This scripture dwells upon various subjects like death, release of the Atman from the body, ascent to the higher worlds, reincarnation and Karma, Atman's relationship with God and so on. In the following Shlokas it is most emphatically stressed when Lord Krishna tells Arjun that the Atman is immortal.

"*avināśhi tu tadviddhi **yena sarvam idaṁ tatam***
vināśham avyayasyāsya na kaśhchit kartum arhati"
(Bhagavad Gita: 2.17).
[Know 'That' (Atman) to be indestructible, by whom all this is pervaded. None can cause the destruction of 'That', the Imperishable.]

The Atman – 'That' – which pervades the entire body – "*yena sarvam idham thatham* – is indestructible. The Atman is 'avinashi' (indestructible) and 'avyaya' (immutable). Therefore, Atman can neither be killed nor it can kill. It is a single individual entity.

"*antavanta ime dehā nityasyoktāḥ śharīriṇaḥ*
anāśhino 'prameyasya tasmād yudhyasva bhārata"
(Bhagavad Gita: 2.18).
[Only the material body is perishable; the embodied Atman within is indestructible, immeasurable, and eternal. Therefore, fight, O descendent of Bharat.]

The body is perishing every day, and the process of such destruction cannot be stopped. Whether Arjun fights or withdraws from the war, the imperishable cannot be destroyed and the perishable cannot be saved from destruction. Sage Narad instructed Yudhisthira along similar lines,

"*yan manyase dhruvaṁ lokam adhruvaṁ vā na chobhayam*
sarvathā na hi śhochyās te snehād anyatra mohajāt"
(Bhagavad Purana: 1.13.44).
[O King, in all circumstances, whether you consider the Atman to be an eternal principle, or the material body to be perishable, or everything to exist in the impersonal Absolute Truth, or everything to be an inexplicable combination of matter and spirit, feelings of separation are due only to illusory affection and nothing more.]

Atman is eternal, and pervades everywhere. Atman is unconditioned by anything other than itself. There cannot be any place or period of time where the Atman was not there before.

"*nainaṁ chhindanti śhastrāṇi nainaṁ dahati pāvakaḥ*
na chainaṁ kledayantyāpo na śhoṣhayati mārutaḥ"
(Bhagavad Gita: 2.23).
[Weapons cannot cut It, fire cannot burn It, water cannot wet It, wind cannot dry It.]

"*achchhedyo 'yam adāhyo 'yam akledyo 'śhoṣhya eva cha*
nityaḥ sarva-gataḥ sthāṇur achalo 'yaṁ sanātanaḥ"
(Bhagavad Gita: 2.24).

[This Atman cannot be cut, burnt, wetted or dried up. It is eternal, all-pervading, stable, ancient and immovable.]

Being subtler than the material energy, the Atman is also inconceivable to our intellect. The material intellect can only comprehend material concepts, but can never reach the divine Atman by the power of its contemplation.

"*avyakto 'yam achintyo 'yam avikāryo 'yam uchyate*
tasmādevaṁ viditvainaṁ nānuśhochitum arhasi"
(Bhagavad Gita: 2.25).
[The Atman is unmanifest, unthinkable and unchangeable. Therefore, knowing it to be as such, you should not grieve.]

"*dehī nityam avadhyo 'yaṁ dehe sarvasya bhārata*
tasmāt sarvāṇi bhūtāni na tvaṁ śhochitum arhasi"
(Bhagavad Gita: 2.30).
[This Atman, the indweller in the body of everyone, is always indestructible.]

"*anāditvān nirguṇatvāt paramātmāyam avyayaḥ*
śharīra-stho 'pi kaunteya na karoti na lipyate"
(Bhagavad Gita: 13.32).
[The Super Consciousness is imperishable, without beginning, and devoid of any material qualities, O son of Kunti. Although situated within the body, It neither acts, nor is It tainted by material energy.]

"*yathā sarva-gataṁ saukṣhmyād ākāśhaṁ nopalipyate*
sarvatrāvasthito dehe tathātmā nopalipyate" (Bhagavad Gita: 13.33).
[As the all-pervading ether is not tainted because of its subtlety, so too the Atman that is present in every body does not suffer any taint.]

He who thinks 'I slay' or 'I am slain' really does not comprehend the true nature of the Atman. The indestructible Atman exists in all periods of time – past, present and future. It is the existence itself. The agent of slaying is the 'Ahamkara' (ego) and the object of slaying is the 'Sharira' (body).

"*ya enaṁ vetti hantāraṁ yaśh chainaṁ manyate hatam*
ubhau tau na vijānīto nāyaṁ hanti na hanyate" (Bhagavad Gita: 2.19).
[He who looks on the Self to be the slayer and he who looks on the Self as the slain – neither of them apprehends correctly. The Self neither slays nor is slain.]

"*na jāyate mriyate vā kadāchin*
nāyaṁ bhūtvā bhavitā vā na bhūyaḥ

ajo nityaḥ śhāśhvato 'yaṁ purāṇo
na hanyate hanyamāne śharīre" (Bhagavad Gita: 2.20).
[The Atman is neither born, nor does it ever die; nor having once existed, does it ever cease to be. The Atman is without birth, eternal, immortal, and ageless. **It is not destroyed when the body is destroyed**.]

"*vedāvināśhinaṁ nityaṁ ya enam ajam avyayam*
kathaṁ sa puruṣhaḥ pārtha kaṁ ghātayati hanti kam"
(Bhagavad Gita: 2.21).
[O Partha, how can one who knows the Atman to be imperishable, eternal, unborn, and immutable kill anyone or cause anyone to kill?]

In all the above Shlokas, Lord Krishna explains the nature of immortal Atman in a variety of ways giving several illustrations so that anyone can grasp the underlying idea. Six kinds of modification – birth, subsistence, growth, transformation, decay and death – are inherent in every living being, but absent in the Atman. This concept has been repeatedly emphasised in the Vedas. The Katha Upanishad contains two similar passages.

"*na jāyate mriyate vā vipaśhchin nāyaṁ kutaśhchin na babhūva kaśhchit*
ajo nityaḥ śhāśhvato 'yaṁ purāṇo ***na hanyate hanyamāne śharīre***"
(Katha Upanishad: 1.2.18).
[The Atman is not born, nor does it die; it did not spring from something, and nothing sprang from it. It is unborn, eternal, immortal, and ageless. **It is not destroyed when the body is destroyed.**]

"*hantā cenmanyate hantu hataścenmanyate hataṃ*
ubhau tau na vijānīto nāya hanti na hanyate"
(Katha Upanishad: 1.2.19).
[The slayer who thinks of slaying this and the slain who thinks this slain, both these do not know. This slays not, nor is slain.]

Brahmam is the macrocosm while Atman is the microcosm of the same Reality. They both exhibit the same Absoluteness. Hence the Atman is superior to everything else in the human being.

"*indriyāṇi parāṇyāhur indriyebhyaḥ paraṁ manaḥ*
manasas tu parā buddhir yo buddheḥ paratas tu saḥ"
(Bhagavad Gita: 3.42).
[The senses are superior to the gross body, and superior to the senses is the mind. Beyond the mind is the intellect, and even beyond the intellect is the Atman.]

The embodied Atman is caught in the trap of 'Samsara' (the causative world) through desires and attachment, whereas the liberated Atman with adequate spiritual effort and divine help is forever free from this control. At the time of death, the Atman leaves the body and goes to a higher world depending upon its Karma. Only the 'Seers of the truth' know what it does and where it stays in its liberated state. Even though the Atman is within everyone, people cannot feel its presence because they remain distracted by the activity of their senses and minds. If they succeed in withdrawing their senses and look inwards, they have a chance of coming into contact with it. Briefly, this is the concept of the consciousness we find in the Bhagavad Gita.

1.3: NDE, Consciousness and Advaita Vedanta Philosophy

In this scientific age, it seems death is no longer Shakespeare's undiscovered country, the one "*from whose bourn no traveller returns*" (Hamlet, act III, scene 1.13). With due respect to Shakespeare, travelers sometimes return back from the other side and tell us fascinating stories. These are collectively termed as Near-death experience (NDE). Thus, an NDE is an incomplete process of dying. Exceptional reports of NDEs go back to the dawn of history but modern medicine has democratised them. NDEs are mostly triggered by a life-threatening situation, under conditions of intense medical monitoring, and while these are happening, the electrical activity of the brain is entirely flat-lined. The experiencers often report a subsequently increased sense of spirituality, and a connection with their inner self and the world around them. Once thought to be rare, the NDEs have been estimated to occur to a third of people who came close to death.

The account of Pam Reynolds has been widely acclaimed by the researchers as the best instance they have in the literature on NDEs which came closest to providing solid, scientific evidence suggestive of the post-mortem survival of consciousness. A weakness in the walls of two arteries in her brain had caused the arteries to swell, and rupture was considered imminent. Anesthesia was induced, and soon her NDE began with the buzzing noise of the bone saw motor. She remembered seeing a lot of tools and instruments in the operating room when she was looking down.

After the operation, Pam was placed on cardiopulmonary bypass to quickly cool her core body temperature. As her temperature fell to sixty degrees F, her heart stopped, her EEG flattened into complete electro-cerebral silence, and her brainstem and cerebral hemispheres became unresponsive. The cardiopulmonary bypass machine turned off, and the blood drained from her head. In this critical condition she saw passing through a tunnel-like passage and heard her grandmother calling her. At the end of the passage, she saw an incredibly bright light. As she began to discern, she noticed different figures in the light. They were all covered with light as if they were light themselves, and had light permeating all around them. The figures began to form shapes soon and restricted Pam to go further though she wanted to go into the light.

According to the 'whole brain' definition (Uniform Determination of Death Act, 1981) of death, life ends with the "*cessation of all functions of the entire brain*". During Pam's surgery, her brain had been drained of blood and found 'dead' by all clinical tests of brain function. From a clinical perspective Pam was by all definition be dead. However, in her own words, "*[I was] the most aware that I think I have ever been in my life*".

Can science explain the Pam Reynolds case? Materialistic science cannot explain these otherworldly experiences because our knowledge of science is not enough to explain the laws of the Universe. Advaita Vedanta can explain NDE cases in a fine manner.

Researchers say that the near-death experiencers are accessing a dimension where the time-based and space-based constraints are transcended. Based on the evidence, this nonlocal consciousness has no biological basis. This is exactly what Advaita philosophy asserts that the unborn and undying Atman is the same as the underlying absolute reality of the whole Universe, which is called Brahmam. We are all one 'thing' and one awareness – Brahmam.

There are moments when we feel that we are 'one' with the Universe. This is something what we all want to explain but we cannot. This expression of cosmic unity is what we call love and sympathy, and it is the basis of all our ethics and morality. A person in his NDE experiences it in the most profound way. In NDE, people generally pass through a dark tunnel, and then emerge from the tunnel to a brilliant light, brighter than any they had encountered before. This, as they describe, is an 'infinitely loving' being of light. The light is incredibly bright, like sitting in the middle of a light bulb. Pam Reynolds narrated,

> "*To me the Light doesn't need a word. So, if someone needs to call it Buddha or Jesus or God, I would say 'yes', but for me, it was love. I knew that I was forgiven for anything and everything. I was loved and I knew that would never, ever change. Bliss is a word that doesn't even come close to describing that moment.*" (Sharp, 1995, p. 163).

> "*Very rapidly I was enveloped within this most divine, living, golden-white light, my HOME. The joy, bliss, humility, and awe were beyond human capability to bear. The LIGHT was an infinite, loving, accepting BEING without form. IT had personality. IT communicated with me telepathically. IT was pure TRUTH.*
>
> *I was the LIGHT and the LIGHT was me. I was still a unique, separate, point of consciousness with the same sense of humor and*

> *awareness that I had always had, but the paradox is that I was MORE. I had become homogeneous with the LIGHT. I was all love, wisdom, truth, peace, joy, for all eternity. Human words fail to express this experience. Not only was the message of my true nature conveyed to me telepathically, but I experienced the SPIRIT of the message – I felt IT with every speck of my being. There was absolutely no possibility of hiding, distorting information, or lying in communicating with the LIGHT. I fell madly in love with the SPIRIT OF TRUTH! There was no concept of space or time in the GREATER REALITY. All takes place or exists in the ETERNAL NOW. That is my last conscious memory of the experience.*" (Atwater, 2007, pp. 27-28).

All that exists in the afterlife seems to exist within this 'all-ness', this oneness, as if there is only 'One Mind', yet many thinkers. A favourite phrase the near-death experiencers come to use is – **We are one with 'The One' who teaches us that a moment taken to show another human being selfless and unconditional love without thought of reward and recognition can give incredible meaning to our lives.** It is more fulfilling than becoming the President of a state or becoming a billionaire. Likewise, moments that are simply spent on oneself, without a thought of service to another or without a thought of bringing something good into the world are as if they never existed. Our every action and every choice are incredibly powerful and significant. This is also the very basic understanding of the law of Karma.

This kind of love and the deep feeling of oneness with the Universe are summed up in the Vedanta Philosophy by the celebrated aphorism **Tat Tvam Asi** – You Are That! All that exists is seen to exist within this 'all-ness', this oneness, because every living creature is an extension of 'The Divine'.

Ruth Montgomery (1913 - 2001), a journalist by profession, had the gift of 'automatic writing' (trance typewriting) by which she could communicate with various deceased personalities. She was able to channel a great deal of information from the other side specifically from her deceased friend the famous spiritualist and medium, Arthur Ford. Montgomery received amazing information regarding Karma, reincarnation, soul realm, Maya, time and space delusion from the other side and documented these revelations in a series of books.

> "***We are as much God as God is part of us.... For if each of us is God, then taken together we are God****; and since it takes all of us to make a complete God, we know that other person is as necessary to us and to the common welfare as we ourselves. Therefore, it behooves each of us*

to concern ourselves mightily with others, for they are as necessary to us as our own arms and legs and eyes and ears.

Each of us is incomplete without the totality of humanity, both living and dead. Don't forget that ***this all-for-one-and-one-for-all applies equally to the living and so-called dead, for it is the totality that makes us the whole of the Universal Spirit which we want to call God.*** *The clergy may not like this concept, but....*" (Montgomery, 1972, pp. 12-13).

In sum, anyone who had undergone an NDE first and foremost talk about 'God'. This is their first discovery that God exists. Their next discovery is what is deep-rooted in Advaita Vedanta Philosophy that we, as souls, are extensions from the same source unified and one. We are of 'The One' with the same creative potential in consciousness as our creator. (Atwater, 1999a, p. 165). Every sentient being is a co-creator of the Universe with the Divine because the Atman is actually identical to Brahmam. The power which is making billions of stars go around galactic centres, within billions of such galaxies... the same power is within us, albeit in miniature, in a very different form. And when we understand this, we find that the entire energy of the Cosmos – and of the sacred, of the absolute – is ours. Carl Gustav Jung writes that following discovery came to him while meditating alone amidst the rampant natural life at Africa.

"*...man is indispensable for the completion of creation, that in fact he himself is the second creator of the world, who alone has given to the world its objective existence.*" (Papadopoulos, 1992, p. 237).

NDEs reflect what quantum physics and Vedanta Philosophy seek to uncover and explain. Wave-particle duality is the concept in quantum physics that every particle or quantum entity may be described as either a particle or a wave, and both experiments are true. During life, our consciousness has an aspect of particles, but when we die our consciousness will no longer have an aspect of particles, but only an eternal aspect of waves. Even after almost fifty years of research into NDE phenomena, there is no final opinion among the scientific community with regard to its interpretation. It is high time they read and understand the Advaita Vedanta Philosophy.

1.4: Conclusion

"*Consciousness is that in which all experience appears, it is that with which all experience is known and it is that out of which all experience is made.*"

Rupert Spira

"***We are eternal spiritual beings having a physical experience.***"
Craig Hogan

Quantum physics is inevitably converging towards Advaita Vedanta. By following the revolutionary scientific contributions to the theory of Einstein's relativity and quantum physics many scholars have been inspired to discover striking parallels between the worldviews of Vedanta and modern science.

Schrödinger (1961) claims that the Vedic slogan "All in One and One in All" (Isa Upanishad: Mantra no. 6) was an idea that led him to the creation of quantum physics. However, even before Schrödinger, the idealist philosophical tradition in Europe had long been moulded by Vedic ideas. Many parts of the Vedic literature are still not properly understood although considerable progress has recently taken place. Undoubtedly, with advent of quantum physics many questions have been successfully answered, but with every answer many new questions come up. And thus, the search for answers doesn't seem to end. Some of the questions cannot and will not be answered by science because they are outside the scope of science. This is the reason many famous quantum physicists are avid readers of various Dharmic scriptures, mainly the Upanishads. Neils Bohr commented, "*I go into the Upanishads to ask questions.*" (Prothero, 2010, p. 168). The Upanishads are the most remarkable spiritual documents of all time. Arthur Schopenhauer declared,

> "*In the whole world there is no study so beneficial and so elevating as that of the Upanishads. It has been the solace of my life – it will be the solace of my death.*" (Durant, 1942, p. 410).

Conventional science still does not accept the presence of timeless and spaceless soul but quantum physics does. Hence we call it the 'Quantum Consciousness' or 'Quantum Soul'. From both scientific and Dharmic standpoint, the Quantum Soul or Atman is a life force that connects to everything that exist in the Universe from distant stars and galaxies to microscopic atoms within our body. The fourth Mantra of the Isa Upanishad explains this in a very straightforward manner.

> "*anejad ekaṃ manaso javīyo nainaddevā āpnuvanpūrvamarṣat*
> *taddhāvato'nyānatyeti tiṣṭhat tasminn apo mātariśvā dadhāti*"
> [Unmoving, one (and speedier than the mind), the senses reach it never, (for) it (Self) goes before. Standing, it outstrips others that run. In virtue of it, does 'mātarisvā' (He who moves) allot functions (separately to all).]

John E. Mack, Professor of Psychiatry and Pulitzer Prize-winning author pointed out that, both modern physics and depth psychology are revealing to us a Universe where "*all that we can perceive around us is connected by resonances, both physical and non-physical...*" (Weiss, 2004, p. 17). The moment we realise the Divine Self within us, we understand that the realm of the same Atman extends to the sun, moon, stars, and even to the most distant planets – the light from which takes billions of years to reach us. Physicist and astronomer Victor J. Stenger commented,

> "*The physical Universe is the product of* ***a cosmic mind to which the human mind is linked.*** *This interpretation has provided an ostensibly scientific basis for various mind-over-matter claims, from ESP to alternative medicine.*" (Oakley, 2011, p. 93).

The notion of Atman – "*a cosmic mind to which the human mind is linked*" – is called 'monism'. The monistic thinkers of the present age, like Ernst Haeckel and others, admit this one eternal substance as the source of mind, matter and all forces. Some new age scientists and modern mystical literature writers call it 'Quantum Mysticism' (Leane, 2007, p. 33). Swami Abhedananda (1905, pp. 25, 40) commented that the Vedanta Philosophy repeatedly says that,

> "*From that infinite substance or Brahmam, the Absolute Being, have evolved life-force or Prana, mind, all the mental activities, and the sense powers, which are included in the meaning of the term 'spirit' or subject on the one hand, and, on the other, space or ether, and all gaseous, liquid and solid objects which are understood by matter!*"
>
> "*Wherever there is existence, whether on the physical or mental plane, there is also the manifestation of this Divine Self.*"
>
> "*akṣharaṁ brahma paramaṁ svabhāvo 'dhyātmam uchyate*
> *bhūta-bhāvodbhava-karo visargaḥ karma-sanjñitaḥ*"
> (Bhagavad Gita: 8.3).
> [Brahmam is the Imperishable, the Supreme. **Dwelling in each body, Brahmam is called the individual Atman.** The offering of the sacrifice, which brings into existence all beings and supports them, is called action.]
>
> "*kathyate jīva nāṁnaitac cittaṁ pratanuvāsanaṁ*
> *śānta deha camatkāraṁ jīvaṁ viddhi kramāt paraṁ*"
> (Yoga-Vasistha: 3.91.23).
> [That individualised consciousness itself is known as the jiva, or the individual Atman – when the potentialities are in an extremely subtle state. And when all this jugglery of the jiva ceases – **that itself shines as the Supreme Being.**]

If a light is enclosed within a semi-transparent globe, it reveals the globe. If the globe is removed the light reveals itself. Likewise, after bodily death the Atman exists in a state of full consciousness and continues evolving towards truth with a new identity. The Atman obeys the laws of the astral world, and the rules by which success is measured in the next world are quite different from the rules of materialistic world.

Scientists focused solely on matter and energy cannot understand the Quantum Consciousness – it's beyond their reach because they are not open to studying it. The Bhagavad Gita knows the limitations of human mind to gauge the true nature of the Atman.

> "*āśhcharya-vat paśhyati kaśhchid enan āśhcharya-vad vadati tathaiva chānyaḥ*
> *āśhcharya-vach chainam anyaḥ śhṛiṇoti śhrutvāpyenaṁ* ***veda na chaiva kaśhchit***" (Bhagavad Gita: 2.29).
> [Some look on the Self as a wonder, some speak of It as a wonder, some hear of It as a wonder, while others even after hearing **do not understand It at all**.]

This Shloka explains why the learned professors of materialistic science are in a dilemma to understand quantum physics – "*If you are not completely confused by quantum mechanics, you do not understand it.*" (John Wheeler), "*I think I can safely say that nobody understands quantum mechanics. If you think you understand quantum mechanics, you don't understand quantum mechanics.*" (Richard Feynman) and "*Quantum mechanics makes absolutely no sense.*" (Roger Penrose).

> "*prajñāvānapi paṇḍito'pi caturo'pyatyantasūkṣmātmadṛg*
> *vyālīḍhastamasā na vetti bahudhā saṃbodhito'pi sphuṭam*
> *bhrāntyāropitameva sādhu kalayatyālambate tadguṇān*
> *hantāsau prabalā durantatamasaḥ śaktirmahatyāvṛtiḥ*"
> (Vivekachudamani: Shloka no. 114).
> [Even the wise and the learned, and those who are expert in the understanding of the supremely subtle meaning of the scriptures, are overpowered by ignorance and cannot comprehend Truth, even though it is clearly explained in various ways. They consider as real what is simply superimposed by delusion and attach themselves to its effects. Alas! How powerful is the great veiling power of dreadful ignorance!]

Quantum theory still isn't taught in high schools because who can teach what makes no sense? But if we wait to use quantum physics until we understand it, then we would be stuck back in the 1940's. The quantum world is definitely a weird one, but we do recognise the significance and potential it has to help transform our world. In the next chapter I will provide more explanations from the ancient Dharmic scriptures which will dispel many doubts of the quantum physics. The whole of our physical existence is really a mystery because we live in a MAYA world.

CHAPTER - 2

Quantum Physics and the doctrine of MAYA (Cosmic Illusion)

"*As the world is perceived through the images formed and stored in the minds of individuals, the question is whether these images, which are just pictorial representations of objects and not the actual objects, truly represent reality and how they influence the perception and interpretation of reality.*"

Ben G. Yacobi

"*Along with philosophers' reduction of all objective reality to a shadow world of perceptions, scientists have become aware of the alarming limitation of man's senses.*"

Lincoln Barnett

Many of us have seen the movie 'The Matrix' which had popularised the idea that we may be living in a virtual reality. In this fictitious movie people think they are living in a modern city but they are actually bodies stored in vats wired to a central computer that immerses them in a world of illusion. This work of fiction may contain a core of truth – one's understanding of reality depends solely on their subjective feelings, and we cannot confirm the actual existence of anything except our consciousness. Could we already be living in a virtual reality? If so, what is the 'real' reality? Investigation into this phenomenon has only recently been explored by quantum theory and to some extent by the science of consciousness. The ancient texts of Upanishads had once strongly pursued this investigation. One concept that appears to unite the ancient monistic philosophy of the Upanishads and quantum theory is the phenomenon of filtration – cognitive filtration for the Upanishads and quantum filtration for physics.

2.1: Introduction

"*Our observable reality is merely the shadow play of an underlying truth.*"

Plato

"*Reality is merely an illusion, although a very persistent one.*"

Albert Einstein

We take our world to be an objective reality that exists in and of itself. An objective reality should just 'be' and unchanged in space and time, but Einstein's relativity theory had proved that space contracts and time dilates. The sun bends light by curving the space around it. The earth's gravity slows down time and atomic clocks tick faster on tall buildings than they do on the ground. Movement slows down time, so an atomic clock on an aircraft ticks slower than a synchronised one on the ground, and moving objects become heavier with speed as well. In our world, space, time and mass are not constant. How can a space that defines the term 'expand', itself expand? How can a time that defines all change, itself change? An objective reality should not behave this way.

Objective things should just inherently exist, but double-slit experiment shows that electrons behave in various physically impossible ways. This is like a cop detected a car doing 200 mph on the expressway, but not being able to locate it to give chase. String theory has six extra dimensions curled up and hidden from view. In M-theory (a variant of String theory), the Universe floats on a fifth dimension "brane" (short for 'membrane') we can't see (Gribbin, 2000, pp. 177-80). If an electron can exist as a quantum wave unless observed, it is logical that the physical world is just another view – an unreal view – generated on demand by a quantum world. Fairytale physics cannot describe objective reality.

In the past, the scientists thought that atoms were unbreakable, so the hydrogen atom was considered the smallest particle. But at the beginning of the twentieth century, it was discovered that atoms are made up of protons, neutrons and electrons. The electron is indivisible and fundamental, but protons and neutrons appear to be built out of much smaller particles called quarks. Quarks are believed to be made of vibrating loops of energy, i.e., 'strings' of light energy. If we compare an atom to the whole solar system, the vibratory strings would only have the size of a small electric bulb. The living body of a giant animal, or a bacterium, or a virus, or a lifeless rock – all is nothing more than vibrating strings of energy.

Cosmologists suggest that the entire physical Universe just popped up out of nothing about 13.5 billion years ago. How did the entire Universe come from nothing? If matter just popped out of space, what did space pop out of ? A Universe that began must be dependent, and therefore it is a valid question – what it depends on? If at the big bang the Universe started from a dimensionless point, and if our time and space were created, then how the space started and time began? How the Universe started expanding when the space was 'zero'? A world of only objects has no basis for movement in 'zero' space. Point particles with no extent cannot have mass. A trillion numbers of point particles of no extent take up no more space than one. Then how do extended objects form? Would space still be there if every physical particle in the Universe disappears? What exactly do space and time do? What is there at the 'edge' of the space? Could space and time suddenly be 'stopped' at any moment? Does multiverse of parallel worlds exist? Is the three-dimensional world that surrounds us a three-dimensional surface of a higher dimensional world? Today, there are many questions like these which do not belong to philosophy alone but science also.

Doubting the age-old ideas of physical reality is not denying science but engages its very spirit of inquiry. The questions may be beyond the scope of Newtonian science but the theory is not as it is about our world. In ancient Dharmic scriptures this is called 'Maya' whose mystery I will unveil here. In this chapter, I have restricted my inquiry to the Vedic literature, especially the Upanishads, Yoga-Vasistha, Bhagavad Gita, Patanjali's Yoga Sutras and have carried my investigation down to Adi Shankaracharya.

2.2: The concept of MAYA in Sanatan Dharma

"*The whole Cosmos is a projected thought of the Creator.*"

Yogi Mahavatar Babaji

"ātmā vā idameka evāgra āsīnnānyatkiṃcana miṣat
sa īkṣata lokānnu sṛjā iti" (Aitareya Upanishad: 1.1.1).
[The self, indeed, is this, one only, the first; no other blinking one whatsoever was present. He thought, 'Now let me send out the worlds'.]

The term 'Maya' is one of the most important words in the history of Indian Dharmic thought. Etymologically the term 'Maya' is derived from the Sanskrit verbal root 'ma' which means measure, mere out, arrange, build, form, make etc. Hence, the literal meaning of Maya is that which measures, arranges, forms, builds, makes. The English word 'magic' is derived from the word Maya. The word Maya, in the sense of illusion, occurs for the first time in the Svetasvatara Upanishad.

"*chandāṁsi yajñāḥ kratavo vratāni bhūtaṁ bhavyaṁ yacca vedā vadanti*
asmānmāyī sṛjate viśvametattasmiṁścānyo māyayā sanniruddhaḥ"
(Svetasvatara Upanishad: 4.09).

[The Lord of Maya projects the Vedas, sacrifices, spiritual practices, past and future, religious observances, all that the Vedas declare, and the whole world including ourselves. The other (Jivatman) again is bound by Maya in this (world).]

"*māyāṁ tu prakṛtiṁ vidyānmāyinaṁ ca maheśvaram*
tasyāvayavabhūtaistu vyāptaṁ sarvamidaṁ jagat"
(Svetasvatara Upanishad: 4.10).
[Know then that the Nature is Maya, and that the great God is the Lord of Maya. The whole world is filled with beings who form His parts.]

Life is an auditorium, Maya produces a play, an enchantment and spell in which we are not the spectators but the unsuspecting puppets. To advance from puppets to conscious actors requires that we understand how our mind is working. Maya is the illusive power of Brahmam.

"*prapañco yadi vidyeta nivarteta na saṃśayaḥ*
māyāmātramidaṃ dvaitamadvaitaṃ paramārthataḥ"
(Mandukya Upanishad: 1.17).
[If the perceived manifold were real then certainly it would disappear. This duality (that is cognised) is mere illusion (Maya). **Non-duality is (alone) the Supreme Reality.**]

We live our lives believing that we are special, unique and important individuals. We think we control the world but the exact opposite is the truth. The sun rises, the sun sets – it's impossible to hold onto the day or night. The average physical human body is a group of over sixty trillion living cells that do what they do by themselves. Every second, trillions of things are happening inside our bodies that keep us alive, and we have no control over it. Blood is being pumped, cells are being created, hormones distributed, the nails and hair grow without our authorisation. An average size and mass of a human body could contain at most about 300 billion billion billion billion (four times) megabytes of information (Tipler, 1994, p. 407). It means, a trillion things out of our control have to happen just for us to take a single breath, and we are not even aware that it is happening right now. Hence, control is an illusion, and our life is full of contradictions. There are contradictions in knowledge, thought, relationships, in our search for God, and above all there are self-contradictions. Though we are truth-seekers, when we take few sincere steps an extremely determined and strong wall stands in front of us which we cannot pass. This is because we cannot go beyond our intellect.

"*icchā-dveṣa-samutthena dvandva-mohena bhārata*
***sarva-bhūtāni sammohaṃ sarge yānti** parantapa*"
(Bhagavad Gita: 7.27).

[O scion of Bharata, O Parantapa, **all living entities are born into delusion**, bewildered by dualities arisen from desire and hate.]

Every child is a born optimist. As he grows, he becomes more optimistic. He does not think much about death. Then old age comes, the life becomes a mass of ruins, and he becomes a pessimist. Thus, we go from one extreme to another without knowing where we are going. All our progress, our wealth, beauty, power, ego, luxuries, status, knowledge have only one end – Death. None can stem the tide; none can hold it back for a second. Yet this tremendous clinging to life exists. Somehow, we don't know why we cling to life, but we cannot give it up.

In the Mahabharat once a question was asked to King Yudhisthira, "What is the most wonderful thing on earth?" The king replied that everyday people are dying around us, yet men think they will never die. The exact Sanskrit words are,

"*ahany ahani bhutani*
gacchantiha yamalayam
sesah sthavaram icchanti
kim ascaryam atah param" (Mahabharat: Vana-parva 313.116).

[At every moment countless numbers of living entities are being dragged to the court of Yamaraja (the God of Death). But those who are remaining here are thinking that they will live forever. **What could be more amazing than this?**]

Death cannot be avoided because it is all-powerful – "*mṛtyuḥ sarva-haraś cāham*" (Bhagavad Gita: 10.34), means, I am all-devouring death. In spite of this 'Dhruvsatya' (the truth that is as immovable and eternal as the position of the polestar), our mind is not capable to conceive our own annihilation. Even to imagine my own annihilation I shall have to stand by and look on as a witness. This serious self-contradiction is caused by Maya.

The forces of affection and love play through us resulting in attachments and entanglements. A mother is nursing her child with great care. All her soul, life, happiness is in that child. The child grows, becomes a man and marries a selfish woman. Under the spell of this evil woman, he becomes brutal. He beats his mother every day and denies her food. The helpless mother still clings to her child, and when her reason awakes, she covers it up with the idea of love. She lives in bondage which she cannot shake off. She is entangled in the web of Maya. What is the way out? Bhagavad Gita provides the answer.

"*daivī hy eṣā guṇamayī mama māyā duratyayā*
mām eva ye prapadyante māyām etāṃ taranti te"
(Bhagavad Gita: 7.14).

[Truly, this divine illusion of Mine (Maya), consisting of the gunas, is hard to overcome. **But those who take refuge in Me (The Supreme Lord) alone shall cross over this illusion**.]

These tremendous contradictions in our intellect and knowledge are the facts of life which face us on all sides. There are objections against this view, but remarkably, the objections generally come from people who possess many of the good things of the life!

The amount of information in the visible Universe is at the most 10^{116} megabytes (Tipler, 1994, p. 221). Every waking second, 400 billion bits of information approach the brain through sensory input channels, but the brain processes only 2,000 of these bits per second (Willis, 2007, p. 66). Since the brain can never catch up, how much of reality is completely unknown or inaccessible to human reason and understanding? Moreover, no two minds pick up the same 2,000 bits. When two persons have observed the same exact event by their five senses, the descriptions do not exactly match to one another. Also, we do not just perceive the bits. The mind plays a trick with us – it takes the bits, passes them through our past memories of those bits, and subconsciously tells us how to think and how to feel about what we observe as per one's needs and desires. Sage Patanjali was aware of this fact.

"*vastu samye chitta bhedat tayoh vibhaktah panthah*"
(Yoga Sutras: 4.15).
[Although the same objects may be perceived by different minds, they are perceived in different ways, because those minds manifested differently.]

The minds get different impressions from the same object because they have followed different paths in their karmic evolution. Hence the 'Vrtti' (Sanskrit word – 'Vrt' means 'to exist', and 'Vrtti' is a way of existing) is different. When the 'Vrtti' of various minds have been eliminated, the mind becomes one with the object.

I pick up a book from the table. But, is this book real? Everyone will reply in the affirmative because the object is within our five sensory perceptions. But the real answer may be no because even the things we can sense may have no substance at all. Atoms are 99.9999 percent empty space (Rutherford's nuclear model of atom). The matter, the 'stuff' we seem to touch and feel, is actually mostly empty space. Our senses do deceive us.

"*dṛśyātyantābhāvabodhaṃ vinā tannānubhūyate*
kadācitkenacinnāma svabodho'nviṣyatāmataḥ"
(Yoga-Vasistha: 1.3.3).

[All visible objects are absolute negation; we have no idea of them save from sensation. Inquire into these apprehensions, and you will never find them as real.]

Our brains cannot accurately tell what is real or not real. As example, schizophrenia – the visions and sounds schizophrenic patients 'see' and 'hear' are just as real to them as this book you are reading, or the chair on which you now sit. The brain has the capacity to construct a spatio-temporal reality (existing in both space and time) as real as the one you are experiencing now. Another example is when we are dreaming. If I am a non-swimmer, and in my dream I find myself in the ocean I am scared. This is because, in that particular moment my brain tells me that the ocean is real, the water is real, and my life is in grave danger. It means, my body is like a robot that is controlled by the mind. What the mind tells the robot is real, the robot will experience. The illusion was in the mind, and bodily sensation was produced to support the illusion. Although nothing was real, my body (robot) thought it was.

Every physician knows that the placebo effect is very useful when faith in 'belief-of-cure' is heightened. But how the healing takes place? Healing really begins with the mind, and the human body just obeys the mind like a robot.

If the brain can generate a world and populate that world with various objects and the expressions of other seemingly human and non-human personalities, then how can we know whether or not our waking worlds are merely strange lucid dreams? What if the reality as we know it exists only inside a dream then may be our minds could be confused by various deceptions? René Descartes argues that if we cannot even tell for sure whether we are dreaming, then how can we know for certain any truth about the world in which we seem to live? How can we know whether or not other people are merely figments of our imaginations? Where is the certainty that we living beings are not in a 'dream condition' produced by the illusion of some higher and stronger mental power? If so, all of our activities, emotions, fears etc., are unreal, and at the moment of our death we actually wake up from our dreams and experience the 'reality'. Life is as unreal as a bad or pleasant dream.

"*jagadbhramo'yaṃ dṛśyo'pi nāstyevetyanubhūyate*
varṇo vyomna ivākhedādvicāreṇāmunā'nagha"
(Yoga-Vasistha: 1.3.5).

[The conception of this world is a mistake, and though we actually see it, it is never in existence. It appears in the same light, O sinless Sage, as the variegated colours in the sky.]

This is the mysterious nature of reality. In our struggle we are not sure whether we arrive at a deeper understanding of reality or just move from one illusion to another. Therefore, Maya is simply a statement of facts of the Universe as they exist – that the very basis of our being is contradiction, that everywhere we have to move through this tremendous contradiction. And as I have shown, the contradictions are not only mental or philosophical or argumentative, but Maya extends to our known physical world also. In fact, Maya is everywhere and all around us. It is terrible, yet we have to work through it.

Then what is reality? Is there a way out beyond Maya? When a person asks such questions, he is on his way to find the truth.

2.2.1: Understanding MAYA from Advaita Vedanta

"*brahmam satyam jagan mithya, jivo brahmaiva naparah*"
(Brahmajnanavali Mala: Mantra no. 20).
[Brahmam is real; the world is an illusory appearance; the so-called Atman is Brahmam itself, and no other.]

Adi Shankaracharya

"*Whenever I give a lecture on quantum physics, I feel as if I am talking on Vedanta.*"

Prof. Dr. Hans-Peter Dürr
(Quantum Physicist and Philosopher)

The theory of Maya forms one of the pillars upon which Vedanta rests. The scriptures support the view that the known world is an illusion created by God's 'play' (Lila). Adi Shankaracharya, the insightful Sage, commented,

"*samsaarah svapna-tulyah hi, raga-dvesha-aadi sankulah.*
swakaale satya-vat bhaati, prabodhe satiasatbhavet"
(Atma Bodha: Mantra no. 6).
[The world is truly like a dream only, full of its attachment and aversions, and so on. While the dream continues it appears to be real and when we awaken its unreality is seen.]

"*taavat satyam jagat bhaati, shuktikaa rajatam yathaa;*
yaavat na jnaayate, sarva adhishthaanam advayam"
(Atma Bodha: Mantra no. 7).
[As long as the world appears to be real, like the mother-of-pearl appears as silver; so long Brahmam cannot be realised, which is the substratum of all and one without a second.]

Maya, in the opinion of Shankaracharya, is "*mahādbhutā anirvacanīyarūpā*" (Vivekachudamani: Shloka no. 109) means, "It (Maya) is most wonderful and cannot be described in words". Maya is caused by 'Avidya' (ignorance). Once the ignorance is dispelled, we can achieve liberation through a practical realisation of the oneness of the Atman with the Brahmam. Shankaracharya compares Brahmam with a spider emitting its threads 'Maya Jaal' (Vedanta Sutra Bhasya: 1.4.26-27). Since Brahmam is beyond all changes or modifications, 'Pariṇama' (the evolution) is only a misleading appearance. Brahmam is thus likened to a magician (Mayavi) creating and maintaining the illusion of the world (Vedanta Sutra Bhasya: 2.1.1, 14). Brahmam, according to Shankaracharya, is beyond all attributes (Nirguna). But the magical creative power of Maya allows Brahmam to manifest Itself with qualities (Saguna) – "*the empirical existence of the Cosmos can be explained, as due to the creative activity of a Lord.*" (Smart, 1964, p. 100). We can know about Nirguna Brahmam and Its Absolute Oneness only by a higher sort of realised knowledge. I will discuss more on this in the next chapter.

Shankaracharya was preceded by Gaudapada who was a believer of very strict form of monism. He asserted categorically that the external world is unreal and the only reality being the Brahmam. Dreams are not much different from our wakeful experiences. The whole world is a vast dream-like illusion and nothing exists other than the Brahmam. Gaudapada denied the possibility of change or the validity of causation.

> "*na nirodho na cotpattirna baddho na ca sādhakaḥ*
> *na mumukṣurna vai mukta ityeṣā paramārthatā*"
> (Mandukya Karika: 2.32).
> [There is no destruction, no creation, none in bondage, none endeavouring (for release), none desirous of liberation, none liberated – this is the absolute truth.]

Shankaracharya took a less extreme position. Though he asserted the identity of the Brahmam with Atman, he did not accept the description of the world as a pure illusion. He explained the appearance of the world with an analogy. A person may mistake a rope for a snake. The snake is not there, but it is entirely not an illusion for there is a rope. The appearance of the snake lasts until we closely examine the rope. The world can be compared with the snake and Brahmam with the rope.

> "*rajju sarpavad aatmaanam jeevam jnatvaa bhayam vaheth*
> *naaham jeevah paraatmeti jnateschet nirbhayo bhaveth*"
> (Atma Bodha: Mantra no. 27).

[As one who regards a rope as a snake, so too one regarding oneself as an ego, is overcome by fear; I am not the ego, but the Supreme Self – if he realises this, he becomes fearless.]

The world is neither real nor quite unreal because it is an appearance based on the existence of the Brahmam. In the desert, water appears in the distance though it is really sand. As long as one is under the influence of Maya, one takes such visions to be real. A snake in the dream is also real, but as long as the dream lasts. In our worldly life, such experiences as birth-death, pain-pleasure, good-evil etc., – all seem so real, though the waking state and the dream state are both a mirage. The Self does not change. Sand is not changed into water, nor is the rope changed into a snake. This is all Maya. We are all born in Maya because ignorance surrounds us ever since we come to this world.

2.2.2: Understanding MAYA from Yoga-Vasistha

Yoga-Vasistha teachings are based on a philosophical foundation very similar to those found in Advaita Vedanta though Advaita has a slightly different way of looking at reality. It is the crest-jewel of all the works on Vedanta. Every advanced student of Vedanta keeps this book for constant study. Many teachings are notable for expounding the principles of Maya and Brahmam as well as the principles of non-duality. Sage Vasistha has seen the nature of reality. He recognises the false perceptions and worthless attractions of conventional life, yet is unable to live with quiescence of mind.

"*śrīvālmīkiruvāca*
bhramasya jāgatasyāsya jātasyākāśavarṇavat
apunaḥsmaraṇaṃ manye sādho vismaraṇaṃ varam"
(Yoga-Vasistha: 1.3.2).
[Valmiki replied: 'Know, holy Sage'! **This world-appearance is a confusion**, even as the blueness of the sky is an optical illusion. It is better not to let the mind dwell on it, but to ignore it.]

"*yataḥ sarvāṇi bhūtāni pratibhānti sthitāni ca*
yatrai 'vo paśamaṁ yānti tasmai satyātmane namaḥ"
(Yoga-Vasistha: Prayer before study).
[Salutations to that reality in which all the elements, and all the animate and inanimate beings shine as if they have an independent existence, and in which they exist for a time and into which they merge.]

The world is unreal to its core. Water in the mirage does not come into being and go out of existence. Similarly, this world does not come out of the absolute nor does it go anywhere.

"*anubhūtānyapīmāni jaganti vyomarūpiṇi*
pṛthvyādīni na santyeva svapnasaṃkalpayoriva"
(Yoga-Vasistha: 3.15.6).
[The ideal world is but an aerial castle, and this earth (with its contents), is as unreal as a dream, and as false as the objects of our desire.]

"*piṇḍagraho jagatyasminvijñānākāśarūpiṇi*
marunadyāṃ jalamiva na saṃbhavati kutracit
jagatyapiṇḍagrāhesminsaṃkalpanagaropame
marau saridivābhāti dṛśyatā bhrāntirūpiṇī"
(Yoga-Vasistha: 3.15.7-8).
[The earth appearing as solid, is in the light of philosophy, no better than the liquid water of a river, in the mirage of a sandy desert, and is never in existence
The illusive forms of the visibles, in this supposed substantial form of the world, resemble at least, but aerial castles and rivers in the mirage.]

"*tasmānna kiṃcidutpannaṃ jagadādīha dṛśyakam*
anākhyamanabhivyaktaṃ yathāsthitamavasthitam"
(Yoga-Vasistha: 3.15.14).
[Know therefore this visible world to be no production at all; it is as nameless as it is undeveloped, and as inexistent as its seeming existence.]

The main theme of Yoga-Vasistha is that the Atman is undergoing a dream from which it must awake. There is no difference between the waking and dream experiences. The waking state is a long dream. The dream experiences become unreal as soon as man comes back to his waking state. Even so, the waking state becomes unreal for a sage who has attained self-realisation.

"*śrīrāma uvāca*
yaccedaṃ dṛśyate kiṃcijjagatsthāvarajaṃgamam
tatsarvamasthiraṃ brahmansvapnasaṃgamasaṃnibham"
(Yoga-Vasistha: 1.28.1).
[Lord Ram said, 'whatever we see of all movable or immovable things in this world, they are all as temporary as things viewed in a dream'.]

"*na puṁsa iva jīvasya svapnaḥ saṁbhavati kvacit*
tenaite jāgrato bhāvā jāgratsvapnakṛto 'tra hi"
(Yoga-Vasistha: 6.1.52.2).
[The dream of the jiva (the embodied Atman) is not like the dream of a person The former's dream is experienced as the wakeful state. Hence, it is that the wakeful state is considered a dream.]

The world exists with all its objects as the very meaning of materialisation of the infinite consciousness. Hence, even the form, its seeing and the thought concerning it are all the same pure consciousness and nothing else. The diversity of dream objects is a dream, not diversity. It is the indivisible consciousness that has the appearance of diversity.

"*yathā svapnapuraṃ svacchaṃ jāgratpuravaraṃ prati*
tathā jagadidaṃ svacchaṃ sāṃkalpikajagatprati"
(Yoga-Vasistha: 3.15.12).
[As a city in a dream, is finer than one seen in the waking state, so this visionary world is as subtle as an imaginary one.]

In dream, the objects are really immaterial and subtle yet they are seen to be significant. Similarly, the objects in this world appear to be solid and perceptible, but only pure consciousness exists. We should struggle to liberate ourself by shedding ignorance with the help of pure and right understanding. When the truth is realised, this objective Universe ceases to bother us even if it continues to be seen and even if it is full of restlessness.

"*ajñāvabuddhaḥ saṁsāraḥ sa hi nāsti manāgapi*
avaśiṣṭaṁ ca yatsatyaṁ tasya nāma na vidyate"
(Yoga-Vasistha: 6.2.43.21).
[The ignorant regard this Samsara as real. In reality, it does not exist at all. What does exist after this appearance is rejected, is in fact the truth – but it has no name.]

"*manaḥ sarvamidaṃ rāma tasminnantaścikitsite*
cikitsito vai sakalo jagajjālāmayo bhavet" (Yoga-Vasistha: 4.4.5).
[The mind is all (i.e., the agent of all actions). It is, that by the healing of your heart and mind, you can cure all the troubles and diseases, you may incur in the world.]

"*vivartameva dhāvanti nirvivartāni santi ca*
cidvedhitāni sarvāṇi kṣaṇātpiṇḍībhavanti ca"
(Yoga-Vasistha: 3.12.30).
[Such is the growth and multiplication of things by pervasion of the intellect, until they are put to a stop by its contraction and when weakened in their bodies by its desertion, they sink down in the end.]

Yoga-Vasistha leads to spiritual liberation and this is among those rare conversations which directly leads to Truth. One unusual thing about this scripture is that Sage Vasistha is teaching none other than Ram, God-incarnate and Avatar of Vishnu. In the following Shlokas the scripture provides understanding, scientific ideas and philosophy; it explains consciousness, the creation of the world, our perception of the world, the liberation of the Atman and the non-dual approach to creation.

> "*svapnāddṛśyeva jagatāṃ tulādeśena kena ca*
> *tulitā kalanonmuktā dṛśyaśrīrvyoma jṛmbhate*
> *varjayitvā jñavijñānaṃ jagacchabdārthabhājanam*
> *jagadbrahmasvaśabdānāmarthe nāstyeva bhinnatā*"
> (Yoga-Vasistha: 3.15.9-10).
> [The visionary scenes of the world being taken to the scales, will be found when weighed, to be light as air and as hollow as vacuum. The ignorant that are taken away by the sound of words in disregard of sense, will find when they come to sense, that **there is no difference between the world and Brahmam**.]

> "*na dṛśyamasti sadrūpaṃ na draṣṭā na ca darśanam*
> *na śūnyaṃ na jaḍaṃ no cicchāntamevedamātatam*"
> (Yoga-Vasistha: 3.4.70).
> [In reality; neither the objective Universe, nor the perceiving self, nor perception as such, nor void nor inertness, exists – **only one is, Cosmic Consciousness.**]

> "*jagadbhānaṃ na bhātīdaṃ brahmaṇo vyatirekataḥ*
> *jālasūryāṃśujālaṃ tu vyatirekānubhūtidam*" (Yoga-Vasistha: 3.15.5).
> [The fancied world is no more than an exact copy of the mind of its Maker, just as the sun-beams under the water, are but reflections of the light above; and no other than a negative notion.]

The sum total of pleasures of the whole world is a mere drop when compared to the bliss of Moksha. When all the desires are destroyed, the extinction of the mind is Moksha.

2.2.3: Understanding MAYA from Bhagavad Gita

Bhagavad Gita says that people with low spirituality (those who indulgence in evil actions) cannot overcome this delusion, and hence cannot realise the Divinity in themselves. Because of this total ignorance the world fails to recognise the presence of the Eternal, the Imperishable, the Spirit as distinct from the gross matter.

> "*na māṃ duṣkṛtino mūḍhāḥ prapadyante narādhamāḥ*
> *māyayāpahṛta-jñānā āsuraṃ bhāvam āśritāḥ*" (Bhagavad Gita: 7.15).
> [Those contaminated by fruitive action and fools who are devoid of discrimination, who are the lowest among human beings, whose knowledge has been completely covered by Maya, and who have a demoniac nature, do not surrender unto Me.]

On the other hand, the wise are those who pray for others demanding nothing, expecting nothing. They offer themselves in total surrender. Their only wish is that they should become one with The Supreme.

"*nāhaṃ prakāśaḥ sarvasya yogamāyā-samāvṛtaḥ*
mūḍho 'yaṃ nābhijānāti loko mām ***ajam avyayam***"
(Bhagavad Gita: 7.25).
[Veiled by My Maya born of the gunas, I am not revealed to all. **This deluded world does not know Me as the unborn and eternal.**]

Maya is unfathomable to human reason. It is hard to overcome Maya by self-effort if unaided by divine grace. The relationship between Brahmam and the Maya world is not reversible. There will be no world without the Brahmam, but the existence of the Brahmam does not depend on the appearance of the world. The appearance of the snake depends on the existence of the rope but the opposite is not true.

"*mayā tatam idaṁ sarvaṁ jagad avyakta-mūrtinā*
mat-sthāni sarva-bhūtāni na cāhaṁ teṣv avasthitaḥ"
(Bhagavad Gita: 9.4).
[By Me, in My unmanifested form, this entire Universe is pervaded. All beings are in Me, but I am not in them.]

"*ye caiva sāttvikā bhāvā rājasās tāmasāś ca ye*
matta eveti tān viddhi na tv ***ahaṃ teṣu te mayi***" (Bhagavad Gita: 7.12).
[Know that all states of existence – goodness (sāttvika), passion (rājasika) and ignorance (tāmasika) – are manifested by the modes of My material nature. **I am not subject to these modes, for they are all under the control of My energy**.]

This Shloka says that all things (including the different states of mind) are in Brahmam but He is not in them just as all waves are in the ocean but the ocean is not in them. The Universe is only an appearance, like a mirage in the desert. From the standpoint of the onlooker, the illusory water exists in the desert but the desert does not depend upon or exist in the mirage. Similarly, none of the properties of the Universe touches the Brahmam, just as the waters of the mirage cannot soak a single grain of the desert sand.

"*tribhir guṇa-mayair bhāvair ebhiḥ sarvam idaṃ jagat*
mohitaṃ nābhijānāti ***mām ebhyaḥ param avyayam***"
(Bhagavad Gita: 7.13).
[Deluded by these threefold Gunas (modes of nature) of Prakriti **the whole world does not recognise Me as distinct from them and imperishable**.]

Many people are comfortable with a formless God who is all-pervading, incorporeal, and subtle, and thus they revolt at the idea of a God who possesses a form. God is definitely incorporeal and formless, but that does not mean that He cannot simultaneously have a form as well. Since God is all-powerful, He has the power to manifest in a form if He wishes. Therefore, to say that God cannot have a form actually means that God is not all-powerful.

The Vedic scriptures describe seven planes of existence lower than the earthly plane, and also seven planes of existence starting from the earthly plane and above. All the planes are within the realm of Maya, and the residents of these planes are still subject to Maya.

For a long time, the concept of Maya made little sense to the scholars in the Western world. For the materialists it is downright ridiculous. Not many people, even if curious about Vedic thought, gave serious attention to Lord Krishna's doctrine of illusion. However, this is changing in recent years. Many scholars well-versed in Bhagavad Gita try to reconcile Lord Krishna's doctrine of illusion with the physical sciences, and many books on this theme have gone over well with the public. The prime objective of these science-and-spirituality books has been to show similarities between the theoretical subatomic world of quantum physics and the Vedic worldview.

2.3: The illusion of time and space in the MAYA world

"*To me every hour of the light and dark is a miracle, every cubic inch of space is a miracle.*"

Walt Whitman

"*If you try to get your hands on time, it's always slipping through your fingers. People are sure time is there, but they can't get hold of it. My feeling is that they can't get hold of it because it isn't there at all.*"

Julian Barbour

"*Time, space and causation are like a glass through which the Absolute is seen: in That there is neither time, space, nor causation.*"

Swami Vivekananda

"*Actually, space and time are modes by which we think and not the conditions in which we live.*"

Albert Einstein

The Dharmic scriptures have always declared that what binds us to the wheel of 'Samsara' (transmigration world) are the three mental conditionings known as 'Akasa' and 'Antariksha' (sky and outer space),

'Kaal' (relative time) and 'Nimitta' (causality) and that these are purely mental bonds which we have created ourselves! Within 'Mahakaal' (the timelessness of eternity) all events take place in relative time. All souls want to return to Mahakaal's timeless eternity from within the bondage of Kaal time. Mahakaal is self-originated; nothing generates it. In contrast, Kaal is always 'gatisila' (moving on); it can never be stopped. Mahakaal is not bound by Maya, but Kaal is.

> "*yugavatsarakalpākhyaiḥ kiṃcitprakaṭatāṃ gataḥ*
> *rūpairalakṣyarūpātmā sarvamākramya tiṣṭhati*"
> (Yoga-Vasistha: 1.23.7).
> [Time pervades all things, but has no perceptible feature of his own, except that he is imperfectly known by the names of years, ages and Kalpas.]

> "*anantāpāraparyantabaddhapīṭhaṃ nijaṃ vapuḥ*
> *mahāśailavaduttungamavalambya vyavasthitaḥ*"
> (Yoga-Vasistha: 1.23.29).
> [As the high and huge rock supports its body upon the basis of the earth, so does time rest itself in endless and interminable eternity.]

The mystery of space and especially time had thickened with Einstein's discovery of relativity in the beginning of the twentieth century. Einstein first discovered that time and space are not at all universal but relative to the observer. This is exactly what the Dharmic scriptures had repeatedly said. Therefore, to unveil the mystery of time and space first we will look to quantum physics and then to Dharmic scriptures.

Quantum theory suggests an underlying wholeness of the Universe. Quantum entanglement is a phenomenon in which pairs or groups of particles that have been in contact with each other (they share a wave-function according to quantum theory) seem to remain connected over vast distances. When actions are performed on one of the particles, corresponding changes are observed on the others. They can fly apart – even across the width of the galaxy – and yet they still retain this connection, this knowledge of each other. If one is interfered so that it loses its 'anything is possible' nature and has to decide instantly to materialise with, say, a horizontal polarisation, its twin will then instantly materialise too, and with a vertical polarity. If one becomes an electron with an up spin, the twin will too, but with a down spin as if endowed with a kind of ESP. They are eternally linked in a complementary way that acts as if there's no space between them and no time influencing their behaviour.

Yoga-Vasistha speaks about the relativity of time and space in a variety of ways.

> *"bhidyate nāvabhagno'pi dagdho'pi hi na dahyate*
> *dṛśyate nāpi dṛśyo'pi dhūrtacūḍāmaṇirmune"*
> (Yoga-Vasistha: 1.23.16).
> [O Sage, time is the subtlest of all things. It is divided though indivisible, it is consumed though incombustible, it is perceived though imperceptible in its nature.]

> *"saṃlīnāsaṃkhyasaṃsārasārayā svātmasattayā*
> *urvyeva bhāraghanayā nibaddhapadatāṃ gataḥ"*
> (Yoga-Vasistha: 1.23.31).
> [As the earth is the great support of hills which are fixed upon it, so is time the support of all the innumerable ponderous worlds that constitute the Universe.]

> *"kevalaṃ jagadārambhalīlayā ghanahelayā*
> *pālayatyātmanātmānamanahaṃkāramātatam"*
> (Yoga-Vasistha: 1.23.33).
> [Time is never proud to think, that it is he who without the least sense of pain and labour, brings this world into play and makes it to exist.]

In 1997, a team led by Swiss researcher Nicolas Gisin created entangled photons and sent them ten miles apart along optical fibers. One encountered an interferometer where it could take one of two paths, always chosen randomly. Gisin found that whichever option a photon took, its twin would always make the other choice 'instantaneously' – **faster than the speed of light**. The second photon's reaction was not even delayed by the time light could have traversed those seven miles but instead occurred less than three ten-billionths (limit of the testing apparatus's accuracy) of a second later (Lanza, 2009, p. 52). Repeated experiments have produced same result. Hence, Einstein's insistence that nothing can influence anything else at superluminal speeds is wrong.

Living cells can instantly communicate over distances. One simple experiment involves a batch of algae cells grown in a Petri dish. After few days, the researchers divide the cells into two batches. One batch remains in the original dish and the other one is shifted to a different laboratory few miles away. When the original group of cells is stimulated by a low-voltage current, the other group reacts in precisely the same way, to the same degree, at the exact same instant that the stimulated cells react to the charge. And when the separated batch is stimulated the home team cells react instantaneously as well. Various new experiments have furnished the most powerful evidence to date that the quantum point of view of the world is correct at the level of living organisms. Thus, the actual 'reality' is different. Philosophers of our ancient past were right; our senses really do deceive us. It means, space and time are Maya. The illusive Maya-Shakti ('Shakti' is energy. Maya-Shakti is the power of Maya) has invaded every human activity and experience.

> "*śrīrāma uvāca*
> *atraiva durvilāsānāṃ cūḍamaṇirihāparaḥ*
> *karotyattīti loke'smindaivaṃ kālaśca kathyate*
> *kriyāmātrādṛte yasya svaparispandarūpiṇaḥ*
> *nānyadālakṣyate rūpaṃ na karma na samīhitam*"
> (Yoga-Vasistha: 1.25.1-2).
> [**Time stands the foremost of all deceitful players in this world.** He acts the double parts of creation and destruction, and of action and fate. **Time has no other character but those of action and motion by which his existence is known to us, and which bind all beings**.]

The speed of light in a vacuum is constant no matter how we measure it. As example, light shone from a spaceship going at nearly the speed of light still leaves it at the speed of light. Einstein's special theory of relativity claimed to explain this 'invariance of the speed of light'. Instead of considering space and time independently, he proposed a unified vision of space-time where time dilation (the faster you go slower your time gets) and space contraction (shortening distance for fast moving objects) play a significant role.

Let us start with the time dilation formula. In the theory of relativity, time dilation is the phenomenon of time passing slower for an observer who is moving relative to another observer. Einstein gave an exact formula for calculating this which forms the backbone of relativity, and shows us the fickle nature of space, distance, and time.

$$\Delta T = t.\sqrt{1-\left(\frac{v}{c}\right)^2}$$

ΔT is the change in your passage of time – what you yourself perceive. Small 't' represents the time passing for those you left behind on Earth, 'v' is your speed, and 'c' is the speed of light (186,282.4 miles per second). In physics the term '(v/c)' is called 'beta' – the Greek letter β (which looks like a B with a tail).

Time dilation is an unnoticeably small effect. The Hafele-Keating experiment of 1971 involved flying planes around the world with atomic clocks on board. Upon the trips' completion the clocks were compared to a static, ground based atomic clock. It was found that 273 ± 7 nanoseconds had been gained on the planes' clocks. It means, even at the 'slow' velocity of airplanes, the equation works. For airplanes moving at 675 miles per hour, the effect is only about 5×10^{-13}. That means, if a person travelled at this speed for one day, he would lose forty-three nanoseconds. If he flies for a year without stoppage, he would experience sixteen microseconds less time than the other person who was stationary. When radioactive atoms move, their radioactive decays slow down due to time dilation. Super-accurate atomic clocks onboard the earth-orbiting satellites, are 'pre-corrected' as per the above time dilation formula prior to launch so that it will run at exactly the same frequency as an identical clock left behind on the Earth's surface.

Time dilation becomes large if the velocity approaches the speed of light. Let's consider, an astronaut is traveling at a very high speed. At 99.999999999 percent of speed of light (perfectly allowable by the laws of physics), he will experience a dilation effect of 22,361. It means, when he spent one day on his spaceship, on Earth 22,361 days have passed for everyone else. We can insert any number for 'v' and the formula will yield how much time passes for the astronaut while a given time passes on Earth. If the astronaut travels at the speed of light, 'v' becomes equal to 'c' and ΔT equals to zero, means **time has been frozen for him**.

Therefore, when a person travels at the speed of light, he takes "NO TIME" to travel from any point of the Universe to another. This also means that he will find himself everywhere in the Universe at the same time. **This is the realm of Mahakaal where the time dimension is terminated.** Light consists of photon particles, and if a photon were sentient, it would have experienced the same.

The neuroscientists could not locate a single clock in the brain that is responsible for detecting time passing. Flow of time is created by Maya-Shakti that gives us the false impression that 'I was born, grew old, and will die; there is a future and a past'. Sage Patanjali gives us an excellent concept of the three-fold nature of time (Trikala) in his Yoga Sutras. One who knows all three aspects of time is called 'Trikala Jnani'.

> "*atita anagatam svarupatah asti adhva bhedat dharmanam*"
> (Yoga Sutras: 4.12).
> [Past and future exist in the present reality, appearing to be different because of having different characteristics or forms.]

The above Sutra says that neither time flows nor do we live at the edge of time. Within the Cosmos, there are time cycles of differing lengths for each planetary system. Sense of time is greatly altered during NDE. Albert Heim who had an NDE while falling on a ski trip reported that "*time became greatly expanded*" during his fall. Heim's fall lasted less than ten seconds during which he experienced a life-review and other elements which he claims will take a very long time to describe. Ray Kinman, after an incident of accidental overdose had an NDE, where he had experienced timelessness, and past and future were completely nonexistent – "*I was traveling in an intense, burning 'now'. 'Now' was everything. I ceased to be a noun (person, place, or thing) and became a verb (an action)*" (Atwater, 2007, pp. 35-36). Arthur Ford explained that time and space limitations in the afterlife realm are completely eliminated.

> "*Since we are able to will ourselves to be anywhere at any moment of earth time and are able to look ahead so far into what you call the future that this also transcends the earthly idea of time.*" (Montgomery, 1972, p. 14).

Speed of light is the barrier, and once the barrier is crossed, we come out of much of the deception of Maya and time ceases to have any hold on us. We will immediately feel oneness with the Universe.

Anyone with a minimum of scientific culture today has heard of Einstein's theory of relativity. This theory predicts a curved Universe. In a curved Universe anyone traveling in a 'straight line' across the Cosmos would eventually return to where they started. Also, the future leads to the present and then the past. The past affects the present, the present affects the future and the future affects the past, and so on in a cyclic way. Past, present and future – all are one extending in multiple directions and dimensions until perceived by a conscious mind. It means, retrocausality or backwards causation is a hard fact, means, a later event in time can affect an earlier event in time. The future exists before it arrives and some people consciously perceive a future before it becomes the present; phenomenon which can be classified as evidence of entanglement and which are variably experienced as deja vu, premonitions, and precognition.

Another Sutra throws some light on the nature of the manifested world and time. This is remarkable because a whole scientific theory is presented in a definite philosophical model in just few words.

> "***ksana** pratiyogi parinama aparanta nigrahyah **kramah***"
> (Yoga Sutras: 4.33).
> [The sequencing process of **moments** and impressions corresponds to the moments of time, and is apprehended at the end point of the **sequence**.]

The above Sutra gives such details about time that is unknown to modern science. Before the advent of modern science matter was considered to be continuous, but research showed that it is discontinuous, being composed of discrete particles separated from one another by enormous empty spaces. Similarly, the apparently continuous series of changes which are taking place in the phenomenal world and by which we measure time, are not really continuous. The changes consist of a number of successive states which are quite distinct and separate from one another.

In this Sutra two words are of utmost importance – 'Ksana' (moments, units of time) and 'Kramah' (succession). The interval of time corresponding to each of these successive states is called a 'Ksana'. So 'Ksana' may be called the smallest unit of time which cannot be broken up further. 'Kramah' stands for this process consisting of a relentless succession of discontinuous changes underlying all kinds of phenomena. This process is ultimately based upon the 'Ksana'. As example, we are watching a movie on the screen. The projector is on, the film rolls move, one picture goes out of focal point, the next picture comes into place and is projected on the screen in less than one-tenth of a second and we get the impression of a continuous picture. Likewise, as one 'Ksana' succeeds another 'Ksana' the whole manifested world passes from one distinct state to another distinct state, but the succession is so rapid that we are not conscious of the discontinuity – this explanation is beyond the realm of modern science today. The scientists are yet to discover this fact which the ancient sages knew several thousand years ago.

However, in recent years, some physicists are proposing about the 'quantisation of time', means that time exists or is available only in discreet or fixed amounts. The 'Chronon' is one proposed quantum of time, same as 'Ksana'. This is the time taken for light to travel the classical radius of the electron. This is calculated to be equal to 6.27×10^{-24} seconds, an infinitesimal value relative to every day time durations. Time is perceived by us through transmittal of electric impulses by neurons. The impulses are not themselves Chronons, yet their transmission could be considered an interaction of neurons and Chronons. Hopefully, in the coming few decades, the scientists will get clear concept about 'Ksana' or 'Chronon' whatever they would call it.

The above two Sutras (4.12 and 4.33) clear the concepts of the 'Block Universe Theory' which modern scientists are still struggling to comprehend. Dr. Kristie Miller, the joint director for the Centre for Time (University of Sydney), suggests that our Universe may be looked at as a giant four-dimensional block of spacetime containing all the things that ever happen. In the Block Universe all moments that exist are just relative to each other within the three spatial dimensions and one time dimension. One end of this block holds the big bang, and at the opposite end is the conclusion of the Universe. Our sense of the present is just reflecting where in the Block Universe we are at this instance. The 'past' is just a slice of the Universe at an earlier location while the 'future' is at a later location. It means, we spread through time just as we spread through space. We are not located in a single moment and there are changes, but the past does not 'disappear'; it simply exists in different parts of space-time, much in the same way that our current location doesn't exclude the existence of other locations. The past, present and future all exist simultaneously, and are equally real. This is 'timelessness' in NDE cases.

The materialistic manifestations are essentially based on a hidden, essentially mechanical process (the projector of a motion picture). The whole manifested Universe and everything in it changes from moment to moment by a persistent law which is inherent in the very nature of manifestation. Two serious questions – who is controlling this mechanical process (the projector operator), and from where (the projector room)?

Beyond our known world there is a reality which transcends time and yet expresses itself as time in the world process. Does the manifested world in time and space rigidly express a predetermined pattern of Divine Thought, just as a picture on a cinema screen is the result of a mechanical projection of the photographs in the film roll? Does the procession of events in the phenomenal world merely conform to a plan which exists in the Divine Mind in the same way as the construction of a building follows the plan of the architect? The first question suggests most rigid form of determinism while the second question leaves some room for free will.

> "*kṣaṇakalpaṃ jagatsarvaṃ tvattāmattātmajanmanām*
> *yathāvatpratibhāsasya vakṣye kramamimaṃ śṛṇu*"
> (Yoga-Vasistha: 3.20.30).
> [Attend to what I tell you about the manner in which we form the idea of time, and its distinct parts of a moment and an age, in the same way as we make the distinction of individualities in me, thee and this or that person (which are essentially the same undivided spirit and duration).]

Along with time, space is also a human construct. In this space-time premise, space contraction is the counterpart of time dilation.

Suppose an astronaut wants to travel from Earth to a destination one light year away. If he travels close to the speed of light, his time will slow down significantly compared to someone who remained on Earth. For an earth-clock he still takes a year to reach, but his clock having slowed down might show only one day has passed. Hence, he will assume that the distance was one light day only. The faster he travels, the shorter the distance will be. This is called 'space contraction'. Now, if he travels at a speed extremely close to that of light, he could even cross the Universe in the fraction of a second. So, the Universe itself could be just a few meters wide for him in that kind of extreme velocity situation.

> "*śrīdevyuvāca*
> *deśadairghyaṃ yathā nāsti kāladairghyaṃ tathāṅgane*
> *nāstyeveti yathānyāyaṃ kathyamānaṃ mayā śṛṇu*"
> (Yoga-Vasistha: 3.20.28).

[The Goddess replied: There is neither any limit of space or duration, nor any distance of place or length of time in reality: hear me now tell you the reason of it.]

"*yathaitatpratibhāmātram jagatsargāvabhāsanam tathaitatpratibhāmātram kṣaṇakalpāvabhāsanam*" (Yoga-Vasistha: 3.20.29).

[As the Universe is the reflection of the Divine Mind, so are infinity and eternity but representations of himself.]

If we travel outbound at a high speed, the distant stars would lie at an entirely different distance. By mathematical calculation it can be shown that if we head toward the star Sirius at ninety-nine percent of light's speed of 186,282.4 miles per second, we would find that it was barely more than one light-year away, and not the 8.6 light years. If we cross a living room twenty-one feet in length at that speed, every instrument and perception would show that it was actually now three feet in length. The amazing thing is that the living room, or the intervening space from Earth to Sirius, is now not artificially shrunk by some illusion. The star is REALLY that far away. The living room is REALLY only three feet across. And if we could move at 99.9999999 percent of speed of light, which is perfectly allowable by the laws of physics, the living room would now be 1/22,361th of its original size or just a hundredth of an inch across (Lanza, 2009, p. 115). All items, furniture, or people in the room would be likewise Lilliputian, and yet we'd notice nothing wrong.

Earth's eighteen miles per second motion around the sun causes stars to shift position by several seconds of arc from their actual locations. If we increase our speed this effect will become more dramatic. At very close to speed of light,

"*The entire contents of the Cosmos appear to hover in a single blindingly bright ball, dead ahead. If one is looking out any other window, there appears nothing but a strange, absolute blackness.*" (Lanza, 2009, p. 126).

This consequence is called aberration. The entire Universe has no inherent external structure. Every single particle of this Universe, living or non-living, is connected even if they are billion light years apart. The mysterious quantum entanglement phenomenon is explained.

Quantum entanglement theory has a philosophical aspect. Two particles are mysteriously linked that they will always remain bonded together beyond space and time, means that since we are too made of particles, we are also connected beyond space and time, so quite literally what we do unto others we do unto ourselves. This is the very basic concept of the law of Karma which I will discuss later.

At the speed of light, the space shrinks to nothing. If a photon particle were sentient, it would have experienced no movement at all (movement is impossible if space shrinks to nothing). **Time and space both are frozen for a space traveler travelling at the speed of light.** This is Maya-Shakti – the great deceptive power of Maya. Space-time is a subjective ordering device used by Maya-Shakti for living beings to make sense of their world. If the deceptive power of Maya is removed, we will find that we exist in a timeless, spaceless world – Mahakaal – a unified field of pure consciousness that permeates the whole Cosmos. There is not a single law of traditional physics that depends on time and space factor (i.e., they are symmetric as time 'passes' and space 'changes'). This fact has profound implication and unleashed a flood of papers from the academic world.

The ancient sages possessed much more superior scientific knowledge that modern science has yet to get even in theories. When the physicists discovered the wave-particle nature of all matter and energy, and when Einstein doubted the very basic concept of time and space, we knew that **Maya has unexpectedly entered even the field of hard practical science.** Our whole concept of reality became questionable at a fundamental level. The result of double-slit experiment is in every way physically impossible, so physicality cannot be its base – **the entire observable Cosmos is cloaked by the activities of Maya.**

2.4: Various components of Maya-Shakti

Maya-Shakti has three components – Avaran, Adhyasa and Vikshepa Shakti. Avaran Shakti means veiling power which does not allow us to realise our divine Sat-Chit-Ananda nature. Names (nama) and forms (rupa) by which things are wrongly identified are because of Adhyasa Shakti. As example, all dolls made of sugar are sugar itself but name and form are our perceptions. Likewise, all deities that we worship are actually different aspects of the same Supreme God. Conflicts arise when we fail to understand this. We can find the famous metaphors in Chandogya Upanishad likening Brahmam to clay and gold as the material sources (Prakriti, upadana-karaṇa) of earthen pots and gold ornaments, and to the potter and goldsmith as their efficient causes (nimitta-karaṇa) in Shankara's Bhasya.

> "*yathā somyaikena mṛtpiṇḍena sarvaṃ mṛnmayaṃ vijñātam*
> *syādvācārambhaṇaṃ vikāro nāmadheyaṃ mṛttiketyeva satyam*
> *yathā somyaikena lohamaṇinā sarvaṃ lohamayaṃ vijñātam*
> *syādvācārambhaṇaṃ vikāro nāmadheyaṃ lohamityeva satyam*"
> (Chandogya Upanishad: 6.1.4-5).

[O Somya, it is like this – By knowing a single lump of earth you know all objects made of earth. All changes are mere words, in name only. But earth is the reality.
O Somya, it is like this – By knowing a single lump of gold you know all objects made of gold. All changes are mere words, in name only. But gold is the reality.]

Vikshepa Shakti means projecting power, which projects the Universe and the body causing 'Abhimana' (arrogance, pride etc).

The holographic principle is the idea that the Universe around us, which we are used to thinking of as being three dimensional is actually at a more fundamental level two dimensional and that everything we see that's going on around us in three dimensions is actually happening in a two-dimensional space. This is Vikshepa Shakti – the projecting power of Maya.

Theoretical physicists ask a question – why the entropy of a black hole is proportional to the area of its horizon? Since entropy is an extensive quantity, one would have expected the entropy to be instead proportional to the volume the black hole occupies. This question leads to a new paradigm for physical reality – the holographic principle – the consequences of which we are only just beginning to understand. At a conference in Stockholm on August 28, 2015, Stephen Hawking announced that he had resolved the information paradox, that all the information about the matter and energy within the three-dimensional volume of a black hole is encoded as a hologram upon its two-dimensional surface, the event horizon (the boundary between the black hole and the rest of the Universe). Calculations show that on just the two-dimensional surface of a black hole enough information can be stored to completely describe any seemingly three-dimensional objects inside it. And the mathematics works just as well whether we are talking about a black hole, a planet, or the entire Universe.

This idea although at first might seem like a completely absurd idea, it actually helps us to solve some of the puzzles that arise when we try to combine quantum physics and general relativity. A team of physicists had provided some of the clearest evidence that our Universe could be just one big projection, and the information content of the entire Universe is captured by an enveloping surface that surrounds it. Leonard Susskind (theoretical physicist at Stanford University in California), Gerard Hooft (Nobel Laureate theoretical physicist) and Donald Hoffman (Cognitive scientist and popular science author) were among the first theoreticians to explore the idea of holographic Universe. American author Michael Talbot's research on the holographic principle is a landmark work whose exciting conclusions continue to be proven true by today's most advanced physics, cosmology, and string theory. Several NDE researchers have also pointed out that the holographic model offers us a way to understand these experiences scientifically. Dr. Kenneth Ring (Professor of Psychology at the University of Connecticut and one of the first NDE researchers) believes that NDEs are journeys into a holographic realm of higher frequencies – "***just as the holographic image appears to be fully real when illuminated by a laser beam, so the images produced [during NDE] by interacting thought-forms appear to be real***" (Ring, 1980, p. 247). The ancient sages knew about the projecting power of Maya several thousand years ago what Stephen Hawking and other researchers just began to understand. There are many elements in the illuminating scriptures of Sanatan Dharma that can deepen and straighten science.

Stephen Hawking, in his 1988 mega-bestseller 'A Brief History of Time' predicted that physicists would soon find an 'Ultimate Theory' that would explain how our Cosmos came into being. He compared this achievement to knowing 'the mind of God'. This statement was ironic because Hawking, an atheist, wanted science to eliminate the need for a divine creator. Richard Dawkins, another diehard atheist, declared in his 1986 bestseller 'The Blind Watchmaker' that the mystery of life had already been solved. Like Hawking, Nobel Laureate Steven Weinberg hoped that the final theory would crush, once and for all, our superstitious faith in an all-powerful, beneficent deity. However, all the attempts had been unsuccessful to formulate a 'Theory of Everything' that unifies the fundamental forces into a single, all-encompassing, coherent theoretical framework of physics that fully explains and links together all physical aspects of the Universe. This is because scientific omniscience itself is a delusion caused by 'Abhimana' (arrogance, pride). If all our knowledge comes from natural selection for survival, how would we know that our insights into a world we don't even naturally perceive are not an illusion?

Yoga-Vasistha explains why Maya is divine. Dream is a delusion but it has some truth, that it is the effect of our intellect. In the similar way, Maya has the intelligence of Divinity. In other words, though Maya is delusion, it has the truth of all-powerful God in it. Maya is the power which belongs to Brahmam and is not independent of it.

> "*ajñānameva yadbhāti saṃvidābhāsameva tat*
> *yajjagaddṛśyate svapne saṃvitkacanameva tat*"
> (Yoga-Vasistha: 3.11.16).
> [Whatever appears as ignorance or delusion (as this world), has some appearance of intelligence or truth (of the Divinity) in it, as **the delusion of the world seen in a dream, is the effect of the intellect within us.]**

"*asmādacetyacidūpaṁ jagadvyomeva kevalam
śūnyau vyomajagacchabdau paryāyau viddhi cinmayau*"
(Yoga-Vasistha: 3.15.13).
[Know therefore the insensible world to be the inverse of the sensible Atman, and the substantive world as the reverse of the unsubstantial vacuum. The words plenum and vacuum are both as absurd as airy breath, because **these opposites are but different views of the same Intellect.]**

Mahavatar Babaji, a highly developed Indian Yogi, once said,

"*The substance of a dream is held in materialisation by the subconscious thought of the dreamer. When that cohesive thought is withdrawn in wakefulness, the dream and its elements dissolve. A man closes his eyes and erects a dream creation, which, on awakening, he effortlessly dematerialises. He follows the divine archetypal pattern. Similarly, when he awakens in cosmic consciousness, he will effortlessly dematerialise the illusions of the cosmic dream.*" (Yogananda, 2021, p. 320).

"*yaṁ pratyudeti sargo 'yaṁ sa evainaṁ hi cetati
padārthaḥ sanniveśaṁ svamiva svapnaṁ pumāniva
iti māyeyamādīrghā prasṛtā pratyayonmukhī
satyāvalokamātrātivilayaikavilāsinī*" (Yoga-Vasistha: 6.2.13.4, 6).
[Just as one's dream is experienced only by the dreamer, this creation is experienced only by the one in whose mind it arises…. **This Maya or world-appearance will continue to flow with ever-changing appearance until the truth is realised – and only then will Maya cease to operate.**]

Now I have a very serious question – if the power of the mind to self-deception is the very same power of Maya which creates any reality, then how we can be sure that our understanding of Maya is not another deception of Maya? In other words, is the physical Universe actually part of a Matrix-like computer simulation?

2.4.1: Maya-Shakti, the quantum indeterminacy – The real Matrix

"*We are asleep. Our Life is a dream. But we wake up sometimes, just enough to know that we are dreaming.*"

Ludwig Wittgenstein

"*tadevaṁ svapna evā 'yaṁ jāgradbhāvamupāgataḥ
sarve vayamiha svapnapuruṣāstava suvrata*"
(Yoga-Vasistha: 6.2.151.9).

[Thus, your dream has materialised into the waking state reality. **All of us here are your own dream-objects.**]

In the movie, the character Neo (played by Keanu Reeves) realises that his entire life, including his job, the building he lived in, and everything else, was part of an elaborate video game. He ultimately wakes up in a world outside of the game. The fundamental question is – how can the knower know himself? When I am awake, I am actively doing something with the physical body. But while asleep, I am not doing anything physically, but I dream as if I am travelling, running, laughing. In my dream, I am doing all these things 'physically' while actually the physical body is lying in bed – a mysterious Matrix-like movie plot in real life that we experience every day but do not pay serious attention to it. Sometimes when we wake up from deep sleep, we take quite some time to realise where we are and what time of day it is. It means during sleeping state the mind had stopped functioning. What happened to the mind? Was the mind functioning in another space-time? Was the mind in process of reconditioning by a controller from another dimension?

At the point of creation of the Cosmos, all possible 'alternative histories' (all the future evolutionary possibilities through which the Cosmos would evolve to its present state) were projected into a kind of cosmic possibility space, but none of these possibilities were 'actualised' because it required the presence of conscious beings to perceive and experience. For the readers who could not understand the logic, I will use a simple metaphor. The words on the pages of a closed book are 'information', but they are not doing their job of meaning something until someone opens the book and starts reading. It requires the active intervention of consciousness to bring inert information into life and meaning. But the information is there. Similarly, if the Cosmos starts empty but potentially with a huge amount of information, it is logical to conclude that the existential information of the entire Cosmos starting from big bang to big crunch is actually a program stored on someone else's hard drive.

If the entire Cosmos is a computer simulation and there is nothing outside it, then our known world must be finite, because what is infinite can't be computed. All the laws of physics are calculable, and our world is lawfully specifiable. It means the Cosmos is a mock-up. This theory could be falsified by at least one non-computable law of physics, but there is none. Indeed our world has an algorithmic simplicity beyond all expectations. It means, there is some mysterious controlling mechanism outside the entire Cosmos – "*The enormous usefulness of mathematics in the natural sciences is something bordering on the mysterious and that there is no rational explanation for it*" (Wigner, 1959). The Universe is a digital system which began when it was booted up at big bang. The physical world is just an 'output', and Planck limits (the Universe's minimum limit beyond which the laws of physics break) exist because space and time really are digital. Calculus (a branch of mathematics that involves the study of rates of change) works because infinitesimals, in the limit, really do create physical reality. This is a very strong view no doubt.

The speed of light in vacuum (186,282.4 miles per second) is a constant value. We know that light propagates as wave, similar to water wave. The movement of water wave depends on the elasticity of the water medium. This is true of every wave in every physical medium. Light, as a wave, should move at a speed defined by the elasticity of ether that fills all space. Our earth is not stationary in such ether because the earth orbits the sun at 108,000 km per hour and orbits the galaxy even faster. So, the speed of light should vary with direction, but in 1887 Michelson and Morley found it was the same in every direction. Does the speed of light define the elasticity of space, like some kind of 'physics in reverse'? This is quite a disturbing question to ask. Is ether physical? Einstein saw that space has to be something for objects to move in it.

> "*According to the general theory of relativity space without ether is unthinkable; for in such a space there would not only be no propagation of light, but also no possibility of existence for standards of space and time ...*" (Einstein, May 5, 1920, address at the University of Leiden).

Nothing can travel faster than light. This is impossible but true for no known reason. The current view of physics, after almost a century of consideration, is that, "... *the speed of light is a constant because it just is, and because light is not made of anything simpler.*" (Laughlin, 2005, p. 15). Such a silly comment proves that science does not have a satisfactory answer. In an objective world, things could just go faster and faster because there is no one to set the limit. What makes the speed of light a maximum for our Universe? Does the processing rate of the Universe define the speed of light? As an object approaches the speed of light, its mass rises quickly. With the increase of mass and speed, the network load also increases causing a reduction of frame rates. This is time dilation. When the object tries to travel at the speed of light its mass becomes infinite, and so does the energy required to move it. Time comes to a standstill, means the simulation hangs, and our known physical reality collapses. The spell of Maya-Shakti is over. For this reason, no physical object can travel as fast as or faster than light otherwise the magic trick would go horribly wrong.

From the double-slit experiment it seems that our simulation is conserving its resources and rendering certain things only when it knows we're looking at them. In a simulation if the same processing gives position and momentum, we can't get both together.

Human DNA is like a computer program but much more advanced than any software ever created. Who 'wrote' the code? Mainstream science tells us that life developed over millions of years by a process of time and chance. How could one molecule in each cell of a randomly generated life-form be so complex?

In the future, may be thousands of years from now, it is possible that we will be able to create technology capable of running convincing simulations of reality. It is likely that we will create many such simulations and hence there will be lots of simulated realities and only one 'base reality'. Are we already living in a simulation right now which is indistinguishable from reality amongst uncountable number (may be one in billions) of parallel universes? A super-computer can be so powerful that it can run a great many such simulations simultaneously.

Today we cannot create conscious mind, but if technological progress continues at the current rate, then these deficiencies will eventually be overcome. In fact, a computer does not need to be conscious. What is required is a simulation that is programmed in such a way that it behaves like a human in all situations (including passing Turing tests – a test of a machine's ability to exhibit intelligent behaviour equivalent to, or indistinguishable from that of a human, etc.). Moreover, the physical environment does not need simulation because a realistic simulation of human central nervous system can be too perfect to ensure that the simulated humans, interacting in normal human ways with their simulated environment, don't notice any irregularities. This is Maya-Shakti. Now it makes sense if I say that the 'real' reality is in quantum level and the physical Universe is the work of Maya. In a double-slit experiment, when the 'director' of Maya-Shakti notices that a human is about to make an observation of the microscopic world, he fills in sufficient details in the appropriate domain in the simulation on an as-needed basis. This is how the millennium-old Dharmic Philosophy can explain the strange quantum indeterminacy in a fairly straightforward manner. Quantum physics is postmodern science, but Sanatan Dharma is eternal.

Can we explain the 'errors' of history, such as, Chernobyl meltdown, rise of dictators like Hitler, Genghis Khan etc., with malfunctioning simulation or whoever is pushing the buttons is messing up the things? Lastly, the 'characters' within a simulation will never know that they are living in a bondage because any evidence that they are 'allowed' to get could also be simulated. In the science-fiction movie 'The Matrix', people lived in a virtual reality that appeared real to them as long as they stayed within it, knowing their world only by the information they received from it, as we know ours. It is not easy to come out of Maya.

The divine magician is continuously editing the states of any brains that have become aware of an anomaly before it spoils the simulation. He can even skip back or move forward in time and replay the simulation in a way that avoids the problem.

A simulator with enough computing power can simulate the entire mental history of humankind (ancestor-simulation) even while using only a tiny fraction of its resources for that purpose. Hence not only our future but our past is also changeable. Retrocausality is a science fact. Hawking and Mlodinow (2010, pp. 82-3) explained,

> "*Quantum physics tells us that no matter how thorough our observation of the present, the (unobserved) past, like the future, is indefinite and exists only as a spectrum of possibilities. The Universe, according to quantum physics, has no single past, or history.*
>
> *The fact that the past takes no definite form means that observations you make on a system in the present affect its past.... the Universe doesn't have just a single history, but every possible history, each with its own probability; and our observations of its current state affect its past and determine the different histories of the Universe, just as the observations of the particles in the double-slit experiment affect the particles' 'past'.*"

This is the amazing potential of Maya-Shakti. From the timeless point of creation, a spontaneous universal creative act projects all possible futures into a universal possibility or potentiality space. At the point of creation everything that possibly can happen becomes potential, so all possible future histories of the Universe come into being as potentialities, although not yet experienced realities. Some people can make a great mystery of this idea, sometimes called the multiverse or parallel Universe concept, but these are just different expressions of what the ancient Dharmic wisdom had revealed.

2.5: Conclusion

"*The history of the universe is, in effect, a huge and ongoing quantum computation. The universe is a quantum computer.*"

Prof. Seth Lloyd,
designer of the first feasible quantum computer

"*A long time ago, the Great Programmer wrote a program that runs all possible universes on His Big Computer.*"

Jurgen Schmidhuber, pioneer in artificial intelligence

> "*Not only is the Universe stranger than we imagine, it is stranger than we can imagine.*"
>
> Sir Arthur Eddington

This whole idea of Maya has been profoundly well explored metaphysically in the Dharmic scriptures, and has let to psychological insights which are open to the western scholars to investigate systematically. This wisdom is not an end but a beginning which allows new thinking, new perception and new actions. Sadly, in the Christian Western world such a view was not really taken seriously except a few. The Muslim world with a magical view of 'hope for heaven and the fear of hell' is even less fortunate.

But one thing is for certain. The Maya-Shakti gives us complete freedom because without uncertainty there cannot be any freedom. It means, the Atman or Quantum Consciousness has the power to overcome Maya-Shakti if properly trained. Many of the ancient sages have done it. In that sense they were more scientific and more advanced than many of the Learned Professors of modern world of space flight, computers, robots, and genetic engineering who believe that they command the world with science and technology.

> "*nāsato vidyate bhāvo nābhāvo vidyate sataḥ*
> *ubhayorapi dṛiṣhṭo 'nta stvanayos tattva-darśhibhiḥ*"
> (Bhagavad Gita: 2.16).
> [The unreal has no existence. The Real never ceases to be (to exist). Men possessed of the knowledge of the Truth fully know both these.]

There is a question. A profound sense of reality pervades the near-death experience, both while it is happening and later (in its recollection). Many experiencers state that their experience was hyper-real – not dream-like, not hallucinatory – more real than the experience on Earth. Also, there were increased powers of logic, clarity of thought, overall visual and auditory clarity, vividness of colours, and control of cognition.

> "*It's reality. I know for myself that I didn't experience no fantasy.* ***There was no so-called dream or nothing. These things really happened to me****. It happened. I know. I went through it.*"

> "*[The experience is] realer than here, really. After that* ***the world seemed like a mockery to real life – make-believe****. Like people playing games. Like we are getting prepared for something but we don't know what.*" (Sabom, 1982, pp. 32, 33).

Swiss geologist Albert Heim who had an NDE while falling on a ski trip refers to this aspect during his mountain fall.

> "*All my thoughts and ideas were coherent and very clear, and in no way susceptible, as are dreams, to obliteration ... The relationship of events and their probable outcomes were viewed with objective clarity, no confusion entered at all.*" (Laureys and Tononi, 2009, p. 313).

The question is why is the experience of the self during NDE so real? People in the spell of Maya are eager to squeeze out gross pleasure from the senses. During NDE, the consciousness is separate from the body, and therefore some of the spell of Maya is removed. But the afterlife realm is still Maya. Arthur E. Yensen had an NDE in 1932. He described,

> "*Everything over here is pure. The elements do not mix or break down as they do on earth.* ***Everything is kept in place by an all-pervading Master Vibration, which prevents aging.*** *That is why things do not get dirty, or wear out, and why everything looks so bright and new.*" (Atwater, 1994, p. 50).

The highest afterlife abode is paradise (Swarg). For a true Dharmic, even the happiness of paradise is unsatisfying because this is also an annexure to the material manifestation (holographic realm of higher frequencies) – a product of Maya. Thus, when the Universe dissolves, the paradise also dissolves. The happiness of paradise is the same as the happiness of this world which is an illusion of the mind. Brahmam alone exists and hence the aim of a true Dharmic is to attain Moksha. Attaining Moksha is not to be confused with reaching paradise.

CHAPTER - 3

Fine-tuning, Biocentrism and the concept of BRAHMAM (Eternal Consciousness)

"I believe the Universe has a purpose, and our greatest intellectual challenge as human beings is to glimpse what this purpose might be."
Owen Gingerich

"If there wasn't a reason to exist, existence wouldn't happen."
Eric Weiss

World's greatest philosophers have wrestled with the question of God. Is there a mysterious supernatural power that created the Universe and is the source of all moral goodness? Even atheist philosophers, e.g., Jean Paul Sartre and Albert Camus had recognised that the question makes a tremendous difference. Today's education system does not encourage the students to ask questions on this issue.

There is an age-old question in natural theology first formulated perhaps 1,600 years ago by the great thinker St. Augustine of Hippo and 800 years ago by St. Thomas Aquinas – Can God's signature be seen in the Universe He created? In this scientific era, we can find God's signature in the fine-tuning of the Universe.

3.1: God's signature – fine-tuning of the Universe

"The more I examine the Universe, and the details of its architecture, the more evidence I find that the Universe in some sense must have known we were coming."

Freeman Dyson

> "*The more we discover about the Universe, the more we find that it is governed by rational laws... You still have the question, why does the Universe bother to exist? If you like, you can define God to be the answer to that question.... If we find the answer to that, it would be the ultimate triumph of human reason –* ***for then we should know the mind of God.***"
>
> Stephen Hawking

Fine-tuning refers to the surprising exactness of nature's physical constants at the beginning state of the Universe which converge as potential pointers to an Eternal Consciousness. The slightest variation from their actual values results in an early Universe that never becomes capable of hosting life. For this reason, the Universe seems finely-tuned for life. There are more than two hundred fine-tuned physical parameters within the solar system and the Universe. Recent studies in biological evolution also reveal that extreme fine-tuning did exist in the beginning of life and evolution process. Since the early 1970s hundreds of articles and dozens of books are written on the topic.

Oxford physicist and Nobel Laureate Roger Penrose has noted that a single parameter, the so-called 'original phase-space volume', requires such precise in tuning that the "*Creator's aim must have been [precise] to an accuracy of one part in $10^{10^{123}}$ [ten to the power ten to the power 123, which is ten billion multiplied by itself 123 times!]*". Penrose goes on to remark that, "*one could not possibly even write the number down in full ...[since] it would be '1' followed by 10^{123} successive '0's!*" – ***more zeros than the number of elementary particles in the entire Universe***". (Penrose, 1989, p. 344). Such is the accuracy required to set the Universe on its course. It takes far more 'faith' to believe that this happened by chance than to believe that it was initiated by an incredibly powerful mind.

Many other physical parameters are balanced on a razor's edge for the life to occur, such as (parameters: maximum deviation), electrons: protons is $1{:}10^{37}$, electromagnetic force: gravity is $1{:}10^{40}$, expansion rate of the Universe is $1{:}10^{55}$ mass density of the Universe is $1{:}10^{59}$ and cosmological constant is $1{:}10^{120}$. These numbers represent the maximum deviation from the accepted values that would either prevent the Universe from existing now, not having matter, or be unsuitable for any form of life. As example, electrons: protons ratio is $1{:}10^{37}$. This perfect balance establishes the role of gravity in relation to the electromagnetic force. A certain number of protons and electrons were able to survive the primordial annihilation between matter and antimatter at the big bang. Strangely the number of protons and electrons that were left intact were equivalent to with one part in 10^{37} (Corey, 1993, p. 62). Had this primordial balance between protons and electrons been any different, the electromagnetic force would have so completely dominated the gravitational force that stars and planets could never have evolved. How accurate is this (one part in 10^{37}) 'lucky accident'?

> "*Cover the entire North American continent in dimes all the way up to the moon, a height of about 239,000 miles (in comparison, the money to pay for the U.S. federal government debt would cover one square mile less than two feet deep with dimes). Next, pile dimes from here to the moon on a billion other continents the same size as North America. Paint one dime red and mix it into the billions of piles of dimes. Blindfold a friend and ask him to pick out one dime.* ***The odds that he will pick the red dime are one in 10^{37}***." (Ross, 1995, p. 115).

Even a staunch atheist like Stephen Hawking (1998, p. 144) expressed his doubt, "*It would be very difficult to explain why the Universe should have begun in just this way, except as the act of a God who intended to create beings like us*".

If the initial explosion of the big bang had differed in strength by as little as one part in 10^{60}, the Universe would have either quickly collapsed back on itself, or expanded too rapidly for stars to form. (Davies, 1982, pp. 90-91). In either case, life would be impossible. Calculations show that if gravity had been stronger or weaker by one part in 10^{40}, then life-sustaining stars like the sun could not exist and life would be impossible. (Davies, 1984, p. 242). If the neutron was not about 1.001 times the mass of the proton, all protons would have decayed into neutrons or all neutrons would have decayed into protons, and thus life would not be possible. (Leslie, 1989, pp. 39-40). The mass of the neutrinos (subatomic particles similar to electron but electrically neutral) is fine-tuned by one part in 10^{35} (Davies, 1982, p. 61). The additional gravitational mass would result in a contracting rather than expanding Universe because of their great abundance in the Universe.

Simply, the laws of nature seem to have been designed so as to move the Universe towards the emergence and sustenance of life. This is known as 'Anthropic Principle' (Australian theoretical physicist Brandon Carter coined this term in 1970 – Anthropic means 'relating to human beings or their existence'. The Anthropic Principle is the 'Law of Human Existence') which had been popularised by great thinkers, such as Martin Rees, John Barrow and John Leslie.

> "*If, then, there were aspects of nature's workings that appeared very fortunate and also entirely fundamental, then these might well be seen as* ***evidence specially favouring belief in God***." (Leslie, 2001, p. 213).

How nature came packaged in this fashion? The English philosopher Antony Flew commented, "*This is certainly the question that scientists from Newton to Einstein to Heisenberg have asked – and answered. Their answer was the Mind of God*". (Flew, 2008, p. 96). Flew renounced his atheism due to the argument for intelligent design. American Philosopher Robin Collins commented,

> "*Imaginatively, one could think of each instance of fine-tuning as a radio dial: unless all the dials are set exactly right, life would be impossible. Or, one could think of the initial conditions of the Universe and the fundamental parameters of physics as a dart board that fills the whole galaxy, and the conditions necessary for life to exist as a small one-foot-wide target: unless the dart hits the target, life would be impossible. The fact that the dials are perfectly set, or the dart has hit the target, strongly suggests that someone set the dials or aimed the dart, for it seems enormously improbable that such a coincidence could have happened by chance.*" (Murray, 1999, p. 49).

The laws of physics that govern a major part of the natural world are simple enough for a mediocre graduate student to grasp, and the mathematical concepts of these laws can be fully explained in a few ordinary textbooks. But why they are so simple? These laws could be formidably complex so that they would require millions of textbooks or a super computer to define. They might even be an indigestible chaos of special cases and exceptions that could not be reduced to a rational system. This particular fact has led many prominent scientists to conclude that God must be a mathematician. Nobel Laureate Physicist Paul Dirac (1933, shared with Erwin Schrödinger) commented, "*God is a mathematician of a very high order and He used advanced mathematics in constructing the Universe*". (Dirac, 1963, p. 53). Dr. Paul Dirac was right. The spirit guides from afterlife realm revealed the same truth through Ruth Montgomery.

> "*The Guides say that 'the earliest souls brought with them the science of Mathematics, which is* ***a divine law of harmony and balance'****.*" (Montgomery, 1976, p. 48).

The elegance of the laws of physics is also one of the conditions for the existence of life as we know it.

We know that the atoms and molecules are stable because all electrons and all protons have exactly the same charge but opposite. If these charges varied randomly from one particle to another, neutral atoms would not be possible, and our world would never have the chance to form at all. The perfection is one part in one hundred billion. (Corey, 1993, p. 62). Can we dismiss these coincidences as 'lucky incidences', or do they confirm the presence of an Eternal Consciousness even before the big bang? Though the individual calculations of fine-tuning figures may differ slightly, the fact that the Universe is fine-tuned for life is beyond question – "*Clues heaped upon clues can constitute weighty evidence despite doubts about each element in the pile*" (Leslie, 1988, p. 300). How to explain this perfect degree of balance?

The combination of matter and energy in the Universe accurately fits the future needs of the lives to survive and to grow both intellectually and spiritually. This means that the initial state of the Universe must have been very carefully chosen. The second law of thermodynamics concerns about 'Entropy' (the measure of the level of disorder in a closed but changing system). Things disintegrate and they fall apart over time. How our Universe began with order and is gradually becoming less orderly? Why there was not chaos at the beginning? Hogan (2008, p. 50) explains,

> "***One analogy is that expecting to get our uniquely designed living environment out of an accidental explosive expansion in the Universe is like expecting to get a dictionary out of an explosion in a printing shop.***"

There are many remarkable pieces of engineering around us, e.g., the gravitational pull of the Sun and Moon perfectly stabilises the Earth's tilt of rotation axis that results in a stable climate, and Moon has the perfect size to cause ocean tides that mix nutrients from the land and oceans to make life possible. The motions of the planets can be explained by gravity, but it cannot explain who sets the planets in motion. The Earth is at the perfect distance from the Sun so water can stay liquid with temperature ranges such that human beings can live, and a size sufficient to have an atmosphere. The Earth is also set up remarkably precisely to provide the water and oxygen the planet needs to support life.

Our Universe is set up not only to allow us to exist but also allows us to have maximum opportunities to discover how it works. As example, the moon is just the right size and just the right distance from the Earth moving in just the right orbit to cover the sun precisely so we can have perfect solar eclipse. As a result of the moon exactly covers the sun from where we are standing, we have made discoveries about the sun's corona and the warping of light by gravity that couldn't have been made without this incredible set of matched conditions. We are far enough from the center of the Milky Way Galaxy and the galaxy disk is flat enough that it doesn't excessively obscure our view of the distant Universe. We can see a wonderful diversity of nearby stars, other galaxy structures and the unique cosmic microwave background radiation that shows us that the Universe is expanding and finite in age

Such fine-tuning requires a fine-tuner with incredible knowledge and power. Sceptics may find this idea a bit unscientific. For them I have a question – What happens after an explosion, order or disorder? The answer is always that disorder results. My next question – So why after the big bang, which was the biggest explosion ever, has so much order been created? Some intelligence must be organising its energy and matter into form and unifying all the forces of nature to create such a masterpiece.

The fine-tuning argument is probably the most powerful argument for the existence of an Eternal Consciousness which is a critical component of the Cosmos even before big bang. In Sanatan Dharma, this Eternal Consciousness is Brahmam, as I will be explaining next.

3.1.1: Dharmic versions of the fine-tuning argument

"*The Universe begins to look more like a great thought than like a great machine.*"

English physicist-astronomer Sir James Jeans

The fine-tuning argument is found in classical Dharmic thought that originated several thousand years before Christ. Yoga-Vasistha contains several teachings which confirm that we live in a fine-tuned Universe.

"*nā 'buddhipūrvaṁ tatkarma saṁkasyacit*
buddhipūrvaṁ tu yad vyarthaṁ kuryādunmattako hi kaḥ"
(Yoga-Vasistha: 6.2.103.69).
[**The world-creation is not the action of ignorance. On the other hand, if it is the action of intelligence**, why will an intelligent being indulge in such futile action like a madman?]

"*nehā ' 'kṛtirna ca bhavābhavajanmanāśāḥ*
sattā na caiva na ca nāma tathā 'styasattā
śāntaṁ paraṁ kacati kevalamātmanītthaṁ
brahmā 'thavā kacanamapyalamatra nāsti"
(Yoga-Vasistha: 6.2.178.62).
[There are no forms. There is no existence or non-existence, no birth and no death. There is nothing known as reality nor something which can be called unreal. **The Supreme, which is absolute peace, perceives this creation within Himself – it is not independent of Brahmam the infinite consciousness – so why create the false notion of an independent manifestation?**]

"*saṅkalpasya vapurbrahma saṅkalpakacidākṛteḥ*
tadeva jagato rūpaṁ tasmād brahmātmakaṁ jagat"
(Yoga-Vasistha: 6.2.184.19).

[The content or the reality of notions and thoughts is Brahmam or the infinite consciousness, and that itself is the content or the reality of the world-appearance, too. **Hence, the world is Brahmam.**]

"*cidvyoma cā 'sti sarvatra sarvaṁ caitajjaganmayaṁ*
sarvaṁ brahmamayaṁ śāntaṁ jagadityapi śabditaṁ"
(Yoga-Vasistha: 6.2.210.31).
[The indivisible consciousness exists everywhere, and **all that is also this creation.** All this, is the ever-peaceful Brahmam or infinite consciousness, which is also known as creation.]

"*jagataḥ pañcakaṁ bījaṁ pañcakasya cid avyayā*
yad bījaṁ tat phalaṁ viddhi tasmād brahmamayaṁ jagat"
(Yoga-Vasistha: 3.13.9).
[The five elements are the seed of which the world is the tree; and the Eternal Consciousness is the seed for the elements. As is the seed, so is the tree. **Therefore, the world is nothing but Brahmam - the absolute.**]

The ancient texts contemplated the Universe as a connected and perfect system, governed by general laws and directed to benevolent ends. This also points to God's unity and wisdom. And since these thoughts originated millennia ago there were no foreign influences. The philosophical question raised by St. Augustine about 1,600 years ago, and by St. Thomas Aquinas 800 years ago had already been explained by the Dharmic texts thousands of years ago before the question was even asked. Without undermining the supremacy of reason, the ancient texts reflected and reinforced the notion of a created Universe that is essentially mechanistic in nature portraying God as an architect or potter – a critical presupposition of any fine-tuning argument. Arthur Ford revealed the same wisdom through Ruth Montgomery.

"*We will first consider the aspect of God, the one abiding force which melds all else together.* ***The force or power is so intense that nothing will survive if it should fail for so much as the batting of an eye.*** *It is the glue of the Universe, the melding together, the complete atom.... a tremendous force for good that knows no other than good... This force or Godhead is the universal truth, the universal good, the universal all-in-all.*" (Montgomery, 1972, p. 29).

The Baptist evangelical missionary William Ward spent many years in India, translating and interpreting many original Sanskrit works with the help of 'Pandits', including the philosophical treatises of the six 'orthodox schools' and the Buddhist scriptures. Ward carefully noted various conflicting opinions about such questions as whether the world was created or had sprung into existence by itself. According to Ward, the Buddhists affirm that the world sprung into existence of itself and there is no creator. Ward then continues,

> "*Against this, the writers of the orthodox 'durshunus' [Darsana – six orthodox schools of Philosophy] insist, that proof equal to that arising from the senses may be obtained from inference, from comparison, and from sounds [Ward's literal translation of the Sanskrit term 'sabda', which refers to the spoken word, and hence to verbal authority, both of a sage and of scripture]. The following is one of their proofs from inference:* ***God exists; this we infer from his works. The earth is the work of some one – man has not power to create it. It must therefore be the work of the being whom we call God.***" (Ward, 1985, p. 117).

This brief passage covers both the design argument and cosmological argument for the existence of a 'self-existing power', and points to a vibrant, rational approach to theology that the great thinkers of Sanatan Dharma were capable of when left to their own wisdom.

Three great Sages, Adi Shankaracharya, Acharya Udayana (975-1050 CE) and Ramanuja advanced elaborate details of the design argument against their opponents. Ramanuja, though accepted the design argument, also put forth some counterarguments. It means, those sages not only had a fully developed natural theology, but they also were keenly interested to debate over it.

Shankaracharya characterised the Brahmam or Ultimate Reality as beyond all activity and transformation, and transcending all rational comprehension. The perceived Universe for him is a misleading realm of multiplicity whose true nature is obscured through the power of Maya. For Shankaracharya, Brahmam is both the material as well as efficient cause of the Universe.

> "*prakṛtiśca pratijñādṛṣṭāntānuparodhāt*"
> (Shankara's Bhasya: 1.4.23).
> [(Brahmam is) the material cause (the aspect of the change that is determined by the material that composes the moving or changing things) and the efficient cause (initiation of the process of change by thoughts, desires, judgments, plans, actions etc.) on account of the absence of conflict with regard to the initial proposition and the illustration.]

In other words, the Universe is fine-tuned because God wants it that way. The ancient sages contemplated the universe as a connected and perfect system governed by general laws and directed to benevolent ends supported by total knowledge of the concepts of divine design.

3.2: BRAHMAM - Dharmic versions of Eternal Consciousness

"*athato brahma jijnasa*" (Vedanta-Sutra: 1.1.1).
[Now one should inquire about Brahmam – The absolute truth.]

"*satyam jnanam anantam brahma*" (Taittiriya Upanishad 2.1.1).
[Brahmam is truth, knowledge, and infinite.]

The earliest inquiries about the Eternal Consciousness are recorded in the Vedas. Vedic tradition is not content merely with belief in God, but to know God within our own minds and hearts. This higher knowledge should come from direct perception, not as a mere mental or emotional connection. It means. Vedic Dharma does not rest upon faith at a mass level, but spiritual practices at an individual level for achieving Moksha – the ultimate goal of life.

The first question that comes in our mind is, what are our available means of legitimate knowledge? This basic question is very important for spiritual studies. The next question is, if something divine, infinite and eternal does exist, through what special means can it be known? Obviously, the ordinary mind and senses of a common man is designed to know limited and temporary objects, but a person, well-versed with the ancient Vedas, can speculate about something much farther beyond. One of the legitimate means of knowledge is 'Samadhi' (Yogic perception born of the meditative mind). Sage Patanjali deals with the concept of the Divine in Yoga Sutras.

"*klesha karma vipaka ashayaih aparamristah purusha-vishesha ishvara tatra niratishayam sarvajna bijam*" (Yoga Sutras: 1.24-25).
['Ishvara' (the creative source) is a particular consciousness who is untouched by the afflictions of life, actions, and the results and impressions produced by these actions.
In that pure consciousness, the seed of omniscience has reached its highest development and cannot be exceeded.]

It means, Brahmam is a special kind of consciousness who had not gone through the evolutionary process. Since the Universe is harmonious, it must be the manifestation of one will.

"*sada jnatah chitta vrittayah tat prabhu purusasya aparinamitvat*" (Yoga Sutras: 4.18).
[The activities of the mind are always known by the pure consciousness, because that pure consciousness is superior to, support of, and master over the mind.]

The God is aware in an unbroken manner of all the changes which are taking place in the mind. No change can escape his notice because he is eternal.

> "*God is total awareness. He not only hears prayer but knows without being asked what the plea is going to be. He is truth supreme, wisdom and all-knowing, and without Him there would be only chaotic blackness.*" (Montgomery, 1972, p. 31).

The most fascinating part of Yoga-Vasistha (3.30.8 to 3.30.34) is that Sage Vasistha had astonishing knowledge about extraterrestrial life on other planets. This is something what the researchers are still struggling to get into theory. Since Eternal Consciousness exists everywhere, creation of these planets and their growth and dissolution also goes on everywhere. All these are held together by a mysterious omnipresent power – Brahmam. Sage Vasistha confirmed that everything exists in 'One Infinite Consciousness'.

> "*utpadyotpadyate tatra svayaṃ saṃvitsvabhāvataḥ*
> *svasaṃkalpaiḥ śamaṃ yāti bālasaṃkalpajālavat*"
> (Yoga-Vasistha: 3.30.8).
> [There is but one indefinite space in nature, as there is but one consciousness in all beings; yet everything moves in its own way, as wayward boys take their own course.]

This light of Brahmam is the true guide. No physical teacher can ever have the knowledge of infinite truth, for such knowledge is available only to the one who transcends time. And because God transcends time, all mysteries are known only to God. It is the light of this Supreme Being that enlightens the mind and heart.

> "*na tat svabhasam drishyatvat*" (Patanjali's Yoga Sutras: 4.19).
> [The mind is not self-illuminating, as it is the object of knowledge and perception by the pure consciousness.]

The Vedas teach the worship of One God who is omnipresent, omniscient and omnipotent Lord of the Universe.

> "*ekam sat, vipra bahudha vadanti*" (Rig Veda: 1.164.46).
> [There is only one truth (or true being) and learned persons call it by many names.]

Sanatan Dharma has often been confused to be polytheistic but this is not true. There are multiple manifestations or personalities of the one Brahmam. This Advaita principle of the infinite divine nature of Brahmam remains forever central, universal and unchanged. This is like a single beam of light separated into colours by a prism. Vedic Sages were attracted by the bright and beautiful aspects of nature and so they worshiped the various forces of nature as manifestations of Supreme Being.

> "*Information is pre-existent because only one mind exists, one source of all things, one power behind and beyond all processes, one force in and though all as all, one intelligence.*" (Atwater, 1999b, p. 164).

This one pure awareness is represented by the symbol of OM. This is the vibratory aspect of God from which the whole of creation emerged. The sound of OM is called 'Anahada Nada' in Sanskrit, meaning 'unstruck sound', i.e., sound produced without striking two things together.

> "*OM tat sad iti nirdeśo brahmaṇas tri-vidhaḥ smṛtaḥ*
> *brāhmaṇās tena vedāś ca yajñāś ca vihitāḥ purā*
> *tasmād OM ity udāhṛtya yajña-dāna-tapaḥ-kriyāḥ*
> *pravartante vidhānoktāḥ satataṁ brahma-vādinām*"
> (Bhagavad Gita: 17.23-24).
> [From the beginning of creation, the three words OM TAT SAT were used to indicate the Supreme Absolute Truth. These three symbolic representations were used by Brahmins while chanting the hymns of the Vedas and during sacrifices for the satisfaction of the Supreme.
> Therefore, with the utterance of OM the acts of gift, sacrifice and austerity enjoined in the scriptures are always begun by the expounders of Brahmam.]

OM is the sound of the Universe, known as the 'Pranava' (the humming). OM serves as a sonic realisation of the Divine, the audible embodiment of Ultimate Reality and the reverberation that sets worlds in motion. While other Mantras are individually recorded in the vast amount of oral texts, OM is at once nowhere and everywhere. The Pranava Japa (repeated utterance of OM with deep feeling for its meaning) can eradiate all the obstacles in the yogic path towards attaining the realised oneness with the Divine.

> "*OM itīdaṃ sarvam*" (Taittiriya Upanishad: 1.8).
> [This whole world is OM.]

Sage Patanjali also stresses the importance of the 'Pranava' and its 'Japa' (repeated utterance).

> "*tasya vachakah pranavah*
> *tat japah tat artha bhavanam*" (Yoga Sutras: 1.27-28).
> [The sacred word designating this creative source is the sound OM, called Pranava.
> This sound is remembered with deep feeling for the meaning of what it represents.]

"*tatah pratyak chetana adhigamah api antaraya abhavash cha*" (Yoga Sutras: 1.29).
[From that remembering comes the realisation of the individual Self and the removal of obstacles.]

Shankaracharya made a place for OM in his inquiry into the metaphysical relations between humanity and Ultimate Reality. For him, OM is the audible realisation of the Absolute – its utterance embodies a transcendent holism that is beyond words. The fact that we are unable to explain the syllable in linguistic, historical, and cultural terms only heightens its power and importance. OM stands alone because this is a 'universal sound', a vocalisation occurring naturally before an infant acquires language.

As per the wisdom of the Vedas, the syllable remains 'Apauruseya' (beyond human origin), eternal, prior to everything. A spirit guide revealed through Ruth Montgomery that the ancient Atlanteans (citizen of the lost continent Atlantis) used OM Mantra to address God. The Atlanteans very rarely used the name of God because God had the greatest command on them. But when it becomes absolutely necessary to write or speak about Him, the guides revealed,

"*... the symbol of a sun with moon at crescent was made, or the lips used to form the sound, so that it becomes a round 'O' for the sun and a 'hum' for the crescent, or 'OM'. ... this would explain the derivation for the mystical incantation 'OM' used in meditation.*" (Montgomery, 1976, p. 97).

In Vedanta, Brahmam is discussed as Consciousness which is 'Sat-Chit-Ananda' (Existence-Consciousness-Bliss). Some spiritualists consider Sat-Chit-Ananda to be the eternal and unified concept of the Atman which is beyond space and time. The core wisdom is that you are one with Brahmam, that you are truly Sat-Chit-Ananda. All beings are in you, and you are in all beings.

"*yas tu sarvāṇi bhūtāny ātmany evānupaśyati*
sarvabhūteṣu cātmānaṃ tato na vijugupsate
yasmin sarvāṇi bhūtāny ātmaivābhūd vijānataḥ
tatra ko mohaḥ kaḥ śoka ekatvam anupaśyataḥ"
(Isa Upanishad: Mantra no. 6, 7).
[And **he who sees all beings in himself and himself in all beings has no disgust thereafter.**
When to a knower discovering unity, all beings become his very Self, what delusion then (to him) and what sorrow?]

Hence, Sat-Chit-Ananda is not a mere philosophical idea but an absolutely unitary idea. Any sense of separation is only Maya.

> "*ajo 'pi sann avyayātmā bhūtānām īśvaro 'pi san prakṛtiṃ svāṁ adhiṣṭhāya sambhavāmy ātma-māyayā*"
> (Bhagavad Gita: 4.6).
> [Though I am unborn, and eternal by nature, and though I am the Lord of all beings, yet subjugating **my own nature, I come into being by my own Maya.**]

'My own nature' means His inherent power of Maya. Maya originates in Brahmam, but Brahmam remains unaffected by it in the same way as the poison of a snake which is in the snake but cannot injure it. This power of Maya deludes the embodied being from recognising the Brahmam who is His true Self. "I come into being by my own Maya" means that it is through Maya the Brahmam appears to be born. His embodiment is not real as are the embodiments of other beings. The all-powerful God has both aspects to his divine personality – the personal form and the formless aspect.

> "*dwe vāva brahmaṇo rūpe mūrtaṁ chaiva amūrtaṁ cha*"
> (Brihadaranyak Upanishad: 2.3.1).
> [God appears in both ways – as the formless Brahmam and as the personal God. They are both dimensions of his personality.]

Shankaracharya spoke that the illusive power of Maya causes Brahmam to be seen as the material world of separate forms – Nirguna Brahmam (higher form) and Saguna Brahmam (lower form). Nirguna Brahmam is without form, quality, attribute and image. Saguna Brahmam is the supreme reality with form, quality, attribute and image. It is the manifested divine presence – changing form of the unchanging formlessness. We can understand it better from the spiritual experience of Goswami Tulsidas.

Tulsidas was a great devotee of Lord Ram. Once Tulsidas went to Varanasi and visited a temple where he saw the image of Lord Krishna. Tulsidas pondered and expressed how he could describe the beauty of Krishna because he would bow his head only if Lord Krishna took up bow and arrow in His hands. To Tulsidas's amazement, Lord Krishna immediately revealed to him in the form of Lord Ram with bow and arrows.

This idea of changing form of the unchanging formlessness is especially significant to Bhakti School of Philosophy wherein the practitioners choose to worship any form or name of God which inspires them the most. Hence, Nirguna Brahmam is not the contrast or opposite of Saguna Brahmam, and neither the vice-versa. The same Nirguna Brahmam appears as Saguna Brahmam for the pious worship of devotees. It is the same truth from two different points of view. Sat-Chit-Ananda however is usually understood as Saguna Brahmam.

3.3: Dharmic interpretation of Biocentrism

"*The Universe could only come into existence if someone observed it. It does not matter that the observers turned up several billion years later. The Universe exists because we are aware of it.*"

Martin Rees

"*We create history by our observation, rather than history creating us.*"

Stephen Hawking

Biocentrism or Biocentric Universe (from Greek – bio, 'life' and kentron, 'center' – life-centric nature-view) is a revolutionary view of the Universe. According to this theory, life is neither an accidental by-product of the laws of physics nor the living beings on Earth are merely the activity of an admixture of carbon and a few other elements. Life is fundamentally immortal that creates the Universe. There is no independent external Universe outside of biological existence. Without consciousness, the Universe necessarily exists in an undetermined state of probability only. Time is not an absolute reality but a feature of our mind. Like five senses and time, space does not exist without consciousness. This is the bold and straightforward explanation of biocentrism.

Hence, biology is the central driving science in the Cosmos and other sciences are dependent on a deeper understanding of biology – "*our current theories of the physical world don't work, and can never be made to work, until they account for life and consciousness*". (Lanza, 2009, p. 2). This core idea, built on established science, demands a rethinking of our current theories of the physical Universe.

The Dharmic scriptures contain many elements of biocentrism and the ancient seers probably had better understanding of biocentrism than the present-day scholars. Ever since the beginning of Vedic era, the seers have acknowledged the importance of consciousness, that all truths and principles of being must begin with the individual mind and self. The Universe is presented as a kind of self-operating machine where humans have no special authority over other creatures because all living things have souls. Those seers had explained the origins of everything with grand unified theories in philosophical terms. They had a clear idea about the central mystery of knowledge, that the observer in a significant sense creates reality and not the other way around. Nothing has existence unless you, I, or some living creature perceives it, and how it is perceived further influences that reality. Even time and space itself is not exempted from biocentrism. From a subatomic particle to trillions of galaxies, from the big bang to the big crunch, everything known to be real is keyed to observation and as such to conscious beings.

Shankaracharya proposed that each cause is hidden in its every effect, but the opposite is not true. In other words, the seed (cause) is hidden in the tree (effect) that produces it. A cause is always part of the effect, hidden within it and so is not different from it. The illusory physical world is 'real' only because Brahmam, who is its cause, is inseparable from it. From this perspective the world disappears when the Brahmam is withdrawn from it. Since individual consciousness is part of super consciousness, the world exists when you, the cause, are present in your mind. When you, the cause, withdraw from it, the world disappears. Therefore, we can conclude that Atman or consciousness causes the Universe to exist.

> "*There is no separate physical Universe outside of life and consciousness. Nothing is real that is not perceived. There was never a time when an external, dumb, physical Universe existed, or that life sprang randomly from it at a later date. Space and time exist only as constructs of the mind, as tools of perception. Experiments in which the observer influences the outcome are easily explainable by the interrelatedness of consciousness and the physical Universe. Neither nature nor mind is unreal; both are correlative.*" (Lanza, 2009, p. 159).

This answers a very important question – why does relativity exist with all its complicated distortions of time and space? Relativity exists because our science is actually a science of what we experience, and not a science of a Universe 'out there' that is 'independent' of us as observers.

The Samkhya-Yoga system had similar biocentric thoughts. The Universe is consisting of two independent realities – Purusha (Atman, pure consciousness) and Prakriti (physical matter in all its countless manifestations, ideas, thoughts and subtle energy patterns). Purusha and Prakriti are 'Anadi' (beginningless) and 'Ananta' (infinite). These two realities exist parallel without affecting each other. All consciousness or awareness is the light of Purusha shining through the forms of Prakriti. Purusha acts as catalytic agent. In fact, the whole process of creation is for the benefit of the Purusha, for their spiritual unfoldment resulting finally in their freedom.

> "*Paradoxical as it may seem, Purusha, though a person, is a mere spectator, at best an observer who does nothing, while the insentient, heartless and brainless Prakriti creates and sustains the Universe on his behalf.*" (Lal, 1978, p. 54).

Consciousness is the invisible creator behind the mask of the physical universe. The ancient seers arrived at this conclusion solely through introspection what the quantum physicists are slowly understanding now.

> "*All matter originates and exists only by virtue of a force... We must assume behind this force the existence of a conscious and intelligent Mind.* ***This Mind is the matrix of all matter.***" (Planck, 1944).

In this close association of Purusha and Prakriti, the latter has no purpose of its own. The whole drama of creation is being played in order to provide experience for the growth and Self-realisation of the Purusha who are involved in the show.

> "*prakasha kriya sthiti shilam bhutendriya atmakam bhoga apavarga artham drishyam*" (Yoga Sutras: 2.18).
> [Nature, its three qualities, sattva, rajas and tamas, and its evolutes, the elements, mind, senses of perception and organs of action, **exist eternally to serve the seer**, for enjoyment or emancipation.]

> "*tad-artha eva drishyasya atma*" (Yoga Sutras: 2.21).
> [The essence or nature of the knowable objects exists only to serve as the objective field for pure consciousness.]

Sentient beings are the 'agents' through which the Universe acquires both meaning and structure. In other words, everything that exists in the material world has a purpose. Atman is not created at a certain stage of material development. Matter fulfils the purpose of the Atman. As example, a machine seems to be working automatically and independently, but actually it is not – there is a driver, someone in control, and the machine is not independent, it fulfils some purpose. The grand biocentric design, that has shaken physics to its roots, will be looked upon as a significant milestone along the way.

The Universe is 'designed' with the goal of generating and sustaining 'observers'. Our perception of duality will disappear when we enter the state of non-duality by overcoming the illusion and by developing detachment from the sense objects. This is the state of pure awareness where the knower and known simply vanishes and the Self alone remains – **"And you, Svetaketu, Tat Tvam Asi – You Are That!"**

3.4: Seth Material: A discarnate spiritual teacher speaks the truth of Sanatan Dharma

A self-proclaimed psychic and spirit medium, Dorothy Jane Roberts (1929 - 1984) channeled a spirit teacher who called himself 'Seth'. Seth spoke through Jane (while in a trance state) in many sessions for twenty-one years and these are recorded and known today as the "Seth Material".

Seth indicated he had completed his earthly reincarnations and was speaking from an adjacent plane of existence. He described himself as a 'teacher', and said that he along with many other spiritual teachers had given this material to each successive generation in many parts of the world through the centuries. (Lewis, 2004, p. 584). The following Sutra confirms the source of knowledge of the Seth personality.

> "*purvesham api guruh kalena anavachchhedat*" (Yoga Sutras: 1.26).
> [From that Consciousness the ancient-most teachers were taught, since it is not limited by the constraint of time.]

In the field of divine wisdom and philosophy of the Universe, the Brahmam is not only considered to be the source of all knowledge and wisdom but the real and the only teacher existing in the world timelessly. For the Western Philosophers, the relationship between God and the Sages of the East had been the source of confusion for millennia. Sage Patanjali was evidently aware of this type of confusion and thus devoted an entire Sutra to put the issue to rest.

In the material, Seth had given many references of consciousness, reincarnation, karmic cycle, spirit world, illusion of time and space etc., in a very objective way. These wisdoms are extraordinarily parallel with those the ancient sages had said millennia ago. I briefly mention below some of the wisdom which are relevant to our topics, and put my comments in square brackets

1. Consciousness creates physical reality. Our beliefs (both individual and collective) form reality, and the intensity of a belief is extremely important. We cannot escape our beliefs. [The Maya world of quantum physics – The strange behaviour of quantum particles confirms that the apparent 'materiality' of the world is no more and no less 'real' than a dream-image.]
2. God exists as a self-replicating and inexhaustible mental energy whom Seth referred to as 'All That Is' and described as a 'primary energy gestalt'. The mental energy of God is the composite substance of all things, including all beings, all Universes, and all events and phenomena. God contains all of creation within Him. God is a gestalt of all existence (a gestalt, as a whole, is greater than the sum of its parts), as in Pantheism and Panentheism (Pantheism means that all is God; Panentheism, that all is in God). God's consciousness extends into all things as they are created and is therefore omnipresent. God experiences existence in all His

forms and consequences through its creations. God is therefore dynamic and ever-changing and shares in the failures, triumphs, perfections and imperfections of His creations. **Every creature, though part of God, has free will and self-determination.** Seth personality was not aware if there is any reality outside of God. [This explains why the Universe is fine-tuned for life. The life of each and every living being has a purpose.]

3. There was a creation, but it differs noticeably from the Christian and Muslim versions. Initially the Universe existed in a state of potentiality within God's dreams. The power of God's consciousness was so great that the individuals in His dreams had self-awareness, and they appealed to be made real. The creation occurred when God made His dreams real. [The Atman is eternal. It existed even before big bang.]
4. No event is predestined. Any given event can be changed not only before and during but after its occurrence also. An individual's future actions are not dependent upon a concrete finished past, for such a past never existed. [If time and space are illusions of mind, then past, present and future – all are changeable. The parapsychologist Helmut Schmidt has performed PK experiments which showed that actions in the present can influence the past. This is called retrocausality. Past is neither written on stone nor it is immune to further influence.]
5. No one is at the mercy of the unexplainable, or at the mercy of events (psychological or physical) over which we have no control. [The free will of the soul is always honoured.]
6. The human race is a stage though which various forms of consciousness travel. [We are multi-dimensional beings more than our physical bodies.]
7. After death we travel in other dimensions where we will find ourselves in another form, an image that will appear physical to us to a large degree as long as we do not try to manipulate within the physical system with it. [The spirit realm is beyond our three-dimensional understanding where we can manipulate by thought process.]
8. Death will not bring us an eternal resting place. After death we are judged by how we treat people, and what we do for others. In answer to someone arguing against reincarnation, Seth replied that all of us will reincarnate whether or not we believe that we will. Our personal beliefs and choices will not change the nature of reincarnation one iota. The purpose of reincarnation is to purify the soul. Purification does require change, and the soul needs the

trials of a new physical life. Often past-life memories come to the surface but are not recognised as such, since they appear in fantasy form, or are projected into art creations. But below the fantasy form and projections there is authentic material. The past-life memories enrich the present live. [Reincarnation is not a hypothesis but a hard science fact. It's a natural law.]

9. All probable worlds and all probable variations on the minutest aspect in any reality exist now. Seth referred this as a 'spacious present'. We live all of our reincarnations at once though we may find this difficult to understand. Time, as we think of it, does not exist. [The multiverse theory fits well with quantum physics that all possibilities can coexist. Also, both past and future coexist with the present ('Trikala', three-fold nature of time) – Patanjali's Yoga Sutra: 4.12. When we think in terms of reincarnation it seems that one 'tracing' exists before the other, but the entire 'chart' exists at once, with all the individual life tracings.]
10. If we release ourselves from hatred then we automatically release ourselves from any bad relationships in the future or any experiences that are based upon hatred. The entire structure of our existence will begin to change with these realisations, and an acceleration of spiritual and psychic growth will develop. [This is how we can work out our Karma faster.]
11. Illness and suffering are not thrust upon us by any supernatural power. They are by-products of the learning process. Our all mishaps have a purpose for the growth of the soul. [The miseries and rewards that our life gives us have meaning. The earthly life is a continuous learning process for the development of the soul. In that sense the Earth is a training ground for the soul.]
12. A human is actually his entity (your Atman). He is its materialisation in space and time as he understands it. There is no division between your entity and what you are. [We are all spiritual beings in a human body.]
13. There is never any justification for violence. Those who indulge in violence for whatever reason are themselves changed, and the purity of their purpose adulterated. [Only love is real.]

In sum, Seth's teachings are full of wisdom that echoes the Dharmic thought and are now proven to be true. Seth wants us to doubt as he had confirmed that his messages are for doubters. The Seth wisdom withstood the test of time and affected the lives of people in every corner of the globe. By now the material had been translated over a dozen languages and sold over eight million copies.

3.5: Conclusion

Scientists are trying to resolve the mystery of the origin of the Universe. Most prominent theory of the origin of the Universe is that this entire Universe is only matter which exploded with a 'big bang'. However, the duration of the material Universe is limited. The expansion of the Universe will eventually stop and it will start to contract until all the matter in the Universe collapses to a final singularity. This is called 'big crunch'. The following Shlokas confirm that the Cosmos itself undergoes an immense, indeed an infinite number of deaths and rebirths – the big bang and big crunch theory.

> "*avyaktād vyaktayaḥ sarvāḥ prabhavanty ahar-āgame*
> *rātry-āgame pralīyante tatraivāvyakta-saṃjñake*
> *bhūta-grāmaḥ sa evāyaṃ bhūtvā bhūtvā pralīyate*
> *rātry-āgame 'vaśaḥ pārtha prabhavaty ahar-āgame*"
> (Bhagavad Gita: 8.18-19).
> [At the approach of the day all manifest objects come forth from the unmanifested and at the approach of the night they merge again into that which is called the unmanifest.
> The same multitude of beings, coming forth again and again, merge in spite of themselves, O Partha, at the approach of the night and remanifest themselves at the approach of the day.]

This 'memory' of the Universe is explained in the above Shlokas. In the below NDE, the entirety of the Universe from its big bang to big crunch is experienced that authenticates the above Shlokas.

> "*I was in the Void. I was in pre-creation, before the big bang. I had crossed over the beginning of time/the First Word/the First vibration. I was in the Eye of Creation. I felt as if I was touching the Face of God. It was no religious feeling. Simply I was at one with Absolute Life and Consciousness... When I say that I could see or perceive forever, I mean that I could experience all of creation generating itself. It was without beginning and without end. That's a mind-expanding thought, isn't it?* ***Scientists perceive the big bang as a single event which created the Universe. I saw that the big bang is only one of an infinite number of big bangs creating Universes endlessly and simultaneously.*** *The only images that even come close in human terms would be those created by supercomputers using fractal [a fractal is an object or quantity that displays self-similarity on all scales] geometry equations.*" (Bailey and Yates, 1996, p. 44).

Therefore, the Eternal Consciousness and the interpretation of the physical fine-tuning of the Universe for life are interlinked. NDEs should be explored through science because these are real experiences. The entire cosmic manifestations are manifested by different activities of Lord Krishna's energy.

> "*pitāham asya jagato mātā dhātā pitāmahaḥ*
> *vedyaṃ pavitram oṃkāra ṛk sāma yajur eva ca*
> *gatir bhartā prabhuḥ sākṣī nivāsaḥ śaraṇaṃ suhṛt*
> *prabhavaḥ pralayaḥ sthānaṃ nidhānaṃ bījam avyayam*"
> (Bhagavad Gita: 9.17-18).
> [I am the father of this Universe, the mother, the support and the grandfather. I am the object of knowledge, the purifier and the syllable OM. I am also the Rig, the Sama and the Yajur Vedas.
> I am the goal, the upholder, the master, the witness, the abode, the refuge and the dear friend. I am the creation and the annihilation, the basis of everything, the resting place and the eternal seed.]

Stephen Hawking can take the Universe all the way back to the instant after the big bang through his 'Unified Singularity Theory', but he can't figure out what it was that caused the bang itself. He believes that bodies such as stars or black holes cannot just appear out of nothing, but a whole Universe can (*creatio ex nihilo* – creation out of nothing in the big bang theory). Also he cannot explain the infinite nature of the Universe. It is believed by many religionists that God created the world in six days about 6,000 years ago and destroyed the world in a global flood. Sanatan Dharma alone thinks in terms of billion of years' time-scale about the repeated cyclical creation and annihilation of the Universe.

> "*sarva-bhūtāni kaunteya prakṛtiṃ yānti māmikām*
> ***kalpa-kṣaye** punas tāni **kalpādau** visṛjāmy aham*
> *prakṛtiṃ svām avaṣṭabhya visṛjāmi punaḥ punaḥ*
> *bhūta-grāmam imaṃ kṛtsnam avaśaṃ prakṛter vaśāt*"
> (Bhagavad Gita: 9.7, 8).
> [O son of Kunti, **at the end of a 'Kalpa'** all material manifestations enter into My nature, and at the **beginning of another 'Kalpa'**, by My potency, I create them again.
> The whole cosmic order is under Me. Under My will it is automatically manifested again and again, and under My will it is annihilated at the end.]

The Sanskrit word Kalpa means a vast cosmic period of time related to the lifetime of the Universe, and the words 'Kalpa-kṣaye' (the end of a Kalpa) and 'kalpādau' (the beginning of a Kalpa) is about 4.32 billion earth years. Shlokas 8.17 and 8.18 of Bhagavad Gita explain the cycles of Kalpas, and states that the duration of material Universe is two Kalpas, i.e.,

8.64 billion years ("*sahasra-yuga*", i.e., a thousand cycles of the four ages, and one cycle equals 4,320,000 years).

> "*na khidyate nādriyate nāyāti na ca gacchati*
> *nāstameti na codeti mahākalpaśatairapi*" (Yoga-Vasistha: 1.23.32).
> [Hundreds of great Kalpa ages (of the **creation and dissolution of the world**) may pass away, yet there is nothing that can move eternity to pity or concern, or stop or expedite his course. It neither sets nor rises.]

After the big crunch, Kaal (relative time) comes to a standstill and rests in Mahakaal (eternal time), and waits for the next big bang. Here "creation and dissolution of the world" is what we know as big bang and big crunch. No one really knows what this time is. In the realm of Mahakaal (the timelessness of eternity), time waits for a new creation of the world. No doubt the teaching of this scripture is revolutionary.

> "*kalpakelivilāsena piṣṭapātitajantunā*
> *abhāvo bhāvabhāsena ramate svātmanātmani*"
> (Yoga-Vasistha: 1.23.43).
> [Time after sporting for a Kalpa period in the act of killing and crushing of all living beings, comes to lose its own existence and becomes extinct in the eternity of the Spirit of spirits.]

The Eternal Consciousness will always remain a mystery. Montgomery (1972, p. 31) explained,

> "***God is the core of the Universe from which all else flows forth.*** *He is truth and energy. He is matter and spirit, and all things of heaven and earth. He is eternity itself, wise and all-knowing, ... He is also the essence of our being, without which nothing would exist. It is His total harmony which melds together the Universe and all therein and thereon, so that* ***without His perfect Being the Universe would instantly fall apart****. God is! The eternal I Am.* ***He is so sublime that we are unable to grasp His full.*** *Without God there is nothing and no thing.... there is no life or being without Him.* ***Thus, we are as much a part of Him as He is of us,*** *and because we are imperfect in our reactions and behavioural pattern, we must strive enough onward through many earth cycles until we achieve sufficient perfection to rejoin God as co-creators.* ***It is the [immutable] law, for no imperfect being will ever have the opportunity to become a part of the Godhead which would not function properly if full of imperfections.*** *Thus our ceaseless attempts to return to the physical state in order to erase our rough edges and be able to fit into the Godhead as perfect segments of the whole.*"

The highlighted words "we are as much a part of Him as He is of us" is exactly what the Advaita Vedanta Philosophy repeatedly tells us.

> "*Time has no meaning here. We are ageless, having existed since the beginning, and we are without end. Thus, we are here, and that is all there is to time.*" (Montgomery, 1972, p. 65).

The body-linked waking consciousness only has a subjective reality. One near-death experiencer commented.

> "*The Light explained to me that there is no death.* ***We are immortal beings****. We have already been alive forever! I realized that* ***we are part of a natural living system that recycles itself endlessly****.*" (Ariel, 2010, p. 193).

> "*God revealed to me that* ***I had been created as a spiritual being at the beginning of the creation of the Universe****. ...* ***It was also part of God's plan to create a physical world as a place of learning and growth.***" (Gibson, 2006, p. 236).

That is the basic idea. The following chapter will spell it out more carefully.

Chapter - 4

The science of Punarjanam (Reincarnation) and Karmfal (Action of Karma)

"*If you don't believe in Karma or reincarnation, don't worry. Probably you will in your next life.*"

Bruce Goldberg

"*The goal of man is to preserve his Karma and to develop it further – when man dies, his Karma lives and creates for itself another carrier.*"

Erwin Schrödinger

'Punarjanam' (Reincarnation) and 'Karmfal' (action of Karma) are two most central beliefs of Sanatan Dharma. Several thousand years ago the wise sages desired to know the mysteries of life and death. There were many basic questions – what happens after death? Why is there so much happiness for some and suffering for others in a lifetime? They searched for answers in their deepest meditation, and many answers to these puzzling questions were given by spiritual powers from the Masters and Guides of the heavenly abode. Many of the constructs of the revealed knowledge are still beyond science.

"*sthūlāni sūkṣmāṇi bahūni caiva rūpāṇi dehī svaguṇair vṛṇoti kriyāguṇair ātmaguṇaiś ca teṣāṃ saṃyogahetur aparo 'pi dṛṣṭaḥ*" (Svetasvatara Upanishad: 5.12).

[The embodied Atman, by means of good and evil deeds committed by itself, assumes many forms, coarse and fine. By virtue of its actions and also of such characteristics of the mind as knowledge and desire, it assumes another body for the enjoyment of suitable objects.]

Reincarnation (repeated incarnation), literally 'to be made flesh again', is the essential life-cycle of the Quantum Soul which may continue for several thousand years. The doctrine of Karma essentially maintains that when a person dies, a record of his actions (good and bad) is imprinted upon his Atman. When that Atman eventually reincarnates into another body, those actions as well as their attendant thoughts, words, and desires, will then manifest in the newborn's genes and determine the quality and conditions of his life. Karmic process is an autonomous process. The concept of Karma is inextricably interwoven with that of reincarnation, and makes reincarnation into an automatic, almost mechanical process. Considering reincarnation and Karma together, this profound issue is an essential part of the evolution of the Universe.

4.1: Sanatan Dharma and the doctrine of reincarnation

"*It is not more surprising to be born twice than once.*"

Voltaire (Francois Marie Arouet)

"*The reincarnation of man is as simple and natural as the reincarnation of Nature in the Spring. And rebirth is no more a miracle than is birth.*"

Frank Homer Curtiss, MD

The Atman leaves the body at death and passes into another physical body which may be human or animal depending on the Karma that the individual has amassed during the lifetime. First we will look at Bhagavad Gita for evidence and analysis of reincarnation. This scripture sheds so much light on the subject of reincarnation and the reasons behind it in just a few words.

In the battlefield of Kurukshetra, Lord Krishna knew that the deep-rooted delusion and grief of the star warrior Arjun cannot be removed without the knowledge of reality of immortality and the transmigration of the Atman. Soon the sinking heart of Arjun heard the divine voice of Lord Krishna.

> "*aśocyān anvaśocas tvaṃ prajñā-vādāṃś ca bhāṣase*
> *gatāsūn agatāsūṃś ca nānuśocanti paṇḍitāḥ*" (Bhagavad Gita: 2.11).
> [Though you are speaking learned words, you lament for that which is not worthy of grief. Those who are truly learned lament neither for the living nor for the dead.]

This is the key Shloka of the Bhagavad Gita. All the subsequent teachings are an elaboration of the principle laid down in this Shloka. The cause for Arjun's nervous breakdown was the feeling of 'me' and 'mine' that became very strong in him when he looked at his relatives, friends and teachers lined up on the opposite side in the battlefield. The central point being the sense of 'I'. A man is grieved when he categorises some objects or persons as his own and some others as not his own. This sense of mine and not-mine is the source of all grief, worry, fear and confusion.

Lord Krishna went to the bottom of the issue and explained that a wise man does not have the sense of 'I', 'me' and 'mine'. Such a man is not bound by any tie or attachment of any kind. Those who are aware of the difference between the real and the unreal (i.e., the Atman and the body respectively) are wise for they have realised the eternal reality behind the phenomenal changes and therefore do not grieve at the decay and death of the mortal physical bodies. The next two Shlokas go deeper into this topic and specify the immortality of the Atman.

> "*na tvevāhaṁ jātu nāsaṁna tvaṁ neme janādhipāḥ*
> *na chaiva na bhaviṣhyāmaḥ sarve vayamataḥ param*"
> (Bhagavad Gita: 2 12).
> [Never was there a time when I did not exist, nor you, nor all these kings; nor in the future shall any of us cease to be.]

> "*dehino'smin yathā dehe kaumāraṃ yauvanaṃ jarā*
> *tathā dehāntara-prāptir dhīras tatra na muhyati*"
> (Bhagavad Gita: 2.13).
> [Just as the embodied Atman gradually passes within this gross physical body from boyhood to youth and to old age, similarly, the Atman receives another body at death. An intelligent person is not bewildered by the destruction and rebirth of the body.]

Childhood dies when youth is born and youthhood dies when the old age sets in. Even when childhood or youthhood no longer remains at the old age, man remembers his early days fairly well. Thus, 'something' is common throughout the various stages of growth which could remember the past experiences. Waves arise, they play and die away. But the ocean ever remains the same. Similarly, there can never be a time when Atman is not there. The all-pervading and eternal Atman moves from one body to another through reincarnation. Birth and death are spoken of with regard to the physical body and not the Atman. Most Eastern Philosophies accept this concept of reincarnation.

Bhagavad Gita (e.g., 2.42, 3.15, 4.32, 9.17 and 10.22) confirms that Lord Krishna advises us to look at the Vedas as a tool of acquiring knowledge. The Vedas compiled by Rishi Vyasa are the oldest scriptures. In this large body of vast knowledge and text there is a prayer which speaks of reincarnation.

"*asunīte punarasmāsu cakṣuḥ punaḥ prāṇamiha no dhehibhogham jyok paśyema sūryamuccarantamanumate mṛḷayā nahsvasti punarno asuṃ pṛthivī dadātu punardyaurdevī punarantarikṣam punarnaḥ somastanvaṃ dadātu punaḥ pūṣāpathyāṃ yā svastiḥ*"
(Rig Veda: 10.59.6-7).
[We pray Thee that **we may be happy whenever we may assume another body after death.** Grant us, O God! The eyes and all the other senses, the 'pranas' and the inner senses in our future birth when **we may assume another body after forsaking the present.**]

The belief in reincarnation is much deep-seated, not only exclusive to Bhagavad Gita but also to those who understand the deeper meanings behind the Vedic symbolic language.

"*vāsāṃsi jīrṇāni yathā vihāya navāni gṛhṇāti naro'parāṇi tathā śarīrāṇi vihāya jīrṇāny anyāni saṃyāti navāni dehī*"
(Bhagavad Gita: 2.22).
[Just as a man casts off his worn-out clothes and puts on new ones, so also the embodied Self casts off its worn-out bodies and enters that are new.]

When we discard old garments in favour of new ones, we do not change ourselves. Similarly, the Atman remains unchanged when it discards its worn-out body and takes birth in a new body elsewhere. There is a similar Mantra in Brihadaranyaka Upanishad.

"*tadyathā tṛṇajalāyukā tṛṇasyāntaṃ gatvānyamākramamākramyātm ānamupasaṃharati, evamevāyamātmedaṃ śarīraṃ nihatya, avidyāṃ gamayitvā, anyamākramamākramyātmānamupasaṃharati*"
(Brihadaranyaka Upanishad: 4.4.3).
[Just as a leech supported on a straw goes to the end of it, takes hold of another support and bonds itself, so does the Atman throw this body aside – make it senseless – take hold of another support, and bond itself.]

Lord Krishna dispelled the cause of lamentation in respect to the Atman in Shloka 2.20, and in respect to the body in Shloka 2.27. Now in the next few Shlokas, He includes both, and then the cycle of life is clearly revealed. This is an inevitable process in the material existence, and all beings existing in the material manifestation completely follow this reality.

"*atha chainaṁ nitya-jātaṁ nityaṁ vā manyase mṛitam tathāpi tvaṁ mahā-bāho naivaṁ śhochitum arhasi*"
(Bhagavad Gita: 2.26).

[But even if you think of it as being perpetually born and perpetually dying, even then, O Mighty Armed (Arjun), you should not grieve.]

"*jātasya hi dhruvo mṛityur dhruvaṁ janma mṛitasya cha*
tasmād aparihārye 'rthe na tvaṁ śhochitum arhasi"
(Bhagavad Gita: 2.27).
[Death is sure to happen to that which is born. Birth is sure to happen to that which dies. Birth and death are certainly unavoidable. Therefore, you should not grieve over an inevitable occurrence.]

"*avyaktādīni bhūtāni vyakta-madhyāni bhārata*
avyakta-nidhanānyeva tatra kā paridevanā" (Bhagavad Gita: 2.28).
[Beings are unmanifest in their beginning, manifest in their middle state and unmanifest again in their end. O Arjun, what is there to grieve about?]

The most prominent thought of one's life occupies the mind at the time of death. The thoughts before departure are very significant because they will naturally be determined by what was constantly contemplated and meditated upon during the span of life as influenced by one's daily habits and associations. There is a similar Mantra in Prashna Upanishad also.

"*yaṁ yaṁ vāpi smaran bhāvaṁ tyajatyante kalevaram*
taṁ tam evaiti kaunteya sadā tad-bhāva-bhāvitaḥ"
(Bhagavad Gita: 8.6).
[For whatever object a man thinks of at the final moment, that alone does he attain when he leaves his body, O Son of Kunti, being ever absorbed in the thought thereof.]

"*yaccittastenaiṣa prāṇamāyāti prāṇastejasā yuktaḥ*
sahātmanā yathāsaṃkalpitaṃ lokaṃ nayati"
(Prashna Upanishad: 3.10).
[Of what thought, by that he attains 'prana', the 'prana' combined with the fire along with the Atman, conducts to the world thought of.]

Lord Krishna was aware of the past lives of all the characters of Mahabharat. Merely because He is standing before Arjun in the human form, He should not be equated with human beings. As example, if someone sometimes decides to visit the prison, but if we see him standing in the jail, we do not erroneously conclude that he is also a convict. We know that he is in the jail merely for an inspection. Similarly, God sometimes descends in the material world, but He is never separate from His divine attributes and power.

"*bahūni me vyatītāni janmāni tava chārjuna*
tānyahaṁ veda sarvāṇi na tvaṁ vettha parantapa"
(Bhagavad Gita: 4.5).

[Many births of mine have passed as well as of yours, O Arjun; I know them all but you know them not, O Parantapa (the subduer of the enemies).]

This Shloka also indicates that it is not necessary that all those who had reincarnated remember their past lives and it is also not easy to remind them by just narrating. In his commentary upon this Shloka Shankaracharya states, "*yā vāsudeve anīśhvarāsarvajñāśhaṅkā mūrkhāṇāṃ tāṃ pariharan śhrī-bhagavān uvācha*" (Śhārīrak Bhāṣhya on Shloka 4.5 – Shankaracharya's commentary on the Vedanta Philosophy is called Śhārīrak Bhāṣhya), means, Lord Krishna spoke this Shloka to refute ignorant people who doubt that He is not God.

"*ā-brahma-bhuvanāl lokāḥ punar āvartino 'rjuna*
mām upetya tu kaunteya punar janma na vidyate"
(Bhagavad Gita: 8.16).
[In all the worlds of this material creation, up to the highest abode of Brahma (the God of creation), you will be subject to rebirth, O Arjun. But on attaining My Abode, O son of Kunti, there is no further rebirth.]

There are many planes of existence (in Sanskrit, 'Loka') other than earthly plane, and all these planes are within the realm of Maya. Swarg loka is the highest amongst them. All the residing souls (they are highly evolved souls) in the higher planes are also subject to reincarnation cycle because they are still not released from the bondage of the material energy.

Many other Dharmic texts other than the Bhagavad Gita talk about reincarnation. Though the central theme assumes various forms, the essence is that the birth and death is actually a link in an infinite series of lives, each of which is conditioned and determined by the acts done in previous existences. The belief has been in existence right from the age of the Rig Veda.

4.2: Reincarnation is a science fact

"*We here know each other through many many lives, some having been together at various stages in physical development, but all of us at one time or another crossing paths, here or there. As a consequence there's no such thing as a stranger here, which makes it easier for us to understand that* ***we are all part of one another as well as of God.***"

Ruth Montgomery

"*The knowledge of rebirth is the turning point in the history of mankind.*"
Friedrich Nietzsche

The reincarnation theory provides a comprehensive and intelligible framework in which all the quite dissimilar, seemingly unrelated, and apparently meaningless events of one's life make sense and are seen to have an inner structure. Curtiss (1949, p. 12) is more elaborate on this issue.

> "*Aside from the fact that this doctrine most satisfactorily solves the problems and includes all the facts of our life here on Earth, how else do we know that the doctrine is true? First, there is the testimony of the ages. No doctrine or theory can survive critical examination and application from age to age if it is not founded on truth. Theories of science, religion and philosophy arise, flourish for a time, then pass away, but reincarnation eternally remains. In fact, it reaches back beyond recorded history.*"

Modern-day investigators can demonstrate reincarnation in three basic forms – spontaneous past-life recalls of the children (Sanskrit term 'Jatismara'), spontaneous past-life recalls by adult persons and hypnotic past-life recalls. Each of these three types independently provides us a concrete proof of reincarnation.

4.2.1: Spontaneous past-life memories in children

> "*Young children sometimes report details of a previous life, which upon checking turn out to be accurate and which they could not have known about in any other way than reincarnation.*"
>
> Carl Sagan

> "*The Vedantic school taught that neither the will of God nor the fault of parents formed children's characters. Rather, each child is responsible for his own capabilities, powers and character through conduct in previous life.*"
>
> Ruth Montgomery

In several instances, small children remember and describe their previous life in another body, another place, and with other people. Even the habit-patterns, skills, dislikes, phobias and scars on the skin appear sometimes to be a 'carry-over' from the 'earlier life'. Dr. Ian Stevenson had accumulated massive evidence in his book 'Twenty Cases Suggestive of Reincarnation' that was a result of his painstaking research for about five decades.

Suzanne, a middle-class girl from Beirut remembered the life of a woman who had died undergoing heart surgery in Richmond, Vancouver. When she was sixteen months old, she pulled the phone off the hook and said, "Hello, Leila?" into it over and over. Soon Suzanne claimed that she was Leila's mother. By the time she was two, Suzanne had mentioned the names of total thirteen people including this woman's other children, her husband, parents and brothers. At three, she had recited portions of a funeral oration for the woman's brother and begged her parents to take her to her 'real' home in a Lebanese town. After inquiry, ultimately the parents found the family of Suzanne's past life. And there they learned that shortly before undergoing her heart surgery, the woman in question had tried desperately to call her daughter Leila. This family confirmed much of what Suzanne had been saying – names, places, the funeral oration. Suzanne identified members of the dead woman's family from photographs. Though she was a child, she treated the dead woman's grown children as a mother would. She asked if their uncles, when they returned to Lebanon, had distributed 'her' jewels to Leila and her sisters – which had been a deathbed request known only to the family. The dead woman's relatives gave it, but reluctantly as they had been rocked by Suzanne's claims. That reluctance made their testimony all the more valuable, in Stevenson's view.

A young Druse boy was adamant on meeting someone of whom his parents had never heard. He was eventually tracked down in another village the boy had never visited. The boy knew his way around, embraced his apparently unknown friend as 'his' son in a former incarnation, identified clothing that had belonged to 'him' before his death in action in Lebanon two weeks before the child's birth, and even correctly stated that 'he' had left a cigarette in a pack in a shirt.

There are strange statements that occur in childhood for which reincarnation provides a better interpretation than other alternative theories, as example, a two-year-old girl pointed at the collapsing twin towers on the screen and said very clearly, 'I die'. Many children demand to be called by the name of the previous person, and some seem to expect that they should be recognised as from the previous life. Many of them do not at first distinguish past from present, and they may use the present tense in reference to the previous life. Most often, the child uses the same kind of hand gestures as the deceased person when talking. He is usually better at recognizing persons in photographs taken during the periods when the previous persons knew him than he is in recognizing. Also, he likes and dislikes special idiomatic phrases, and recollects nicknames and names for objects of his past life. No child had claimed the memories of living ones, or the lives of more than one deceased personality living in the same period.

In rare cases, the child remembers animal lives. One child believed she had been a monkey in one or two previous lives anterior to the two human ones she remembered. A Burmese girl claimed an intermediate life as an ox. There was an amazing case of a woman who saved the life of a fawn, believing it to be the reincarnation of her son, and then was sued in court by the hunters who had been pursuing it. The court ruled that either party had made its case, and retained custody.

A very strong and excessive attachment to an animal may cause rebirth in animal kingdom.

> "*yadā sattve pravṛddhe tu pralayaṁ yāti deha-bhṛt*
> *tadottama-vidāṁ lokān amalān pratipadyate*
> *rajasi pralayaṁ gatvā karma-saṅgiṣu jāyate*
> *tathā pralīnas tamasi mūḍha-yoniṣu jāyate*"
> (Bhagavad Gita 14.14-15).
> [When one dies in the mode of goodness, he attains to the pure higher planets of the great Sages.
> When one dies in the mode of passion, he takes birth among those engaged in fruitive activities; and when one dies in the mode of ignorance, he takes birth in the animal kingdom.]

If we develop the mentality of an animal, we will get the body of an animal. But if we live a humane life, we will receive a human body. The Puranas relate the story of King Bharat who lived in the forest as an ascetic and pursued God-realisation by renouncing his kingdom. One day, Bharat felt pity on a baby deer that he had rescued. Slowly, his mind came away from God and became absorbed in the deer. The absorption became so deep that practically all day long his thoughts would wander towards the deer. When he was about to die, he called out to the deer in fond remembrance, concerned about what would happen to him. Consequently, in his next life King Bharat became a deer. However, because he had performed spiritual Sadhana (a Sanskrit term used to refer to a daily spiritual practice), he was aware of the mistake in his previous life, and so even as a deer, he would reside near the hermitage of sages in the forest. Finally, when he gave up the deer body, he was again given a human birth. This time he became the great Sage Jadabharat, and attained God-realisation by completing his Sadhana. Two Mantras from Chandogya Upanishad speak about reincarnation, Karma and animal rebirth of shorter duration.

> "*tadya iha ramaṇīyacaraṇā abhyāśo ha yatte ramaṇīyāṃ*
> *yonimāpadyeranbrāhmaṇayoniṃ vā kṣatriyayoniṃ vā vaiśyayoniṃ*
> *vātha ya iha kapūyacaraṇā abhyāśo ha yatte kapūyāṃ*
> *yonimāpadyerañśvayoniṃ vā sūkarayoniṃ vā*
> *caṇḍālayoniṃ vā*" (Chandogya Upanishad: 5.10.7).
> [Among them, those who did good work in this world (in their past lives) attain a good birth accordingly. They are born as a Brahmin, a

Kshatriya, or a Vaishya. But those who did bad work in this world (in their past lives) attain a bad birth accordingly, being born as a dog, a pig, or as a casteless person.]

"*athaitayoḥ pathorna katareṇacana tānīmāni kṣudrāṇyasakṛdāvartīni bhūtāni bhavanti jāyasva mriyasvetyetat....*" (Chandogya Upanishad: 5.10.8).
[But those who do not follow either of these two paths are born among small animals and insects again and again. (This can be said about those who are born in) this third state: 'Be born and die.'....]

During the British period, a poor Burmese boy named Maung Htun Kyaing preached Buddhism from very early age of four with profound understanding of the subject and better than any religious teacher could have done. He visited a Buddhist Monastery in the local village, where he lived in his previous life as an abbot (the Head of a Monastery) named U. Pandesia. He recognised the present abbot and correctly mentioned his name and showed the room where he meditated, and identified the things that he used. At the Monastery, the child read the scriptures written in ancient Pali language and explained its meaning. People were so impressed by the sermons that they came by thousands to listen and see him.

Our everyday life provides similar examples. We know how to walk, but how many of us remember the days of infancy when we learned to walk? We can have behavioural memories without any imaged memories about the origin of the behaviour. It is possible that some persons may have had previous lives of which they have no imaged memories but from which they have derived important ingredients of their characters. In these cases, some gentle probing may prompt a past-life story.

The Japanese occupation of Burma was the period between 1942 and 1945 during World War II. During this period the Japanese soldiers had shown extreme cruelty to the rather peaceful Burmese Buddhists. As the British defeated the Japanese in the early 1945, the Japanese army retreated in some disorder and many soldiers remained behind. The British army captured some of them, and the Burmese villagers took revenge by capturing and killing many of them. Many Burmese children born during and after this period had shown behavioural patterns which were unusual in Burma, but typical of Japanese people, especially Japanese soldiers during their occupation of Burma.

Stevenson (1983, pp. 216-17) had examined several behavioural characteristics of a group of twenty-four Burmese subjects (sixteen males and eight females – all the female children claimed to have lived last life as male) who said they were Japanese soldiers killed in Burma. The children showed nostalgia for Japan, unusual interest in war games, preference for Japanese food (raw or partially cooked fish, raw eggs, strong tea) and clothing, annoyance with British / Americans, complaints about heat in Burma etc. Moreover, many of them spoke a strange language (assumed to be Japanese) other than Burmese, persistence of 'foreign' accent in adulthood. Many of them also refused to show respect to Buddhist monks, refused to go to Buddhist temples and worshiping while standing up. They preferred to sit on floor with buttocks resting on heels (common Japanese style).

These twenty-four children were much insensitive to pain (three children rubbed salt in wounds to show how little affected by pain) and showed Japanese-like extreme cruelty, such as pulling limbs off live frogs. One child said he needed a pair of pliers to pull out the fingernails of playmates who annoyed him. This is the exact style of the Kempetai (the Japanese military police). They were also greater industrious than other children. Some children had quite clear, distinct and vivid imaged memory for the details of those Japanese soldiers who they claimed to have died at Burma.

There are many coincidences, such as, most of these reincarnated children were born particularly in the triangular area of upper Burma where the major battles and most of the Japanese army casualties of 1945 took place. The Japanese army suffered some casualties when it first invaded Burma in early 1942, and then again suffered too much casualties in the early 1945. After reincarnation, the oldest Burmese child of the group was born in late 1943 or 1944. One child was born in 1945, and all other children were born later. The youngest was born in 1980. Also, in a few cases the child himself or herself stated where the soldier had died. These places were usually close to the subjects' birthplaces – sometimes as close as only ten meters. A girl remembered the life of a Japanese soldier who was killed near her parents' home. It was found after investigation that a Japanese soldier had really died in the same place, same manner and same time.

The strong manifestation of Japanese-like traits and the amazing coincidences can only be explained by reincarnation – the personality of the dead Japanese soldiers reappeared as Burmese children.

Some children like unusual types of plays. In 1918, a three-year-old child from India played the role of a soldier from British army. He gave accurate military commands to his imaginary regiment in English holding a stick as his rifle, though no one taught him. He also had numerous western behavioural traits. When asked, he revealed that he had been a soldier named Arthur who had been killed in the 'German War' (World War I).

A very young boy of Syria had collected five eggplants and two potatoes. He then gave male names to the eggplants and female names to the potatoes. If anyone touched these vegetables, he became angry, and he wanted to keep them forever. He remembered his past-life as one of his deceased relatives who had five sons and two daughters. His collection of eggplants and potatoes had the same names.

Nearly all the children who claim to remember a previous life as a person of the opposite sex engage in cross-dressing when they are young children. Investigation confirms that these cases do not indicate a psychological disorder. Children select these unusual plays because they have done this several times before. Many of them talk spontaneously about previous lives.

Phobias are irrational fears. Sometimes we observe that strong, irrational fear occurs in children. A nineteenth century pioneering American psychologist and educator G. S. Hall, while studying various root causes of fears, gave casual hints towards the 'Platonic idea of metempsychosis', what today we know as reincarnation.

Most of the phobias occurred in relation to violent deaths of all kinds, such as, a child from Turkey remembered the life of a man who had been murdered by a man called 'Hasan'. The child had a phobia of all persons called 'Hasan'. A child from India remembered the previous life of a child who had been murdered near a temple by a barber and a washerman. He had a generalised fear of all barbers and washermen. He also showed strong fear when taken to the area of the temple where the murder had occurred. A boy from Sri Lanka showed a phobia of policemen when he was just beginning to speak at the age of one and a half years. When he was about four years old, he gave details of a previous life that corresponded closely to the events (April 1971, Sri Lanka) when the police and army suppressed a serious insurgency during which they killed hundreds of the insurgents. The child was describing the life of one of the insurgents killed in the uprising. A four-years-old child from Burma was observed to cringe with fear whenever airplanes flew over. When her father asked, she replied that she was afraid the airplanes would shoot her. She was a World War II Japanese soldier in her previous life who had been shot and killed in an airplane attack. In addition, she was markedly masculine in her behaviour and refused to wear girls' clothes that eventually led to her being expelled from her school.

These phobias are past-life wounds to the Atman which are traumatic enough to cross the barrier of death and to reappear to the new life even if the sources exist no more. In case the wounds are not healed by their own, one should contact clinical psychiatrists who have expertise in past-life regression therapy to resolve the brought forward issues so they are not carried into adulthood – or into future lives.

Some past-life memories in children manifest as talents or unlearned abilities – we often call it 'God given gift'. One such investigated case is from India. Swarnlata Mishra, a girl at the age of five or six years had performed unusual songs and dances which she had no opportunity to learn so far as her parents knew. She remembered two of her previous lives – in one life she was a married woman, and in another life she was a boy named 'Kamlesh' from Sylhet (presently at Bangladesh).

Upon investigation the language of the songs was identified as Bengali – two of them derived from poems by Rabindra Nath Tagore, and the third song, also Bengali, was by an unidentified poet. Sylhet is in a Bengali-speaking area whereas in Madhya Pradesh Swarnlata had lived entirely among Hindi-speaking people. Swarnlata always performed the songs and dances together, never one without the other. It was as if she had learned them together and could not (or did not care to) separate them from each other. It means she had actually practiced the songs and dances together in her past life. Swarnlata said that she had learned the songs and dances from a friend, Madhu, during the previous life as Kamlesh. Talents had been carried forward from past life to present life.

A Sri Lankan girl, Purnima Ekanayake remembered the past life of a man whose family was making incense and had no other job. When she was asked if she knew how incense is made, she gave a detailed reply. There are two methods to make it, and Purnima had extraordinary practical knowledge of both the methods. Since her parents had hardly any idea how the incense is made, the knowledge must have been carried forward from her previous birth.

Highly skilled or gifted children, even prodigies, might be experiencing the carryover of spectacular talents from past lives, and are able to utilise and enhance them in their current lives. Mozart played whole pieces of music at four and wrote his first composition at five. Dhanat Plewtianyingthawee from Thailand had his first art exhibition at the age of three and a half. Thomas Greene Bethune, though born blind, played on the piano 'par excellence'. Whatever he performed were his own original compositions because he never took any music lessons. These young talents are simply the result of the reincarnation of passed away singers and musicians who had toiled to expertise their crafts.

A strong evidence for reincarnation is the incidence of striking birthmarks and birth defects that reflects injuries and other events from the remembered life. Cultural influences are out of question for the formation of birthmarks and defects because these are formed in the embryo before the child is born. These are almost always of rare types, i.e., they differ noticeably from the kind of birthmark and defects that almost everyone has. In some cases, the child has two or more birthmarks each corresponding to a wound on the deceased person whose life he remembers.

A Thai child had a major abnormality of the skin on the back of his head and a deformed toe nail of the right great toe. He recalled the life of his uncle who had been struck on the head with a heavy knife and killed almost instantly. The uncle also had chronic infection of the same toe from which he had suffered for some years before he died. A Turkish boy had diminished and malformed ear and underdeveloped face at the right side. He remembered the life of a man who had been shot (with a shotgun) at point-blank range. The shot had penetrated the right side of the skull. An Indian child, Ravi Shankar, was born with a long, stippled mark across his neck. He spoke about a previous life during which he had died after having his throat cut. He related his birthmark to the murder he said he had suffered. Perhaps the most striking birth defect so far published is that of Wijeratne which I will discuss in details later in this chapter. These cases are especially important for two reasons – these birthmarks and birth defects provide an objective type of evidence, and they provide evidence that a deceased personality, having survived death, may influence the form of a later-born baby. In 1997, Stevenson published a weighty two-volume document called 'Reincarnation and Biology: a contribution to the etiology of birthmarks and birth defects'. In this monumental work, Stevenson documented 225 cases of birthmarks and birth defects on children that corresponded to fatal wounds, injuries, or illnesses of the person the children remembered being in their former life.

These birthmarks and birth defects are not medical malfunctions but the Atman is reconstructing the baby in mother's womb in a very specific way. Quantum physics showed us that consciousness creates matter and the quantum double-slit experiment is one way we can see how consciousness affects the physical material world. Also, the core teaching of the Seth material is that the physical reality arises from consciousness. Therefore, within our understanding of quantum physics, the birthmark and birth defects perfectly explain the reincarnation hypothesis. It is quite possible that everything in the normal body is also constructed individually in a unique way by its Atman.

The whole matter has quite practical significance. If birthmarks and birth defects can be carried forward from one life to another, then it is also possible that many of our health problems (both physical and mental) have origins in past lives, that neuroses have a basis in previous life experiences. It is quite possible that many present-life diseases are due to past-life accidents, sickness or ailments. Residues from past lives have critical karmic issues. Newton (2015b, p. 272) explains,

> "*The time we spend in the spirit world between lives should eliminate all residual effects of our past life experiences. In most cases it does but, as I have said, some people do carry physical and emotional body imprints from one life to the next. This is especially true if that imprint bears upon a particular karmic lesson in the life to come*".

Children's past life memories have better scientific credibility and contain more promising evidence in support of reincarnation because these memories lie closer to the surface of consciousness than that of the adults, and therefore be easier to retrieve. Moreover, since children have fewer experiences than adults, any memories of previous lives would have less danger of becoming contaminated with memories of the present life.

4.2.2: The curious 'Ogbanje/Abiku' (spirit-child or repeater-child) cases

The belief of reincarnation is widespread amongst the Igbo tribe of Nigeria. Nearly everyone is thought to be reincarnation of another person because many Igbo subjects have abundant imaged memories of previous lives. They also have a bizarre belief that some children who die in infancy do so deliberately to torment their parents. The 'spirit-child' or 'repeater-child', known as the 'Ogbanje' in the Igbo language and the 'Abiku' in the Yoruba language of Western Nigeria, is imprisoned in an endless cycle of birth, death, and rebirth. Indeed, the Igbo word Ogbanje means "to make several trips to and from a place". The tribal people believe that the child who is unduly linked to the spirit world cannot complete a normal life cycle because these children are unable or unwilling to break ties with the spirit world, thus compromising their earthly existence. So an Ogbanje/Abiku child has 'decided' beforehand when he would die.

Such babies are not only a burden and a sorrow to their parents, but they are also an 'insult' to the tribal community because they break the cycle of fertility and render it useless. Hence, they must be stopped. The most extreme of the ways a suspected Ogbanje/Abiku may be stopped is by mutilating the child's body, perhaps by amputating a portion of a finger.

The belief is that the Ogbanje works in a group. Every member in the group had taken an oath in the discarnate realm that he or she would die as a child and return back to other members in the spirit world. The Ogbanje dislikes ugliness and deformities. Hence, in mutilating a living or dead suspected Ogbanje, other members of the group would expel anyone whose body was disfigured. When an Ogbanje child has died and his body has been mutilated, the parents closely observe the next child born into the family. If a child is born with a birth defect corresponding to a particular mutilation of a deceased Ogbanje such as absence of tip of the left little finger they identify the newborn child as the Ogbanje reborn. They consider that he or she has now returned to stay because the parents have broken a cycle of Ogbanje deaths in infancy.

Whether or not this act has the desired effect of preventing premature deaths, some Igbo children are really born with a missing finger-end or other deformity that seems to correspond to a mark made on a deceased sibling. A Yoruba woman had her first ten children died young. Enraged by the death of the tenth of these children, she threw the dead body on the ground and broke its lower jaw. Her eleventh baby was born with the lower jaw missing (or greatly reduced in size), and she survived into adulthood. Stevenson (1986, pp. 207-08) had investigated many Ogbanje cases and his findings would astonish anyone.

1. One person had been born after the death of two older siblings. He bore two birthmarks that corresponded in location with different marks made on both of the deceased siblings after they had died.
2. One girl was born with severe birth defects of the hands and feet. Though she displayed some past-life memory, her father did not want her to speak because he believed that the girl was the reincarnation of his deceased daughter. After the death of his daughter in infancy, he had been enraged at the child for dying so young, had mutilated her hands and feet. Then he had performed a ritual to prevent her for reincarnating. Later he by mistake neutralised the ritual unintentionally. Soon after, the present girl child was born to his other wife.
3. A boy was said to be the reincarnation of an older sister who had died at the age of eighteen months. When the sister had been born, she was believed to be the reincarnation of her parental grandfather. When she died in infancy, she was judged to be an Ogbanje. Her parents then chopped her body in two places with a hatchet and warned her discarnate soul that, if she again reincarnates in the family, she should remain or would be cut again. The boy had two birthmarks at the exact sites where the older sister had been cut. He had lived up to adulthood.

Generally, an Ogbanje child prefers to die before fifth birthday. However, if the child cannot manage to die early then it lives to an adult age only to die on very important family occasions or on the day of the marriage (marriage in Igbo culture makes one 'complete'). The ultimate aim of choosing such a date is for the child to be at the centre of attraction achieved by his sudden death. After death the cycle is repeated by reincarnation into the same family.

4.2.3: Spontaneous past-life memories in adults

Spontaneous vivid recollection of past-life memories occurs most frequently during unprompted episodes of non-ordinary states of consciousness such as spiritual emergencies. It can also happen in ordinary states of consciousness in the circumstances of everyday life during normal waking state, dreams, fantasies, reiki, drug-induced states and unusually strong deja vu experiences. Most often, these are 'one-timer view'. Deep meditation is another common method, as example, a young Thai woman of twenty, Pratomwan Inthanu, was meditating when she recalled events from two previous lives as well as the intermission between her most recent past life and her present one. During psychiatric treatments past-life memories often appear unsolicited in sessions with therapists who do not aim for them and do not even believe in them, catching them completely off-guard. Professional psychologists and psychiatrists are aware of such memory recollections but treat them indiscriminately as indications of serious psychopathology.

Often we have strange feelings towards others for which we do not find any reason why they last so long in some persons and quickly vanish in others. We are attracted or repelled by certain nations, people, names, food, or other common objects. In all probability, such fondness and fears are related to apparent memories originating from past-lives. Stevenson (1960, pp. 56-58, 60) mentioned two such cases.

The first case involves an American couple who came to Bombay (Mumbai, India) while cruising around the world. While exploring the city they both found themselves extraordinarily familiar with parts of it so that they had no need of a guide and could tell each other in advance of coming to a place, say around a corner, what they would see. Once they visited a particular quarter and looked for a house and a banyan tree they remembered standing in the garden of the house. However, they did not find them there. They asked a policeman standing nearby if the house and the tree had formerly stood there. The policeman recalled having heard from his father that they had been there as this couple described them. The house had belonged to a family named Bhan. This couple had, for some unknown reason liked the name Bhan and given this name as first name to their son.

The second case involves a person who had a strange feeling when he visited the ruined Heidelberg Castle. Though this was his first visit, he was paranormally aware of the existence of a peculiar room in an inaccessible portion of the building. He drew a diagram of the room even to its peculiar floor with perfect accuracy. Still another impression came to him with regard to a book that was kept in the old library of Heidelberg University. He not only knew what the book was, but even felt that a certain name of an old German professor would be found written in it. After a rigorous search the book was found, and surprisingly, there on the margin of one of the pages was the very name he had given in such a strange manner.

Psychiatrist Stanislav Grof had recorded the case of one of his participants in a month-long seminar at Esalen (Grof, 1988, pp. 92-95). This is Karl's case history.

Karl, a talented artist, suddenly started experiencing fragments of dramatic scenes full of powerful emotions and physical feelings that seemed to be happening in another land and time. In his visions, he saw tunnels, underground storage spaces, military barracks, thick walls, soldiers in various defensive positions and ramparts in a fortress situated on a rock facing a sea shore. He felt puzzled because the soldiers looked like Spanish but the scenery looked more like Scotland or Ireland.

As the vision continued, the dramatic scenes started representing fierce combat and bloody slaughter. Karl experienced himself as a priest and at one point saw himself with a Bible and a Cross. He saw a seal ring on his hand and could clearly recognise the initials that it bore.

Karl produced a series of sketches and paintings of this strange process. Some of these depicted different parts of the fortress, others were scenes of slaughter, and a few were his own experiences including being attacked by someone with a sword. The enemy threw him over the ramparts to die on the beach. Among these pictures was a drawing of the seal ring with the initials.

As Karl was recovering bits and pieces of this story, he found more and more meaningful connections with his present life. He noted that many emotional and psychosomatic (involving both mind and body) feelings, as well as problems in interpersonal relationships that he had at that time in his everyday life, were clearly related to his inner process, involving the mysterious sequence of events in the past. A turning point came when he suddenly felt a strong desire to spend his holiday in West Coast of Ireland. After his return, when he saw the photographs that he had shot on his vacation, he realised that he had taken eleven consecutive pictures of the same scenery that did not seem particularly interesting. He took the map and reconstructed where he stood at the time and in which direction he was shooting. He realised that the place that attracted his attention was the ruin of an old fortress called Dunanoir, or Forte de Oro (Golden Fortress).

Karl suspected a mysterious connection between his experiences and his vision. He studied the history of Dunanoir thoroughly and discovered to his enormous surprise that at the time of Walter Raleigh, the Spaniards took over the fortress, and then the British besieged it. Walter Raleigh negotiated with the Spaniards and promised them free exit out from the fortress if they would open the gate and surrender to the British. The Spaniards agreed on these conditions but the British did not hold their promise. Once inside the fortress, they attacked mercilessly all the Spaniards and threw them over the ramparts to die on the ocean beach.

Karl was thrilled and continued his library research until he discovered a special document about the battle of Dunanoir. There he found that a priest accompanied the Spanish soldiers and was killed together with them. The initials of the name of the priest were identical with those that Karl saw in his vision of the seal ring and depicted in one of his drawings.

Spontaneous past-life memories are felt as extremely real and often facilitate access to accurate information about historical periods, cultures, and even historical events that the individual could not have acquired through the ordinary channels. Accuracy of these memories can be objectively verified sometimes with amazing details. Also, the root cause of various emotional, psychosomatic and interpersonal problems can be better understood because there are karmic links among various incarnations. These memories are more powerful than memories from the present lifetime, and often associated with amazing meaningful synchronicities.

The criteria for adult's past-life verification are similar to that of children, except that the memories of a child are more recent, hence easy to verify. For an adult, evidence is harder to come by as they are much older. However, they are still verifiable with independent historical research. In addition, the karmic pattern started to emerge when their past-life memories are compared with the present life situation. For children such comparison is not possible since the child is yet to experience his present life.

4.2.4: Hypnotic past-life regression

Many people can recall past-lives through hypnosis. Logically, any previous life recollection could be brought to the surface by a method that would relax the person sufficiently so that the past-life memories could make themselves known.

> *"If repressed childhood memories can be recovered through hypnosis, perhaps recall of past lives can be obtained through hypnosis as well. Current experimental investigations of the reincarnation hypothesis using hypnotic regression have given no proof, scientifically speaking, but there is enough evocative evidence [e.g., xenoglossy, children who remember previous lives, hypnotic past-life therapy outcomes] to lead*

us to conclude that the reincarnation hypothesis is worthy of further serious consideration." (Cunningham, 2009, p. 133).

Hypnotic past-life recalls have three common features – first, the past-life experiences often mirror issues in the person's present life that have roots in the past lives (i.e., Karma). Regressions develop according to meanings, not historical time. Second, they are usually visual and have a life of their own. The imagery has an uncanny feeling of familiarity, and the person identifies with one character. And lastly, regressions are often followed by a genuine improvement in mental state. It may affect medical conditions also.

Often a simple therapeutic age regression for reliving an early event can lead to a past-life regression. As example, Brian Weiss (1988) documented the account of his treatment in 1980 of a highly hypnotisable young unmarried woman, named Catherine, who suffered from a number of psychological problems. Weiss made a nondirective suggestion to her during one hypnotic session – "Go back to the time from which your symptoms arise". He expected that the woman would go back to her early childhood as expected, but surprisingly recalled a past life 4,000 years ago in which she had lived. There was a big flood that devastated her village and she died by drowning with her baby in her arms. She identified that mishap as the origin of her present difficulties.

After this session, her symptoms gradually went into remission and within months completely vanished. In the hypnotised state, Catherine gave detailed accounts of many past lives spanned a wide range of times and places from ancient Egypt to England in the days of sailing ships. Weiss said his clinical evaluation of her showed she was not making things up and was not delusional at all. Catherine's past lives all involved humble circumstances, including poverty, prostitution and even servitude. Thus, they were by no means complimentary to her ego. Catherine also spoke of personalities called 'Masters' who lived in the intermediate realm and provided wise advice to incarnating souls. Her testimony paints an overall picture of repeated rebirth as a learning process, a school of hardship in which souls gradually progress to higher spiritual destinations.

During 1952, an amateur hypnotist, Morey Bernstein, regressed a young married woman named Virginia Burns Tighe (born 1923, and had never visited Ireland). Tighe recalled several previous lives under hypnosis – one of which was an Irish girl named Bridey (Bridget) Kathleen Murphy, born on December 20, 1798 in Cork, Ireland and died in 1864 at the age of sixty-six in Belfast, Ireland. During 1952/1953, Bernstein regressed her for total six times. Under hypnosis Tighe told Bernstein many Irish stories, sang Irish songs, and spoke Irish colloquialisms. There were many attempts to disprove the accounts of Tighe's past-life regressions. Some of the statements that Bridey made were refuted by experts based on known facts, but these were later shown to be correct after extensive research. Bernstein at one point asked her to regress even before Ireland, whereupon she related that she had led a prior life in America, where she had resided with her parents, Vera and John, in New Amsterdam, as New York City was named between 1626 and 1664.

One final note on this case concerning the last years of her life at Belfast strongly suggests that the case was genuine. Tighe spoke with a weary, half whine and a throaty Irish accent that defies all explanation except reincarnation. These last recordings of her voice under hypnosis illustrating this accent are more convincing of her life as Bridey Murphy than many of the controversial facts she stated that have subsequently been verified.

The 1952 case of Bridey Murphy became a landmark event in the history of hypnotic past-life regression, and the 1956 publication 'The Search for Bridey Murphy' written by Morey Bernstein became an internationally bestselling book written for lay readers. The book was later made into a movie.

Past-life psychotherapist Linda Tarazi describes the case of one client who never visited Spain, and neither speaks nor reads Spanish. This client (non-Catholic) revealed a volume of information over a three-year period and in some thirty-six formal hypnotic sessions about a past-life as a sixteenth century Spanish Catholic woman named Antonia Ruiz de Prado (Nov. 1555 – Mar. 1588).

The 'Antonia' personality provided with astonishing accuracy numerous out-of-the-way, detailed, and highly specialised facts unknown to even the learned professors who teach courses in Spanish history. These facts could only be verified with great difficulty in fairly obscure sources, such as old Spanish books, inquisition records, and municipal records in the town of Cuenca, Spain for which no expert could suggest an easier source. On many occasions the information 'correctly' contradicted the authorities.

Psychotherapist Peter Ramster described the case of Gwen McDonald, a highly hypnotisable Australian woman who had no previous past-life memories, never travelled outside of Australia, and did not believe in reincarnation. However, during a series of hypnotic past-life regressions she began to recall memories of being a young woman named Rose Duncan who was born in 1765 in Somerset, England and died in 1782 of pneumonia. She revealed great many details about her past-life as Rose Duncan that could be checked easily.

After investigation, her revelations proved to be historically accurate, including names of people she had known, descriptions of clothing she wore, places where she had lived and worked, such as her house and the name of the estate it was attached to, the surrounding towns and villages, and the routine of daily life in eighteenth century England.

The evidence supporting the reincarnation hypothesis has been accumulating over the last fifty/sixty years. Today past-life regression therapy represents a growing field of interest in clinical psychology in which there is a specialised peer-reviewed journal, 'Journal of Regression Therapy' that provides a forum for the communication of theoretical and empirical research into past-life therapy. Many professional hypnotists have regressed between them thousands of subjects throughout the world.

An American clairvoyant Edgar Cayce (March 18, 1877 to January 3, 1945) had the uncanny ability to put himself into a sleep-like state by lying down on a couch, closing his eyes, and folding his hands over his stomach. In this meditative trance state, he could place his mind in contact with all time and space and the mysterious super-conscious mind. Though initially he did not believe in reincarnation (orthodox Christianity does not support the doctrine of reincarnation), at the very late in his life he changed his opinion when during one of his trances he provided some 'life readings' that traced the past-life of individuals with its consequences of a karmic past and aided them greatly in understanding their present problems. At the time of his death, he had given about 2,500 'life readings' that traced the client's experience in past lives and the soul's return to Earth in a different body so that it can continue as an instrument of its own development. Sometimes Cayce would trace a portion of the origins of present health problems to a past-life difficulty.

From his perspective, the purpose of reincarnation is to enable the soul to understand the consequences of previous choices and to know that each individual is ultimately responsible for shaping and creating his or her life in the present. In other words, the past merely provided a framework of potentials and probabilities. With free will, we can turn the challenges life presents to us into stepping-stones toward growth, or we can see them as obstacles and stumbling blocks. Either way, we reap what we have sown. We constantly meet the consequences of previous deeds and attitudes. Each soul's wealth of experiences from the past acts as subconscious memory in the present. It is better to make an erroneous choice than to be idle and to do nothing because soul development is only possible through movement, growth, and activity.

Cayce is the most documented psychic of the twentieth century. Since he would get his information while lying down in a self-induced hypnotic trance, he was popularly called 'sleeping prophet'. Some of his 'life readings' took the subjects back to not only such exotic known lands as ancient India, China, Persia, and Egypt, but to such legendary places as 'lost city' of Atlantis and sunken Lemuria in the Pacific. Cayce claimed that he once lived at Atlantis in a previous incarnation. He described that the lost race was a sophisticated technological civilisation whose power source was crystals. The abuse of this power led to three nuclear disasters, the last in 10,000 BC. Cayce revealed that a great number of souls who lived at Atlantis had been incarnating to America for a long time now. Their purpose is to create a new era of enlightened human consciousness. In all, Cayce referred to Atlantis no fewer than seven hundred times over a span of twenty years.

4.2.5: Xenoglossy: speaking an unlearned language

Xenoglossy (also written xenoglossia) is a rare and unusual paranormal phenomenon in which a person is able to spontaneously speak (and/or write) a foreign language without first having learned it, or even been exposed to it during the present lifetime. This term is derived from two Greek words, 'Xenos' (foreign or foreigner), and 'glossai' (tongues or languages). An event in which an individual who knows only English, has never been exposed to any other language, and who suddenly starts speaking in fluent Swahili with appropriate vocabulary, pronunciation, and grammar would be an example of xenoglossy. Here the cause is more mysterious than the phenomenon itself. Charles Richet coined the term xenoglossy in 1905.

There are two types of xenoglossy – recitative and responsive. Recitative xenoglossy refers to the repetition, as if by rote, of phrases and sometimes longer passages in a foreign language. In responsive xenoglossy, subjects can converse intelligibly with appropriate responses in the unlearned language. The person may converse with native speakers sometimes in obscure dialects that have not been in use for centuries. There are also cases when the person under trance have communicated in languages no longer in use or known only to a handful of experts.

1. Harold Jaworski, under hypnosis, wrote down twenty-two words and phrases that he 'heard' himself speaking in a past Viking life. Working independently, linguists identified and translated ten of these words as Old Norse and several of the others as Russian, Serbian or Slavic. All words were associated with the sea.
2. In 1931, Rosemary, a young English girl from Blackpool, began to speak in an ancient Egyptian dialect under the influence of the personality of Telika-Ventiu (lived some time in 1400 BC).

In front of Egyptologist Howard Hume, she wrote down sixty-six accurate phrases in the lost language of hieroglyphs and spoke in a tongue unheard outside academic circles for thousands of years. Today, only a few specialists in the world could even recognise or comprehend this lost language.

3. An eleven-year-old English-speaking boy under hypnosis was taped for eleven minutes as he spoke in an ancient Chinese dialect. When the tape was taken to a professor at the Department of Oriental Studies at the University of California it turned out to be a recitation from a forbidden religion of ancient China.
4. American medium George Valentine under trance conducted séances in Russian, German, Spanish and Welsh. The Brazilian medium Mirabelli spoke and wrote long technical documents in more than thirty languages in the presence of scientists and crowds up to 5,000.
5. In 1977, doctors discovered that a convicted rapist named Billy Mulligan had two additional personalities, both of whom communicated in a different language. Mulligan was born and raised in the USA and spoke no foreign language. But when taken over by Abdul, Mulligan could read and write in perfect Arabic. As Rugen he spoke perfect Serbo-Croat with a thick Slavic accent.
6. Biologist Lyall Watson described the case of a ten-year-old child, an Igorot Indian, living in the remote Cagayon Valley in the Philippines, had no contact with any language or culture other than his own. Yet under trance conditions, the child communicated freely in Zulu, a language he could not have even heard. Watson only recognised it because he had spent his early life in Africa.
7. Jamie, a two-year-old boy from Ohio was very slow to start talking. He made sounds and his parents soon noticed that Jamie had his own vocabulary because if he wants drink, he would say 'iki', for daddy and mommy he would say 'baba' and 'seziz'. A family friend solved the mystery; Jamie was speaking Turkish though no one in the family had ever been to Turkey. At the age of four Jamie reverted to English.
8. A similar case was triggered by a car accident in 2007. Prior to the accident, Czech speedway racer Matej Kus could barely speak broken English. Yet after being knocked unconscious in the accident, paramedics and others at the crash site were amazed that Matej could suddenly speak clear and perfect English with a British accent and stopped speaking Czech, his mother tongue. But the ability didn't last long. Matej retained no memory

of his temporary English fluency after recovery and started speaking Czech.

9. Psychotherapist Peter Ramster found that he could maintain fluid conversations in ancient French with his student Cynthia Henderson when Cynthia was under hypnosis. When she was out of the trance state, she possessed only a basic knowledge of that language.
10. A twelve-years-old American boy could speak fluent German and Persian while in spontaneous trance. Neither he nor his parents could speak any other language other than English. Scholars who studied the youngster declared that his German was that spoken in the early sixteenth century, and his Persian predated the German by two centuries.

A mother of three children observed that her third child, Carol, was different in all her reactions from the other two. Carol did not speak English and formulated a complete language of her own. She was taken to several psychiatrists for treatment of her speech aversion. Her mother said,

> "*This attitude continued until she was four years of age. Several months before her birthday I said, 'Carol, let's go for a walk. Go upstairs and get your hat'. She looked at me blithely [cheerfully] for awhile and trilled [uttered], 'Mais oui, Maman, ou est mon chapeau?'. ... I followed a strong hunch and took Carol to a private kindergarten run by a delightful French woman. Carol joined in the singing of French songs and after a month of joy in an atmosphere peculiarly her own, began to speak English volubly.*
>
> *She is now twelve years of age and continues to reach back to another life and time, with constant references to the beauty of France and her love for Paris. She said to me the other day, 'you must really go to Paris with me, Monie. It is beautiful. Of course, England is lovely too, but I always liked France much more than England'.*" (Curtiss, 1949, pp. 54-5).

Stevenson had investigated several spontaneous child xenoglossy cases, such as, Swarnlata Mishra, Bishen Chand Kapoor, Uttara Huddar, and Kumkum Verma.

One case involved a woman named Dolores Jay. She could not speak German, never studied German in school, whose ancestry did not include any German. However, during a hypnotic past-life regression, she displayed a personality that called itself 'Gretchen' who spoke only German. Over a period of three years (1971-72-73) there were more than nineteen tape recordings of sessions with Gretchen where Dolores could give sensible answers in German to questions put to her in that language.

Psychic investigators used scientific method to illustrate xenoglossy and claim that there is only one possible explanation, i.e., reincarnation, and every alternative explanation has failed. The ability to speak a language is a skill, and no one can acquire skills without practice. It cannot be transmitted either normally or paranormally, and that if it can be shown that a person has not normally learned a foreign language that he can speak responsively, then we have concrete evidence of the existence and influence on him of another personality which at some time has learned that language. The root of human personality is much… much deeper, as Goldberg (2004, p. 24) commented, "*Psychic genetics is more important than biological genetics in determining the character of our lives*".

The Jensen Jacoby case involves a Swedish male personality manifested by a thirty-seven-year-old American housewife from Pennsylvania. The age regression technique moved the woman back beyond her youth to an earlier life as Jensen Jacoby, a Swedish peasant born in the seventeenth century. As Jensen, she had communicated in fluent Swedish though she had never been exposed to Swedish language. She also named many daily artifacts of the place and time in which Jensen Jacoby was said to have lived. Jensen appeared in eight hypnotic sessions, all during 1955-56.

Stevenson and Pasricha (1980, pp. 332, 335, 337, 338) investigated the case of an Indian woman named Uttara Huddar born in Nagpur (India) in 1941. She had no memory of a past-life as a child, never been to Bengal and had not learned its language. However, she began to display memories and knowledge of foods, customs, and places in Bengal allegedly derived from a previous life lived about 150 years ago when a personality that called herself 'Sharada Chattopadhaya' spontaneously emerged in 1974 and continued to do so at intermittent intervals (lasted from one day to about six weeks) until 1979. Strangely, the two personalities (Sharada and Uttara) knew nothing about each other. Uttara seemed to be completely forgetful for what happened during a Sharada phase, and Sharada regarded Uttara's family as strangers.

Sharada could not speak Marathi (Uttara's native language) but could speak and write Bengali very fluently. She dressed and behaved like a somewhat shy, married, Bengali woman. Her Bengali was free of all English loan words and had more Sanskrit words than modern Bengali has, as did Bengali in the eighteen and early nineteenth centuries.

When Sharada first appeared, she was completely unfamiliar with the tools, instruments, and appliances developed after the industrial revolution. For example, she knew nothing about electric appliances, gas stoves, fountain pens, or modern vehicles such as automobiles and trains.

Sharada gave many details about her life and mentioned the names of places in Bengali with which she was familiar, and gave the correct relationship she had to five of the male relatives of Brajanath Chattopadhaya (Sharada's purported father) whose names appear around his on the genealogy. From her information, it seems that she lived during the years between 1810 and 1830.

Goldberg (1982, p. 56) explained,

> "*When children are regressed and speak or write foreign languages fluently, which they have not been exposed to in this life, I consider this proof of reincarnation. One could rationalise a word or a phrase being mastered in a foreign language by a child, but not an entire language. There is no way that a person's subconscious mind could have been exposed to an entire foreign language without conscious awareness of this. When adults or children start writing in hieroglyphics [the picture script of the ancient Egyptian priesthood] or other dead languages, I start thinking about past lives.*"

In the reliable historical sources there is a wealth of examples involving xenoglossy. Religious scriptures and pseudoscience have tried to explain this in various ways but there is not a single adequate explanation except reincarnation theory.

4.2.6: Intermission memories, pre-birth communications

About twenty percent of children who recall previous lives recall events from the intermission (the period between the deaths of the previous persons and their own births) as well. Intermission memories perfectly strengthen the cases of reincarnation by showing the continuation of journey of the Atman from one life to another. There are three stages of the intermission experience – the transitional stage (this stage most often includes the memories of the previous personality's funeral), the stable stage in a particular location (here the discarnate is more relaxed, and lives in a particular location with peace of mind), and the return stage (the discarnate plans for the next life and most often chooses his parents).

The third stage, i.e., the return stage is the most important of the three stages. The Atman sometimes associates with a grain of rice or speck of dust in the water and being ingested by the mother. One Mantra confirms how the departed souls come to their mothers' womb for reincarnation.

> "*abhraṃ bhūtvā megho bhavati megho bhūtvā pravarṣati*
> *ta iha vrīhiyavā oṣadhivanaspatayastilamāṣā iti*
> *jāyante'to vai khalu durniṣprapataraṃ yo yo hyannamatti*
> *yo retaḥ siñcati tadbhūya eva bhavati*"
> (Chandogya Upanishad: 5.10.6).

[Having become mist, it changes into clouds. Then from clouds, it becomes rain and falls to the earth. Finally it grows as paddy, barley, plants, trees, sesame, beans, and so forth. The change from this state is very difficult. Those who eat these things produce children just like themselves]

The Atman does not become the mist or cloud or paddy etc. He merely becomes associated with these things as a person is associated with a vehicle he is riding on. A few went to considerable lengths. One person said that he had waited by the village well for the mother of the previous life to come when his present mother came instead.

Intermission experiences and NDEs have many extraordinary parallels. A near-death experiencer returns to the same body (the brain's hold on consciousness is reduced or impaired temporarily), whereas the recounters of intermission memories have died but were reborn in new bodies (the brain's hold on consciousness is severed permanently, and hence the consciousness adopts a new body). This is the reason the first stages of the NDE are extremely similar to the first stages of the intermission experience. Hence, intermission experiences pick up where NDEs leave off. Intermission memory cases should be carefully examined to understand how the law of Karma regulates the details of our rebirth in the world of mortals.

Pre-birth communications in the form of announcing dreams (before, during pregnancy and after birth) usually occur to pregnant women, but may occur to expected father, other close relatives or friends of the mother. Following these highly significant dreams, strange experiences, such as visions, apparitions, poltergeist activities and messages passed through mediums might occur. Some expectant parents had exactly the same dream content. Occasionally the announcing dreams are so vivid that the person wakes up expecting to see the discarnate beside the bed.

In the 1902-06 Italian case of Blanche Battista (Gustus, 2011, pp. 123-24), the Battista family had a little daughter born in Rome whom they called Blanche. They employed a French-speaking Swiss 'Nanny' called Marie to look after the child. Marie taught Battista to sing in French a lullaby song (for babies to sleep relax). Blanche was very fond of this song and it was sung to her repeatedly. Unfortunately, Blanche died during 1902, and Marie returned to Switzerland. The cradle song ceased absolutely to be heard in the house because it brought to the couple too painful memories of their deceased child. Soon all recollection of it completely escaped their minds.

Three years after the death of Blanche her mother, Signora Battista, became pregnant, and in the fourth month of pregnancy she had a strange vision. She was wide awake when Blanche appeared to her 'with childlike joyousness' and said in her old familiar voice, "*Mother, I am coming back.*" The vision then melted away. Though the family was skeptical, when the new baby was born in February, 1906, they gave her the name Blanche. The new Blanche resembled the old in every possible way. When the second Blanche was six years old, an extraordinary thing happened.

One evening, the couple heard the famous cradle song like a distant echo. The voice was coming from the bedroom where the parents had put their little daughter Blanche fast asleep. In the bed room they found the child sitting up on the bed and singing with an excellent French accent the cradle song which no one had taught her. The mother asked her what it was she was singing, and the child promptly answered that she was singing a French song. The mother asked again, "*Who, pray, taught you this pretty song?*" The little Blanche replied, "*Nobody, I know it out of my own head*".

Similar to announcing dreams, there are also departure dreams in which a deceased person tells his family where he will be reborn or has been reborn. Pre-birth and departure communications are authentic because they involve a 'prophecy' coupled with 'fulfilment' of test.

4.3: Karmic cycle according to Sanatan Dharma

"*You have inherited most from yourself, not from family! The family is only a river through which it [the Atman] flows!*"

Edgar Cayce

All the well-established Dharmic schools of thought except Carvaka (an atheistic philosophy) believe in the doctrine of Karma unquestionably though there are minor variations from one system to another. The word 'Karma' (Sanskrit word 'kri' means 'to do') means action, work or deed. The word Karma is now almost naturalised into English. Sometimes it is described as law of equilibrium, a law of spiritual dynamics, or the moral law of cause and effect.

The earliest texts such as Vedas and the Brahmanas do not disclose much about reincarnation and Karma. The first significant references appear in early Upanishads – the Brhadaranyaka Upanishad probably composed sometime before the sixth century BC, followed by the Chandogya and the Kausitaki. One or two hundred years later these theories appeared in full bloom in Buddhism and Jainism which have Karma and rebirth at the center of their eschatological thinking.

There are three types of Karma – Sanchita Karma, Prarabdha Karma, and Kriyamana Karma. A person's Sanchita Karma is their 'karmic account' or 'karmic reservoir', the storehouse of all their Karma from all the past lives that has not yet been dealt with. Prarabdha Karma is the specific portion of that Sanchita Karma which the person is destined to face and experience in the present lifetime. If successfully dealt with, that portion of their Karma will then be exhausted and wiped out. Kriyamana Karma is generated from day to day. There is a subtle difference between 'Kriya' and Karma. 'Kriya' is just action. Karma is action done with motivation. It is the motivation which seems to affect or bind a person. Some of this is exhausted immediately while the remainder becomes added to our Sanchita Karma.

Many people say that during NDE they had a life-review – a rapid mental display of significant events and actions the person just completed living. Events seen in life-reviews had really happened even if some of them are forgotten. So far no one had reported unrealistic content or hallucinatory feature in their life-review.

The life-review is a very early event in the overall NDE and probably began prior to the full loss of consciousness. In the life-review one experiences first-hand, with compassionate and empathic understanding, how one's thoughts, feelings, and actions affect others. The life-review makes the person aware of his 'karmic account' or 'karmic reservoir'. The unconditional love they report in their NDEs does not excuse their offensive behaviours on Earth. The experiences necessarily end with a feeling of having returned to the body after a 'communication' takes place between the person near death and the other spiritual beings. This communication is later identified as an important reason for the person's return to life.

During earthly existence we work out most of our Prarabdha Karma. The balance is added to our Sanchita Karma and will manifest itself as Prarabdha Karma in future lifetimes. This is the reason the Masters and Guides in the afterlife realm show us life-reviews.

> "*There is no judgment in the next stage of life except by our own consciousness.... **This voice of inner conscience is a part of God,** as we ourselves a part of the Creator, but the judgment which is meted out comes from our own being.... **the vail is withdrawn, and we are able to see clearly where we erred and where we chose rightly and thus advanced perceptibly**.*" (Montgomery, 1972, p. 123).

> "*[During life-reviews] **we serve as our most severe critic in front of teacher-guides.** This is why Karma is both just and merciful. With the help of our spiritual counselors and peers we decide on the proper mode of justice for our conduct.*" (Newton, 2016a, p. 52).

In a discarnate state, the Atman contains the blueprint of our existence with karmic account and accumulation of desires. A piece of computer software contains the same information whether it is stored on a disk or actually being used in the computer's microprocessor. Likewise, the karmic debt of a living person does not change when he dies and subsequently reincarnates. If some predestined Prarabdha Karma is not worked out during lifetime, the experiencer is asked to return back to work it out.

"*And a voice, a clear voice, said, 'you can't go yet.* ***You have unfinished business****'.*"

"*God said in loud, thundering voice, 'Go back,* ***work not done yet****'.*"

"*Spirits push me back and tell me* ***it's not time yet***".

"*All spirits, with their hands up, waving, said, 'Go back...* ***your children and a lot of people are going to need you****'.*"

"*God said, 'You have* ***a little black spot you have to clean up*** *and then I will come get you. Go back'.*"

"*God said,* ***'I am not ready for you yet'****.*"

The above short statements (Sabom, 1982, pp. 282-3) speak a lot about Karma. The words like unfinished business, work not done yet, not time yet, many people need you, a little black spot you have to clean up, not ready for you yet etc, talk about unfinished Prarabdha Karma that is yet to be worked out. Also, these statements clearly imply that some kind of 'life plan' exists.

"*ātmānaṃ satataṃ jñātvā kālaṃ naya mahāmate*
prārabdhamakhilaṃ bhuñjannodvegaṃ kartumarhasi"
(Naad Bindu Upanishad: Mantra no. 21).
[O intelligent man, spend your life always in the knowing of the supreme bliss, enjoying the whole of your Prarabdha Karma without making any complaint of it.]

Prarabdha Karma is responsible for the present body. It cannot be avoided or changed. It is only exhausted by being experienced. We pay our past debts.

Karma Yoga means attaining liberation through the path of 'Nishkam Karma' (selfless action). Karma Yoga is the Yoga of action. It's about purifying our heart by learning to act selflessly in service of others, and learning these lessons helps us to stay away from our ego, freeing us to move one step further on the path to enlightenment. Bhagavad Gita allots three chapters and 113 Shlokas to explain Karma Yoga.

"*na karmaṇāṁ anārambhān naiṣhkarmyaṁ puruṣho 'śhnute*
na cha sannyasanād eva siddhiṁ samadhigachchhati"
(Bhagavad Gita: 3.4).

[One cannot achieve freedom from karmic reactions by merely abstaining from work, nor can one attain perfection of knowledge by mere physical renunciation.]

Action is the outcome of want and desire. The mind continues to engage in fruitive thoughts, and since mental work is also a form of Karma it binds one in karmic reactions just as physical work does. Hence, we must learn to work without any attachment to the fruits of actions. This requires cultivation of knowledge in the intellect. Simply by renouncing the world and becoming a monk does not help us to accumulate positive Karma. One may give up the physical objects of the senses, but true knowledge cannot be awaken as long as the mind remains impure. Good thoughts in an impure mind gets contaminated, and this materially contaminated mind keeps running in the direction of anxiety, stress, fear, hatred, envy, attachment, and other material emotions. Thus, realised knowledge must be accompanied by similar action that purifies the mind and intellect.

"*na hi kaśhchit kṣhaṇam api jātu tiṣhṭhatyakarma-kṛit*
kāryate hyavaśhaḥ karma sarvaḥ prakṛiti-jair guṇaiḥ"
(Bhagavad Gita: 3.5).
[There is no one who can remain without action even for a moment. Indeed, all beings are compelled to act by their qualities born of material nature (the three gunas).]

"*karmaṇaiva hi sansiddhim āsthitā janakādayaḥ*
loka-saṅgraham evāpi sampaśhyan kartum arhasi"
(Bhagavad Gita: 3.20).
[King Janaka and others attained perfection actually by action only; even with a view to the protection of the masses you should perform action.]

Contrary to popular belief, action does not refer only to professional and daily physical work. When we renounce our profession, we are still performing actions because all activities performed with the body, mind, and tongue are actions. Hence, action is inevitable while life remains, and complete inactivity is impossible even for a moment.

"*na hi kaśhchit kṣhaṇam api jātu tiṣhṭhaty akarma-kṛit*
kāryate hy avaśhaḥ karma guṇaiḥ svābhāvikair balāt"
(Bhagavad Purana: 6.1.53).
[Nobody can remain inactive for even a moment. Everyone is forced to act by their modes of nature.]

The Bhagavad Gita (18.23-25) speaks of three 'gunas' (qualities, virtues), which are 'Sattva' (wisdom, harmony, purity), 'Rajas' (passion, activity, ambition), and 'Tamas' (ignorance, chaos, destruction). Sattvic actions help a man to attain liberation. Rajasic and Tamasic actions bind a man to worldliness. Our body-mind-intellect mechanism is compelled by its own make-up of these three gunas to perform work in the world.

> "*karmendriyāṇi sanyamya ya āste manasā smaran*
> *indriyārthān vimūḍhātmā mithyāchāraḥ sa uchyate*
> *yas tvindriyāṇi manasā niyamyārabhate 'rjuna*
> *karmendriyaiḥ* ***karma-yogam*** *asaktaḥ sa viśhiṣhyate*"
> (Bhagavad Gita: 3.6-7).
> [Those who restrain the external organs of action while continuing to dwell on sense objects in the mind, certainly delude themselves and are to be called hypocrites.
> But those **Karm Yogis** who control their knowledge senses with the mind, O Arjun, and engage the working senses in working without attachment, are certainly superior.]

The science of right action and the art of right living are explained in these two Shlokas. The great Seers of ancient days evaluated life on the basis of the quality of activities. Activities are of three types – 'Karm' (auspicious actions recommended by the scriptures for regulating the senses and purifying the mind), 'Vikarm' (which is forbidden by the scriptures), and 'Akarm' (inaction). Attracted by the lure of an ascetic life people often renounce their work only to discover later that their renunciation is not accompanied by an equal amount of mental and intellectual withdrawal from the sensual fields. This creates a situation of hypocrisy where one displays an external show of austerity while internally living a life of low sentiments and base motives. Hence, it is better to face the struggles of the world than to lead the life of a false ascetic.

The word Karm Yoga has been used in this Shloka 3.7. There are two main concepts – Karm (worldly duties) and Yoga (union with God). Hence, a Karm Yogi is one who performs worldly duties while keeping the mind attached to God. A Karm Yogi has no attachment to the fruits of action.

> "*niyataṁ kuru karma tvaṁ karma jyāyo hyakarmaṇaḥ*
> *śharīra-yātrāpi cha te na prasiddhyed akarmaṇaḥ*
> *yajñārthāt karmaṇo 'nyatra loko 'yaṁ* ***karma-bandhanaḥ***
> ***tad-arthaṁ karma kaunteya mukta-saṅgaḥ samāchara***"
> (Bhagavad Gita: 3.8-9).
> [Do your allotted work; for action is superior to inaction. Even the bare maintenance of the body would not be possible if you remain inactive. Work must be done as a Yajna (sacrifice) to the Supreme Lord. Otherwise work causes bondage in this material world. **Therefore,**

O son of Kunti, perform your prescribed duties without being attached to the results for the satisfaction of God.]

This is the path to perfection. Arthur Ford revealed the same wisdom through Ruth Montgomery. What binds one to the law of Karma is not actions, but the attachment to the fruits of those actions.

"*Go through life as an instrument of the Creator, asking nothing for yourself except that for which you work in order to live comfortably. Forget about publicized alms and make yourself a well which will never run dry, because bubbling up from that well is love which, freely given, continuously pumps up more love to overflowing.*" (Montgomery, 1972, p. 124).

"*gata-saṅgasya muktasya jñānāvasthita-chetasaḥ*
yajñāyācharataḥ karma samagraṁ pravilīyate"
(Bhagavad Gita: 4.23).
[They are released from the bondage of material attachments and their intellect is established in divine knowledge. **Since they perform all actions as a sacrifice (to God), they are freed from all karmic reactions.**]

With the help of a beautiful analogy of the 'padma-patram' (lotus leaf), Lord Krishna says (Bhagavad Gita: 5.10) that just as it floats atop the surface of the lake, but does not allow itself to be wetted by the water, similarly, the Karm Yogis remain untouched by sin although performing all kinds of works because they perform their works in divine consciousness.

"*yasya nāhankṛito bhāvo buddhir yasya na lipyate*
hatvā 'pi sa imāl lokān na hanti na nibadhyate"
(Bhagavad Gita: 18.17).
[Those who are free from the ego of being the doer, and whose intellect is unattached, though they may slay living beings, they neither kill nor are they bound by actions.]

"*naiva tasya kṛitenārtho nākṛiteneha kaśhchana*
na chāsya sarva-bhūteṣhu kaśhchid artha-vyapāśhrayaḥ
tasmād ***asaktaḥ satataṁ kāryaṁ karma samāchara***
asakto hyācharan karma param āpnoti pūruṣhaḥ"
(Bhagavad Gita: 3.18-19).
[He has nothing to gain by what he does in this world, nor anything to lose by what he leaves undone; nor is there anyone, among all beings, on whom he needs to depend for anything.
Therefore, always do without attachment the work you have to do; for by performing action without attachment a man reaches the Supreme.]

"*saktāḥ karmaṇyavidvānso yathā kurvanti bhārata*
kuryād vidvāns tathāsaktaśh chikīrṣhur loka-saṅgraham"
(Bhagavad Gita: 3.25).
[As the ignorant men act from attachment to work, O Bharata (Arjun), **so should the wise act without attachment, wishing the welfare of the world.]**

After explaining the wheel of action Lord Krishna asked Arjun to perform actions which are obligatory on his part in his present status in life. Lord Krishna warns him again to keep his mind away from the pitfalls of attachments. In the Shloka 3.25, the expression '*chikīrṣhur loka-saṅgraham*' (wishing the welfare of the world) is of particular importance. Here Lord Krishna again emphasizes that the wise should always act for the benefit of humankind. The idea is that an ignorant person acts jealously for his personal happiness, but a wise man should act with the same zeal for the welfare of others. When we perform selfless actions, no effort is ever lost and there is no adverse effect. This is one of the best methods to attain liberation. In this respect following Shloka is important.

"***karmaṇy-evādhikāras te mā phaleṣhu kadāchana***
mā karma-phala-hetur bhūr mā te saṅgo 'stvakarmaṇi"
(Bhagavad Gita: 2.47).
[**Your right is to work only, but never to claim its fruits.** Do not become an instrument for making your actions yield fruit, nor let your attachment be to inaction.]

This is perhaps the most quoted Shloka of the Gita. This Shloka contains the essential principle of disinterestedness in action. There are four guidelines – first, do your duty, but do not concern yourself with the results. Second, the fruits of your actions are not for your enjoyment. Third, even while working give up the pride of doership, and last, do not be attached to inaction.

The advice is to make the worker release himself from his mental anxieties and make him aware of the divinity through work alone. The work itself is his reward – satisfaction of the job well done is the end in itself. He will be happy with whatever gain spontaneously accrues to him out of his actions.

"*dūreṇa hy-avaraṁ karma buddhi-yogād dhanañjaya*
buddhau śharaṇam anvichchha kṛipaṇāḥ phala-hetavaḥ
karmaja-jaṁ buddhi-yuktā hi phalaṁ tyaktvā manīṣhiṇaḥ
janma-bandha-vinirmuktāḥ *padaṁ gachchhanty-anāmayam*"
(Bhagavad Gita: 2.49, 51).

[Seek refuge in divine knowledge and insight, O Arjun, and discard reward-seeking actions that are certainly inferior to works performed with the intellect established in Divine knowledge. Miserly are those who seek to enjoy the fruits of their works.
The wise, possessed of calmness, having abandoned the fruits of their actions and being **freedom from the bondage of life and death**, attain the state that is beyond all evil (reaches the blissful supreme state).]

"*tyaktvā karma-phalāsaṅgaṁ nitya-tṛipto nirāśhrayaḥ*
karmaṇyabhipravṛitto 'pi naiva kiñchit karoti saḥ
nirāśhīr yata-chittātmā tyakta-sarva-parigrahaḥ
śhārīraṁ kevalaṁ karma kurvan nāpnoti kilbiṣham
yadṛichchhā-lābha-santuṣhṭo dvandvātīto vimatsaraḥ
samaḥ siddhāvasiddhau cha kṛitvāpi na nibadhyate"
(Bhagavad Gita: 4.20-22).
[Such people, having given up attachment to the fruits of their actions, are always satisfied and not dependent on external things. Despite engaging in activities, they do not do anything at all.
Free from expectations and the sense of ownership, with mind and intellect fully controlled, they incur no sin, even though performing actions by one's body.
Content with whatever gain comes of its own accord, and free from envy, they are beyond the dualities of life. Being steady both in success and failure, they are not bound by their actions, even while performing all kinds of activities.]

Intelligent persons may become confused by the apparently contradictory arguments presented by the scriptures and the sages because they try to determine the principles of Dharma by mental speculation. For example, the Vedas recommend non-violence. Arjun wishes to follow the same course of action and shun violence but Lord Krishna says that his duty here is to engage in violence. Therefore, if duty varies with circumstances, then to ascertain one's duty in any particular situation is a complex matter.

"*kiṁ karma kim akarmeti kavayo 'pyatra mohitāḥ*
tat te karma pravakṣhyāmi yaj jñātvā mokṣhyase 'śhubhāt
karmaṇo hyapi boddhavyaṁ boddhavyaṁ cha vikarmaṇaḥ
akarmaṇaśh cha boddhavyaṁ gahanā karmaṇo gatiḥ"
(Bhagavad Gita: 4.16-17).
[What is action? What is inaction? As to this even the wise are perplexed. Therefore, I shall tell you what action is by knowing which you shall be freed from the evil (of Samsara – the continuous flow of birth, death, reincarnation).

One has to understand what action really is and likewise one has to understand what is forbidden action and also what inaction is. Indeed hard to understand is the way of action.]

"*dharmaṁ tu sākṣhād bhagavat praṇītaṁ na vai vidur ṛiṣhayo nāpi devāḥ*" (Bhagavad Purana: 6.3.19).
[Proper and improper actions are difficult to determine even for the great rishis and the celestial gods. Dharma has been created by God himself, and he alone is its true knower.]

The opening line of few Shlokas (Adi Parva, Vana Parva and Anusasana Parva) in the Mahabharat is "*Ahimsa paromo Dharma*" (means, 'Non-violence is the greatest Dharma'). Ahimsa is certainly not cowardice; it is wisdom. One important point to note that in the Anusasana Parva it is Vishma, the foremost warrior of his time, who is talking about 'Ahimsa' because he only fought when his duty demanded.

However, the very next line states, "*Dharma himsa tathaiva cha*" (means, 'So too is all righteous violence'). Unfortunately, we have remembered the first line only. Over-emphasis on this line has weakened initiative and energy in our millions and instead of making us irresistible moral giants, we have been reduced to cowards. So, by uttering the half-truth "*Ahimsa paromo Dharma*" we should not run away from the conflicts. A lot of our ancestors were killed by invaders and looters of the foreign lands during the past centuries because of their misunderstanding. Mahabharat and Ramayan have so much violence because wars were fought for upholding righteousness and saving Dharma.

"*swa-dharmam api chavekshya na vikampitum arhasi*
dharmyaddhi yuddhach chhreyo 'nyat kshatriyasya na vidyat"
(Bhagavad Gita: 2.31).
[Considering your duty as a warrior, you should not hesitate. **For a warrior there is no better engagement than fighting for upholding of Dharma.**]

In the eighth century when Adi Shankaracharya saw that the Islamic invaders (Muslim invasion in India started in the year 711 AD by Mohammad Bin Qasim) are attacking and beheading peaceful men, raping women, enslaving children and demolishing temples and other cultural sites, he decided to form a military force of Naga Sadhus for the sake of protecting the motherland Bharata-Varsha (India) and Sanatan Dharma from the Muslim barbarians. In Sanskrit, the word 'Sadhu' means an ascetic who has renounced the worldly life. This term frequently appears in Rig Veda and Atharva Veda.

The Naga Sadhus mostly live in Himalayan caves where they practice extreme austerities and take penance to an impossible level. They only appear during the time of Kumbh Mela to take a holy dip in the sacred rivers. They are the true devotee of Lord Shiva, with no fear of death and life. After acquiring a tough military training the Naga Sadhus then became the brave and loyal fighters and played havoc on the enemies' army in the battlefield which instilled a sense of fear in many Muslim kingdoms and empires related to them. When Aurangzeb's general Mirza Ali Turang attacked Varanasi in 1664, thousands of Nagas battled his army and helped safeguard the Kashi Vishwanath temple. When Aurangzeb's army attacked Haridwar in 1666, these Nagas again came forward to resist them. When Sardar Khan, an Afghan commander along with 10,000 Afghan soldiers wanted to plunder Gokul Dham (the birth place of Lord Krishna) they saw 4,000 Naga Sadhus standing firmly for the war with them with the battle cry of "Har Har Mahadev". In this battle, more than 5,000 Afghan soldiers died and countless soldiers were injured whereas 2,000 Nagas attained martyrdom. The Naga Sadhus thus not only saved Gokul but rescued many cultural sites also from the unbeatable Afghan army. They are never threat to any other people or faiths. This is righteous violence – "*Dharma himsa tathaiva cha*".

Chhatrapati Shivaji (1630 - 1680 AD) engaged in hostilities with the Mughal Empire, and established a competent and progressive civil rule with well-structured administrative organisations with the help of his spiritual teacher Samarth Ramdas Swami (1608 - 1681 AD). Ramdas said to Shivaji, **"O King, follow the path of Kshatriya (Warrior) Dharma. Do not abandon your Dharma even at the cost of your life. You are born to protect your subjects"**. The Kshatriya must use power to protect the rights of the weak, for that is his Dharma, the truth of his nature. This is "*Dharma himsa tathaiva cha*". Ramdas had developed a muscular style Sun Prostration (Surya Namaskar) to train troupes in defending against the Muslim invasion.

This eternal question – Should I fight or not? – is probably the reason the Bhagavad Gita has remained so popular throughout history. This question is easily relocated into our own time. Should the US fight for peace in Afghanistan and Iraq? Should one interfere in a quarrel? Should one fight for what one believes in, or let it go? Both sides of the question have a point; it's not clear whether fighting for what's right always has a good effect. Perhaps the fighting itself does more harm than the original wrong might have done. In ordinary life, it's wise to pick your battles when righteous violence is necessary because all nonviolent methods had failed. To kill a man who is taking away the lives of many is not violence.

The victory at the battlefield of Kurukshetra is the greatest lived example of the victory of Dharma over Adharma.

Sage Patanjali explained the essential features of the laws of Karma in the following Sutras in a very concise and lucid manner. Patanjali did not attempt to give us a detailed analysis of the laws of Karma. His aim was just to show the underlying cause of human misery so that we may be able to appreciate the means adopted in yogic discipline for its effective removal.

> "*klesha-mula karma-ashaya drishta adrishta janma vedaniyah*
> *sati mule tat vipakah jati ayus bhogah*
> *te hlada-paritapa-phalah punya apunya hetutvat*"
> (Yoga Sutras: 2.12, 13, 14).
> [The reservoir of Karma which are rooted in Kleshas (sufferings) brings all kinds of experiences in the present and future lives.
> As long as the root is there, it must ripen and result in lives of different class, length and experiences.
> Because of having the nature of merits or demerits (virtue or vice), these three (birth, span of life, and experiences) may be experienced as either pleasure or pain.]

Sage Patanjali often used the Sanskrit word 'Klesha' which means suffering. The root causes of sufferings are five obstacles – 'Avidya' (ignorance, lack of insight), 'Asmita' (egoism, e.g., earthly, material possessions), 'Raga' (attachment to our desires), 'Dvesa' (aversion, repulsion, hatred, dislike), and 'Abhinivesa' (clinging to bodily life). These obstacles are the sources of all individual and worldly problems. They are the underlying cause of the Karma we generate by our thoughts, desires and actions. The generated Karma is recorded naturally and automatically in our life's register, and the recording mechanism is 'Karma-ashaya' (reservoir of Karma). This is the permanent record of all that we have thought, felt or done during the long course of evolution extending over a series of lives and provides patterns and contents of the successive lives. We cannot see these impressions and yet we know that they do exist.

It appears that unless extremely required by the law of Karma, the sex change does not take place. The Atman grows through reincarnation, and certain lessons cannot be learnt unless change of sex occurs (Montgomery, 1972, p. 47). Therefore, it is not surprising to discover that some of us were members of the opposite sex in our past-lives.

Since the second personality has no memory of the particular action for which it is undergoing that experience, often a logical question arises – why should the second personality in the later life suffer for the wrongs done by the first personality in the previous life and if it has to, how can the law of Karma be called just? Of course, if this experience is pleasant no question arises in the mind of the second personality as to the justice of the undeserved good luck. But if the experience is painful a grievance is felt against fate for the undeserved pain or suffering. Sage Patanjali had given a beautiful answer in the following Sutra.

> "*jati desha kala vyavahitanam api anantaryam smriti samskarayoh eka rupatvat*" (Yoga Sutras: 4.9).
> [Since memory (Smriti) and the deep habit patterns (Samskaras) are the same in appearance, there is an unbroken continuity in the playing out of those traits, even though there might be a gap in location, time, or state of life (jati desha kala).]

The chains of personalities in the successive lives are temporary expressions of a higher and permanent entity which is called Atman. The 'complete' memory embracing all the successive lives is attached with the Atman and the different personalities which succeed one another do not share the overall continuous memory. Their memory is confined only to the particular experiences gone through by them in each separate incarnation. Seen in this light, reaping the bitter fruits by a personality for the wrongs done by another personality which has gone before does not involve any injustice. We should adopt the virtuous life to ensure in time an uninterrupted series of pleasurable experiences and to eliminate completely all painful experiences.

4.4: The scientific and logical proof of Karma

"*We are the masters of our destiny.*"

Michael Newton

"*Understanding the Law of Karma is enough to live wisely in the world.*"

Jack Kornfield

Psychiatrist Stanislav Grof (with more than sixty years of experience researching non-ordinary states of consciousness) is one of the co-founders of transpersonal psychology movement. This is the branch of psychology that deals with the sense of identity or self that extends beyond (i.e., trans the individual) to encompass wider aspects of humankind, life, psyche, and Cosmos. He had done extensive research on reincarnation and the law of Karma. According to him, all past-life experiences are "karmic experiences" which can complicate life in many different ways, such as incomprehensible and irrational strange emotions, physical feelings, and visions from unknown sources.

> "*When the content of a karmic experience fully emerges into consciousness, it can suddenly provide an explanation for many otherwise incomprehensible aspects of one's daily life. Strange difficulties in relationships with certain people, unsubstantiated fears, and peculiar idiosyncrasies [an unusual and odd temperament] and attractions, as well as otherwise incomprehensible emotional and psychosomatic symptoms now seem to make sense as karmic carry-overs from as previous lifetime. The problems typically disappear when the karmic pattern in question is fully and consciously experienced.*
>
> *Another kind of complication occurs when a particularly strong karmic experience starts emerging into consciousness in the middle of everyday activities and interferes with normal functioning. One might also feel compelled to act out some of the elements of the karmic pattern before it is fully experienced and understood or completed.*" (Grof, 2019, p. 162).

Our karmic paths cross repeatedly through reincarnation. A skilled past-life regression therapist can exactly pinpoint the problem in a relationship by following the karmic thread to reach at the root of the trouble and find out how much karmic debt is yet to be repaid. First, I will discuss few simple examples from Goldberg (1982, pp. 57-58; 2004, p. 7), and then more complicated ones.

1. A middle-aged woman was treated for insomnia. She revealed a previous life as a male civil war sentry. Once he fell asleep at his post, and as a result enemy soldiers killed him and his fellow soldiers.
2. An overweight man remembered a past-life when he starved to death.
3. A man wondered why he was such an overprotective father. He remembered two past lives. In both the times he had deserted his family.
4. A workaholic in present life witnessed his family starving to death in Greece hundreds of years ago because he was not able to adequately provide for them. By overworking himself he was preventing that from ever happening again.
5. A woman suffering from frigidity in present life remembered a past life when she was rejected by her husband because she was raped. Her husband in the past life is also her husband in present life.
6. A man who was a celibate priest always prayed for resistance to sexual urges during the Middle Ages. He is impotent at the present life.

7. A woman who saw her children die of scarlet fever in the nineteenth century and swore she would never have another child, is barren in the twenty-first century.

All these are real life problems. The middle-aged woman, the overactive father, the priest, the workaholic, and the barren woman – all of them are working out their Karma which has been put out for them; it is the only way. The frigid woman is repaying her husband for what he had done to her in a past life.

> "*Accidents seldom exist, for the planning on this side takes care of nearly everything except sheer, monumental evil which grows rapidly in a bad man's soul and overpowers the original plan he had pledged to carry out.*" (Montgomery, 1972, p. 63).

Karma is not the sum of consequences that arise from an action. It is rather the subtle cause arising from the action which produces those consequences. This is indicative in the following short examples from Montgomery (1969, p. 19; 1972, pp. 47, 48, 77, 147). Karma is a mechanism of balancing the ledger.

1. A weak and trembling woman with palsy had a past life when she was a cruel soldier (male) in ancient Rome. He delighted in frightening others until they trembled with fear. He would turn wild beasts loose on tortured Christians to see them shake and tremble.
2. A very kind-hearted man did generous acts. He loved everyone, and in turn loved by others. But people were repulsed by a giant welt on his face and neck. What a pity, they think, that this kindly man has such a heavy cross to bear. In a past life, he struck a child so roughly across the face and neck that the bones were scattered and the child died.
3. A soul reincarnated in such a body so weakened by malformation that it will not sustain life. Hence the soul withdraws itself after a brief struggle for life. In a previous life, the soul had ended the life of a new baby through neglect of its need.
4. Soldiers who die in battle for the nation feel in the afterlife that they are cheated out of their earth phase by events not of their own making. They often reincarnate within weeks of the crossover. They carry back with them burning hatred against wars. These are the ones most likely to lead the revolts, student uprisings etc.
5. Many people today who had devoted their lives to stop racism against black people were white slave traders in various past lives. They were intolerant towards the human rights of their black slaves

and subordinates, and in present life they are in the forefront of the civil rights movement to repay their karmic debts.

In all the above, they are 'correcting' a wrong (a harm or an injustice) that has happened. The concept of right and wrong are not always same to different group of people. But within all of us is the innate knowledge that to deliberately harm another person, physically or mentally, is unethical. We have the power to reason and to know right from wrong. Hence don't lament when the reversal starts playing its role. This case (Newton, 2016a, pp. 230-46) explains this clearly.

A successful businessman, by the name Steve had two failed marriages. He was also an alcoholic and it seemed though he was financially well off, he was unhappy from his childhood because his mother disappeared after abandoning him on the steps of a church in Texas within a week of his birth. After a few lonely and unhappy years in an orphanage, an older couple adopted him, but he was again unhappy with his foster parents as they were stern disciplinarians who seemed to disapprove of him all the time. His frustration was rooted in feelings of isolation and abandonment issues. He felt that he was losing control over his life.

Under hypnosis Steve recollected vivid memories of his babyhood with his mother. His mother was young and not married to his father because his father was already married. She was crying and her tears were falling on the baby's face. Before leaving the baby on the steps of the church she said, "*I must leave you for your own good. I have no money to take care of you. My parents won't help us. I love you. I will always love you and hold you in my heart forever*". Next, he recollected his memory, how his foster parents were never satisfied with him, and how they made him feel guilty about everything by controlling and judging him continuously.

To find the root of the karmic issue, Newton took him to a previous life where the childhood trauma of his present life had originated. The source of the karmic debt between the mother and the abandoned baby was in a past-life thousands of years ago when Steve was a high priest of a tribe. He saw himself wearing a long, white robe and sandals with a stick in his hand with gold snakes on it as a symbol of his authority. Soon it was unfolded that he was a tribal leader in the Kingdom of Sheba or Saba located on the Arabian Peninsula near Red Sea around 2,000 BC. Under deep hypnosis, Steve saw himself on the step of a temple passing death sentence on his own mother. As a high priest he had too much control over the daily lives of his people. The fault of his mother was that she had broken into the storage house and stole food to give to the people. Many people were hungry at that time of the year, but as a high priest he alone could order distribution. The high priest used the distribution of food as a means of control over his people because he wanted them all to be loyal to him. Since his mother had violated his authority, he ordered her death by banging his stick on the stone steps. The mother of the high priest in the past-life is the mother of Steve in the present life. The karmic connection that was established around 2,000 BC resulted in a disordered life between mother and son in the present life. The karmic payment that was due for about four thousand years was ultimately paid when the sacred bond between a mother and her baby was severed – Sanchita Karma manifested itself as Prarabdha Karma.

The enforcer of the law of Karma may take time in preparing an appropriate environment for dispensing just rewards and punishments, but every karmic debt must be paid in full to the last penny. No compensation is made as answer to prayer to a higher source. The Bhagavad Gita makes this point very clear in two Mantras.

> "*na kartṛitvaṁ na karmāṇi lokasya sṛijati prabhuḥ*
> *na karma-phala-saṅyogaṁ svabhāvas tu pravartate*"
> (Bhagavad Gita: 5.14).
> [The Lord creates neither agency nor actions for the world, nor does He bring about the union with the fruits of actions; but it is nature that does all this.]

> "*nādatte kasyachit pāpaṁ na chaiva sukṛitaṁ vibhuḥ*
> *ajñānenāvṛitaṁ jñānaṁ tena muhyanti jantavaḥ*"
> (Bhagavad Gita: 5.15).
> [The omnipresent God does not involve Himself in the sinful or virtuous deeds of anyone. The living entities are deluded because their inner knowledge is covered by ignorance.]

In other words, an individual is responsible to repay his own karmic debt. The belief 'bribe of heaven and threat of hell' of the Western world does not exist. The present condition of each Atman is due to its own progress, development, advancement, unfoldment, or the lack of the same. The soul being is its own fate and destiny; the enforcer of the Law upon itself, under the law of Karma.

Steve's story does not end here. Under deep hypnotic trance, he remembered another life at Germany where he was a high-ranking officer. He neglected his family and was the object of scorn from his wife's influential parents. Steve had a strong desire to control others in that life, but at the same time he had thoughts of escape by self-destruction. Because of this nature he had conflict with the society. He had a karmic lesson to learn – to overcome his selfish desire to control others at any cost and to resolve his disputes with others in the society. He had learned his lesson when during his childhood he was constantly ridiculed by his adoptive parents.

This case makes us pondering over a common issue. Though most of the biological parents are good and kind to their children, there are cases where children are brought up in dysfunctional families with unresolved and hurtful memories of parents who should have offered love and protection but did not. Such children grow up thinking of themselves as victims. Also, many of us have learnt hard lessons from broken relationships. There is nothing called 'true love'. It's a fantasy driven by an addiction to have love at any price. Hence the important thing is to forgive and move on in life to work out the Karma otherwise we will make the same mistakes over and over again. Edgar Cayce stated that **the law of grace supersedes the law of Karma.** Newton (2016b, p. 285) explains,

> "*Each life is a piece of fabric which makes up the whole tapestry of our existence. If a family member or friend is harsh and uncompromising, or perhaps weak and emotionally distant toward us in life, we are only seeing an external portion of the entire true character of that soul. Role assignments in life all have purpose.* ***If you grew up with a particularly difficult parent… ask yourself this question: What did I learn at the hands of this person that has given me wisdom I would not possess if he or she had never been in my life?***"

Hence, Karma is a well-planned design. The better we understand it, the easier our lives will be. If we imagine life as a grand stage play where we have the lead roles as an actor, then whatever we do on the stage influences other minor characters. We have free will and the minor characters also have free will. So, the script is not fixed. Their parts are altered by us and ours by them because the script changes while the play is in progress. Similarly, other souls who share the same stage with us as minor actors are also playing leading roles in another play where we are playing supporting roles for them. Because of these complications, it is often said that '**Unfathomable is the mystery of Karma**'. An associate in one life will often appear repeatedly in future lifetimes. Goldberg (1982, p. 39) explains,

> "*We do not just reincarnate individually. Rather as I have been suggesting, our own separate karmic cycles are intertwined with many others. For example, your parents may have been your children in a former life. Your wife may have been your brother or son, etc. This is not to say that Karma involves any form of incest or other such moral judgment. It simply implies that our lessons are intermingled with the lessons of other entities. These lessons have an effect between entities and among others around them.*"

I wish to explain more. We connect with people on many levels for a multitude of karmic lessons in every earthly life. It's not just the Karma of one or two souls. Rather it's the Karma of each and every soul who interacts (including past several lives across several thousand years) with each other and set up major or minor karmic debts. Our lessons are intermingled with the lessons of other entities. In addition, there are karmic issues of our ancestors who are no more on Earth but left their karmic legacy (as example, if I inherit my late grandfather's ill-gotten wealth then I will incur negative Karma). Collectively, the whole thing can be called a tangled hierarchy. That's the reason the path of Karma is mysterious. But with mathematical certainty it always works in the right direction.

From Edgar Cayce's treasure of past-life readings we can come across many cases where karmic actions are prominently noticeable. Initially Cayce himself had a hard time accepting what he was saying during the trance states. But he gradually understood the basis of reincarnation and Karma, and how they help us comprehend the seemingly incomprehensible aspects of human life.

A woman of forty, suffered from certain allergies since childhood. Eating certain foods, mainly bread and cereal, made her sneeze heavily. Coming in physical contact with shoe leather and plastic glass gave her severe pain in her left side. Doctors could not cure her but a hypnotic treatment at the age of twenty-five gave her some relief. Cayce went deeper into the cause of her allergies. The reading said that in another life she was a chemist, and used many harmful chemicals to produce itching in others. In her present life Karma worked like a boomerang. Those same substances she used to inflict pain on others are now causing pain to her. In her past-life she had also used certain chemical substances that were poisonous to breath. As a consequence, she now finds herself immediately poisoned in the presence of certain metals, plastics, odors and leathers. If these leathers are tanned with oak, they do not trouble her. If they are tanned with the very same things that she once used to hinder someone else, they cause problem.

A man with distressing digestive weakness from infancy came to Cayce for opinion. He was found to be a glutton in his past two lives. In both these lives he could not control his habit of overeating. In another reading of Cayce of a man having chronic anemia revealed that five incarnations back he was a ruthless conqueror in Peru and brutally caused a lot of bloodshed amongst the people he subdued. The karmic reaction had taken over in having his own body struggling for blood. The past bloody slaughter of theirs now encompassed his own present state. The law of Karma awarded him a protracted form of educative justice throughout the present life. Probably he had already paid much of his karmic debt in past few lives.

Souls reincarnate on Earth to work on their own shortcomings. Let us take the Elizabeth/Stanley case from Newton's (2016b, pp. 58-59, 64) file. Elizabeth loved her husband, but Stanley left her alone and went to Africa. During 1919 at the age of fifty-two Elizabeth died of influenza with much loneliness and sorrow. This suffering had started a karmic issue between them and as a result they reincarnated again in an entirely different set up as Belinda (Elizabeth) and Stuart (Stanley).

When Belinda met Newton, she was forty-seven and had never been married because she had strange feelings of abandonment and loss if she would enter in a marital relationship. She moved to California after a painful breakup with Stuart about twenty years before. Belinda cared for Stuart but she had broken off their engagement after making a decision to change her life and to pursue a new career. She asked Stuart to come with her but he pleaded with Belinda to marry him and stay in the area where they had both grown up but she refused. Stuart was devastated by her leaving him.

This is Karma – its blade cuts both ways. Stanley left Elizabeth in a swift, uncompromising and brutal way in the past life. As a result, Stuart felt the emotional pain of rejection in present life. There is a karmic lesson for Belinda as well. Elizabeth did not understand what freedom meant for her husband. So, Belinda has carried the mental imprint (strange feelings of abandonment and loss in a marriage) of the past life into her life today for this realisation. When she abandoned her lover, she understood what freedom means for her. Since the karmic debt is paid, it is likely they will assume a new role together and enter in a very successful relationship unless some other karmic issues in another life need to be resolved and a balance is made.

Spiritual regressionists and past-life therapists have investigated countless number of cases where love was tormented, deprived, cruel, deadly and unforgiving because of strict karmic challenges in one or more previous lives, but the couples are happily married in present life.

A boy H. A. Wijeratne (born on January, 17, 1947) from Uggalkaltota, a remote village of Sri Lanka claimed to have reincarnated in his own family as 'his' previous brother's son. In past life his name was Ratran Hami. At his birth, his parents noticed a marked deformity of his right chest and arm. The entire right arm and the fingers were grossly underdeveloped.

When Wijeratne was around two and a half years old he began walking around the house in a lonely way talking to himself. His mother overheard him saying that his arm was deformed because he had murdered his wife in his previous life – "*He [Ratran Hami] had killed my wife by using my hand*". He mentioned a number of details connected with that murder incident. During 1961, Stevenson interviewed Wijeratne, his parents, and many others, and obtained a certified transcript of the trial for murder of Ratran Hami. This document enabled Stevenson to ascertain certain dates and established facts.

Ratran Hami had murdered his wife, Podi Menike, with a 'kris' (Malay knife) because she refused to leave her parents' home and accompany him to his village. The murder occurred on October 14, 1927, Ratran Hami was tried in June, 1928 and executed in July, 1928. Wijeratne remembered this incident, recognised and pointed out to his father the plank on which he (Ratran Hami) had sharpened the kris that was used to kill his wife and the orange tree under which the plank stood. The orange tree and the plank were in the same place as they had been two decades ago. He also showed other objects and their part in the murder.

Stevenson (1974, pp. 149-71) had thoroughly investigated this case and included in his book 'Twenty Cases Suggestive of Reincarnation'. Even as a child Wijeratne understood the possible karmic origin of his deformities. How could a child, who belongs to a semi-literate poor family, have such an understanding and wise realisation at the age of two or so? Throughout his present life, his physical deformity constantly reminded him of his crime committed decades ago in the past-life.

Wijeratne had an unbearable temper. It is reported that he had abused his first wife as well and she had died at a young age. As a result, in his present life he was so rejected by a girl he loved that he suffered from mental illness and was admitted to a psychiatric hospital for almost a month. On January 1969, Wijeratne wrote a letter to Stevenson where he had expressed his newfound wisdom.

> "*I carefully considered the assertion of what one should do if a wife behaved in an unseemly manner. I thought it is wise that as a primary step she should be made aware of her weakness and advised accordingly. These are common occurrences in society. If, however, a wife disregards [means misconduct by wives] her husband's advice it is wise to divorce her. Or else the sudden anger that can arise in a person* ***can lead to the destruction of many lives****. Thus, according to Buddha's teaching* ***if one's actions are guided by patience and wisdom it can lead to a happy life.***" (Stevenson, 1974, p. 165).

Wijeratne's reference to "the destruction of many lives" needs specific understanding. This is what the enforcer of the law of Karma teaches us repeatedly but we ignore. There is a spiritual urge in every Atman for peace. Even if a person is violent now, he or she inwardly yearns for peace, humbleness, compassion, love and helpfulness. Montgomery (1972, pp. 64, 81) wrote,

> "*We learn, for instance, that the best way to advance is to love, for an unkind or openly hostile thought about another soul retards the progress to such a degree that sometimes more than one future lifetime is required to erase the blot from the record. Speak no evil. Think no evil. There is no evil except that which we create...* ***We are our own devils, with our thoughts and subsequent deeds***."

> "*Growth, development, love, constructive action, and consideration for others are the keys to unlock the kingdom of heaven, and those who use force and anger to destroy, instead of love to rebuild, are earning dire consequences for themselves in this spirit life and in future incarnations.*"

The spirit guides are always ready to help as long as the soul continues to try. But if the soul does not cooperate, everything comes to a standstill in its development.

The law of Karma counts not only our actions but inactions also. Newton (2016b, p. 350) wrote,

> "*Karma does not only pertain to our deeds, it is internal as well, reflecting our thoughts, feelings and impulses – all relating to cause and effect. Karma is more than taking proper actions toward others, it is also having the intention to do so.*"

A grieving mother whose eight-year-old daughter died was put under deep hypnosis for regression. She recalled (Newton, 2016b, p. 382),

> "*I was a wealthy matron in London in the nineteenth century. I paid little attention to the suffering of the young waifs on the street around my townhouse. I callously disregarded their plight because they were not my children; to my mind they were the responsibility of their parents or the state and had nothing to do with me. I looked the other way even though I had plenty of money to support an orphanage and a safe house for young unwed mothers nearby. I knew these services were struggling to make ends meet and I did nothing.*"

This is Akarm (inaction) that Lord Krishna had warned us in Bhagavad Gita, such as, Shlokas 3.8, 2.47, 4.16-18. The inaction of the grieving mother falls under the category of 'tamasic' inactivity, i.e., delusory and selfish action. Sometimes when we empty ourselves of our wealth, we realise that we are actually fulfilled, that we have flowered – "*karmaṇy-evādhikāras te mā phaleṣhu kadāchana…*" (Bhagavad Gita: 2.47) [Your right is to work only, but never to claim its fruits….]. In this most quoted Shloka, Lord Krishna warns that one should be careful not to lapse into inaction thinking that there is no use performing actions without expecting any rewards. Here ignorance is not excused.

> "*karma brahmodbhavaṁ viddhi brahmākṣhara-samudbhavam*
> *tasmāt sarva-gataṁ* ***brahma nityaṁ yajñe pratiṣhṭhitam***"
> (Bhagavad Gita: 3.15).
> [The duties for human beings are described in the Vedas, and the Vedas are manifested by God himself. **Therefore, the all-pervading Lord is eternally present in acts of sacrifice.**]

In the eternal Vedas, the duties of humans have been planned in such a way that through their performances materially engrossed persons may gradually learn to control their selfish desires and slowly elevate themselves from ignorance and selfishness to goodness. This is sacrifice.

> "*iti te jñānam ākhyātaṁ guhyād guhyataraṁ mayā*
> *vimṛiśhyaitad aśheṣheṇa* ***yathechchhasi tathā kuru***"
> (Bhagavad Gita: 18.63).
> [Thus, I have explained to you this knowledge that is more secret than all secrets. Ponder over it deeply, and **then do as you wish**.]

Karma is the ultimate affirmation of the free will of a self-aware Atman. The enforcer of Karma can only illumine the path, but He will not control the free will of the man. I had free will in each of my past-life and my past had determined my present. At present life I again have free will and my present life will determine my future life. Then whom should I blame for my miseries and whom should I thank for my fortunes when at every moment I am exercising my free will? At the best I can say that Karma sets up the situation, but not the choices I make about the situation. A psychologist, Arthur Knight, who has done considerable work on hypnotic regression commented,

> "*Every time a person describes a life of suffering, he will invariably tell us that he has made someone else suffer in a previous life. It should make us pause and think before we act.*
>
> *It happens again and again in prebirth regressions. If a person meets a violent death, he has nearly always taken someone's life in a previous incarnation. It occurs so often that I've learnt to look for it.*"
> (Montgomery, 1969, pp. 36, 41).

It means, I 'pay forward' my 'reactive past'; if life is cruel, it is of our making here on this Earth. Thus, we have to develop our ability to handle free will responsibly. If an irresponsible motorcycle rider lived for speed and essentially got a high from the dangers of his obsession, then he had deliberately put himself in that position by using his free will. Hence, Karma and destiny are opposing forces. Karma was set in motion an unknown long time ago, and it will keep on going till the time a final balance is reached and no soul needs to reincarnate anymore. Perhaps my best efforts that I put in explaining the law of Karma in this chapter have its root in my past lives.

Souls generally prefer to reincarnate in places where they have been before. However, future life selections are based on more due to karmic choices. For this reason, many souls stay within family bloodlines. As example, a dying man is expected to come back as his own unborn grandchild for some unusual karmic circumstances. If two brothers had a close affinity for each other, and one were to die suddenly while still young, the soul of the dead sibling might want to return in the surviving sibling's child to restore this broken life connection to finish an important task. Young children who die early may do so for the parents to learn an important karmic lesson (means, he had no karmic issue but his parents had). Curtiss (1949, p. 32) explains,

> "*Often the whole life of worldly-minded parents is changed to a more spiritual one after a short visit of a more advanced soul as their child. The short incarnation was like the visit of an angel.*"

This type of short life is called 'a filler life' – souls return for a short life to help someone else rather than work on their own issues. Newton (2016a, p. 219) explains,

> "*In this case, the parents had abused and finally caused the death of another child when they were together in an earlier life. Although they were a loving young couple in the last life of my client, these parents evidently needed to experience the grief of having a child they desperately wanted taken away from them. Experiencing the anguish from this terrible loss gave the souls of these parents a deeper insight into the effects of severing a blood bond.*"

All lives are pre-planned, and if the life ends unexpectedly, it has some plan behind it. From karmic point of view a short-life is no way less significant than a long one. A person can live for hundred years but make little progress in his karmic path if he could not learn life lessons utilising his physical existence and exercising his free will.

> "*Souls who become involved in these tragedies are not caught in the wrong place at the wrong time with a capricious God looking the other way. Every soul has a motive for the events in which it chooses to participate.*" (Newton, 2016a, p. 219).

"*These are souls so desperate to pay off karmic debts that are holding them back that they are willing even to undergo that torture in order to advance spiritually. Sometimes they are deliberately assigned to such afflicted bodies as a means of atonement for abuses committed in previous lives. Other times, if they are truly repentant of serious sins, they will voluntarily select such a body, but in most instances it is an assignment by higher forces who compassionately select that body for a soul so troubled and tortured by past misdeeds that he is incapable of making his own choice.*" (Montgomery, 1972, p. 46).

Hence, a poor or hard life or a handicapped person does not necessarily have to be involved in a karmic debt they are paying off because of past-life responsibility for an injury to someone else.

"*When we see people who are victims of great adversity in life, this does not necessarily mean they were perpetrators of evil or wrongdoing of any kind in a former life. A soul with no such past associations might choose to suffer through a particular aspect of emotional pain to learn greater compassion and empathy for others by volunteering in advance for a life of travail.*" (Newton, 2016b, p. 104).

"*The greater the obstacles in the physical body, the more opportunity for a soul to pay off karmic debts and achieve more spiritual growth. The hurdles are stepping-stones.... The reward is not in the physical form but in spiritual development, and the more hurdles that are overcome in a physical lifetime, the less often that soul will thereafter need to return to physical form to round off the rough spots in his character.*" (Montgomery, 1972, p. 46).

By experiencing difficult lives at free will, they learn great life-lessons, that they should be sympathetic to the poor and not to exploit them, that they should help those who are facing hardship in life, that physically challenged people should not be ridiculed, but assisted. These lessons help the souls to make fewer mistakes in the forthcoming lives. These souls accumulate great positive Karma in every life on Earth.

"*Those in the next higher state are more aware of us than we are of them. They progress to that state when their rough earthbound edges are rounded off, and their mental and spiritual progression is such that they are ready for higher learning in the esoteric sense.*" (Montgomery, 1972, p. 152).

As a thumb rule the more advanced one is, the longer he remains in the soul realm unless there is some special reason such as helping humanity in some special way, spiritual teaching, etc. Some advanced souls have to wait for centuries of earth-time for the proper planetary and racial cycles and karmic conditions to arrive which would permit them to accomplish their mission (Curtiss, 1949, p. 34). Or, they incarnate in other worlds where life-forms have great spiritual development. Spiritual regressionists have confirmed that there are different life-forms in many worlds other than our Earth. When a world dies, those entities with unfinished karmic issue move on to another world which has a suitable life-form for the kind of work they have been doing. Yoga-Vasistha (3.30.8 to 3.30.34) described that life exists on other planets also, of which the modern-day researchers have no clue at all. Some life-forms are so advanced that they are purely mental world in a physical setup.

Hence, reincarnation is a purposeful action, not dependent on luck and chance. Newton (2016a, p. 50) described a case where one person had terribly hurt a girl in one life. After returning to spirit world, his spirit guide had exclusively scrutinised his soul and sent the soul back to Earth very soon as a woman (i.e., reincarnated as a woman) amongst many cruel people around. As an abused woman itself, the soul understood its responsibility to realise the damage it had done to an innocent girl. The spirit guides are very strict with those who have been involved with cruelty. This is not a punishment but 'regeneration'.

Negative Karma is not permanent. A person who had displayed negative attitudes towards others can erase his negative Karma if he continuously makes an effort to change – "*... and the only way to erase the bad marks is to perform a kindly act for someone in need*" (Montgomery, 1972, p. 138). The story of Sage Valmiki/forest robber Ratnakar is worth recalling. Ratnakar forgot the human and divine qualities in him, and opted to became a robber to sustain his family. But there was divinity in him. After some time when he came in the company of some great sages, the wisdom within him emerged gradually. His Atman was salvaged and made eligible to receive God's grace. He became a hermit known as Mahrishi Valmiki.

Similar is the story of Angulimal. He was a dreaded dacoit living in the woods in the territory of King Prasenjit. After killing the passers-by, he used to cut off their little finger and used to wear them as a necklace. However, when he came in touch with Lord Buddha he took the attires of a monk and lived a pious life.

Strange parallel to the above stories, Jetsun Milarepa (estimated 1052 – 1135 AD, from Western Tibet, close to Nepal) had a hard childhood and a dark youth. He was only seven when his father died, and relatives took over his father's property and mistreated the bereaved family. Milarepa had learned black magic to wreak revenge on those who had ruined his life, and soon unleashed a tide of destruction, killing about thirty-five people and destroyed the entire crops of a village. But he came to regret his actions, and looked for help in shedding the bad Karma he had acquired during his revengeful actions. Soon he retreated for many years in isolated mountains to purify himself from the negative Karma he had accumulated, and ultimately attained enlightenment.

Namdev Relekar (1270 – 1350 AD), in his youth, had been a bandit and murderer. In one night in the entrance of a temple, he overheard a young mother explaining to her fatherless child that they had to live in extreme poverty because his father had been killed. Namdev realised with sudden horror that it was he who was the killer, and with a disgust of feeling he entered the temple to sacrifice his own life. He was prevented, however, and he devoted the rest of his life to penance and worship. Later in life he became a great ascetic and an enlightened mystic.

Goldberg (2004, p. 267) wrote that many people asked him to help them speed up their karmic cycles so that they won't have to reincarnate again. But only the individual can do that – "*They must be honest, truthful, and faithful to their own code of ethics. If they follow this simple advice, they are well on their way to the higher planes*". The soul guides give tremendous opportunities to the reincarnating souls to speed up their Karma.

Life is hard, but suicide is not an option because suicide by a physically healthy person is not a prearranged karmic option for anyone. Every adverse situation that we face in life has a meaning by which we possess new wisdom.

> "*No person has the right to take the life within himself, any more than that of another person,* ***since all are a part of the Godhead****.*" (Montgomery, 1972, p. 41).

Suicide-related NDEs are often unpleasant though some religions promote terror and suicide in the name of God. The Isa Upanishad condemns suicide in a straightforward manner.

> "*asuryā nāma te lokā andhena tamasāvṛtāḥ*
> *tāṃste pretyābhigacchanti ye ke cātmahano janāḥ*"
> (Isa Upanishad: Mantra no. 3).
> [Malignant are those worlds and enveloped in blinding darkness, into which people who have committed suicide pass after death.]

In one suicide-related NDE account, a male voice asked the experiencer whether he wanted to return to life, and he stated that he wanted to die. Then the male voice said, "*You are breaking my laws to commit suicide. You'll not be with me in heaven, if you die*". (Ring, 1980, p. 76). This scene confirms what the above Mantra from Isa Upanishad had said.

Spiritualists have put forward many theories on how, when and why the reincarnation and karmic cycle started. Arthur Ford revealed through Ruth Montgomery that the souls have originated from another planet. Earth was a testing ground for them. But the souls had misused the human bodies, and as a result the karmic cycle started.

> "*The father [highly evolved souls from other planets] who conceived the earth phase for testing souls put no evil there, but the errant souls who eagerly inhabited bodies lusted, fought, and squabbled, hoping to enhance their own importance, thus establishing a force of evil...*". (Montgomery, 1972, p. 65).

So, the force of evil created by the migratory souls caused the Karma to begin. And since their negative Karma could not be worked out in one lifetime, these souls had to reincarnate once the physical body was worn out. Bruce Goldberg came to a similar conclusion. Some mysterious 'light' people (they are pure energy in the form of light without possessing any physical body) are responsible for the karmic cycle to begin.

> "*The 'light' people are sent to Earth from another galaxy to experience life in human bodies. Their goal is to assist us in our evolutionary development. When 'light' people leave their human bodies, they return to an examination room (although this is not a physical room as we know it). Their progress is evaluated by a group of monitors or Planners. If they do well, their vibrational rate is raised, but if they fail, it's reduced. These Planners are directed by Master Planners who communicate with them from the home planet many galaxies away.*" (Goldberg, 2004, p. 124).

These 'light' people could enter and leave the physical body any time by their will. The Planners trained them to perform certain functions and assist the human they are occupying in its intelligence and social functions. But sometimes these 'light' people got carried away with the physicality of the body and violated moral and otherworldly spiritual codes (such as obsessions with sex or murder or oppression), or merely refused to perform the functions for which they were trained. When this happened, the Planners punished them.

> "*Many of these 'light' people took advantage (or were overwhelmed) by our physicality and ran afoul with what the Master Planners had in store. The Planners, as supervisors to the progress of these 'light' people, had the power to trap these light beings into our physical bodies and remove their memories so they would not be psychologically compromised as they began life as a human*". (Goldberg, 2004, p. 128).

The mechanism of the origin of our karmic cycle is now clear. Advanced ETs from a distant galaxy in the form of light energy experimented with humans to aid us in our evolution. We are fortunate that these aliens tampered with our evolution, or else our present level of technology would not have been possible.

Though there is no historical or scientific proof to support the 'light' people episode, it explains a very important philosophical question that Sage Patanjali also addresses in the Yoga Sutras – when and how does this process of accumulating 'Samskara' (deep impressions, imprints in the unconscious, deepest habits, traces) begin and how can it be ended? The birth of 'Avidya' (ignorance, veiling) is the moment when consciousness comes into contact with matter. With this 'Klesha' (painful, afflicted, impure) begins to work, and 'Samskara' begins to form.

According to Dharmic scriptures a human pass through many animal lives before he reincarnates as human. Hence a human brings with him all the 'Samskara' of the stages through which he has passed, though most of these 'Samskara' lie dormant in a latent condition. Psychologists recognise the animal traits that are ever present in our subconscious mind. The occasional emergence of these traits belonging to the lower stages is due to the presence within us of all the 'Samskara' which we have gathered in our evolutionary development. That is why, as soon as the control of the Higher Self temporarily disappears or slackens owing to heightened emotional disturbances or other causes, humans begin to behave like beasts or even worse than beasts (for which we may have to repent afterwards).

History provides many instances of temporary reversion to the animal stage. The animal kingdom and the human kingdom are clearly defined and are entirely separate stages of karmic evolution. But as far as 'Samskara' are concerned they are continuous and the human stage may be considered as the summation and conclusion of the previous stages. Hence, it is highly necessary for us to keep a rigid control over our minds and emotions and follow the path of 'Nishkam Karma'. This is what we can learn from those 'light' people.

One fundamental question still remains – how Karma propagates? The simplest understanding of Karma is an action which leaves an informational imprint in a deep level of reality which can be activated at some future point in time. This extends to all actions of sentient beings, including perceptions.

All actions and perceptions leave traces which make future similar actions and perceptions more probable. This helps potentiality for the material world to manifest at future points in time. It means the Karma of each sentient being that inhabits the Universe plays a role in shaping the formation of the Universe. This view is fully supported by the evidence of double-slit experiment, and all sentient beings are the 'observers' whose perception manifests the Universe suitable to work out the latent karmic imprints of earlier times. If this theory is correct, Karma propagates in the quantum level.

There is no scientific way to prove or disprove the existence of Karma because it involves the interaction of non-quantifiable parameters like consciousness, free will and motivation that are beyond the grasp of classical physics. But various case studies confirm its strong presence, and that's the reason we can believe in this doctrine without even considering science.

Classical physics confirms that inanimate objects obey laws for any interaction of any kind from the microscopic level to the macroscopic level. Not a single rain-drop falls from the sky except by law. Therefore, if laws govern all of nature, how can we claim that the all-pervading souls alone are the law-exempt odd man out? Karma is the law of cause and effect in the moral dimension. Quantum physics had proven that consciousness is a self-experienced reality. Even skeptics who deny the existence of Quantum Consciousness are conscious beings because they deny – its attempted denial becomes its undeniable proof. If classical physics can explain interactions of objects with mathematical calculations, how can we label interaction of consciousness as unscientific? All we need is a new branch of science that can precisely distinguish, quantify and explain all the human qualities, and then we will be able to explain the doctrine of reincarnation and Karma with mathematical certainty.

CHAPTER - 5

The purification of the SASVATA ATMAN (Eternal Soul)

"If man is not rising upward to be an angel, he is sinking downward to be a devil. He cannot stop at the beast."

Samuel Taylor Coleridge

There is a general belief among the believers of some religions that when an individual has taken to their own particular religion his spiritual destiny becomes assured as long as he does the rituals laid down for him. The wise sages have never subscribed to this view that a person wins liberation simply by calling himself a Dharmic. The sages require everyone to earn his freedom, to be worthy of it, and to check for himself time to time what progress he is actually making as a result of his 'Sadhana' (Sanskrit term means, a daily spiritual practice). The scriptures laid down clear yardsticks for such evaluation. In other words, the scriptures only give guidance and rest is left to the individual.

The common goals of all the scriptures are the well-being of the entire world and all creatures living in it, and the purification of the Atman of each one of us and its union with the Ultimate Reality. With each reincarnation, the Atman becomes more like a lotus leaf in water and moves closer to God. Lotus leaf just can't get wet or dirty though it is born in muddy water, and lives and dies there.

"brahmaṇyādhāya karmāṇi saṅgaṁ tyaktvā karoti yaḥ
lipyate na sa pāpena padma-patram ivāmbhasā
kāyena manasā buddhyā kevalair indriyair api
yoginaḥ karma kurvanti saṅgaṁ tyaktvātma-śhuddhaye"
(Bhagavad Gita: 5.10-11).

[Those who dedicate their actions to God, abandoning all attachment, remain untouched by sin, just as a lotus leaf is untouched by water. The Yogis, while giving up attachment, perform actions with their body, senses, mind, and intellect, only for the purpose of self-purification.]

"yadā viniyataṁ chittam ātmanyevāvatiṣhṭhate
niḥspṛihaḥ sarva-kāmebhyo yukta ityuchyate tadā"
(Bhagavad Gita: 6.18).
[With thorough discipline, they learn to withdraw the mind from selfish cravings and rivet it on the unsurpassable good of the self. Such persons are said to be in Yoga, and are free from all yearning of the senses.]

There is one activity that is in our hands and not in God's hands. When we purify our heart and engage it in devotion to God, it pleases Him more than anything else. Realising this, the great ancient sages make purification of their heart as the foremost goal, not out of selfishness, rather for the pleasure of God.

"yasya sarve samārambhāḥ kāma-saṅkalpa-varjitāḥ
jñānāgni-dagdha-karmāṇaṁ tam āhuḥ paṇḍitaṁ budhāḥ"
(Bhagavad Gita: 4.19).
[Whose undertakings are all devoid of desires and self-will and whose actions have been burnt by the Fire of Knowledge, the wise will call him the Sage.]

Another classical text, Patanjali's Yoga Sutra, also prescribes a common code of conduct for all aspiring toward freedom in its Yamas and Niyamas (moral discipline and observances), the first two steps of an eight-step path to self-realisation. Knowledge purifies the mind.

"*... jñānaprasādena viśuddhasattvastatastu taṃ paśyate niṣkalaṃ dhyāyamānaḥ*
...yasminviśuddhe vibhavatyeṣa ātmā" (Mundaka Upanishad: 3.1.8-9).
[When one's mind is purified by the clearness of knowledge, then alone he sees the indivisible (Brahmam) by thought.
When the Atman is purified, then it shines out of itself.]

Throughout this chapter I will show that in the teachings of Sanatan Dharma there is an extraordinary direct correlation between human ethics and cosmic order. The universal code of ethics (a system of ethics that can apply to every sentient being) shaped the philosophy of education in ancient India. Sanatan Dharma is not a sectarian belief-system but universally applicable to all people at all times.

Dharma is understood in Vedas as duty par excellence. Dharma is also understood as the duties of humans in four age-based life stages which provide training and environment for realising the ideal of our life. The concept of Karma signifies that there is a uniform moral law. Therefore, by infusing the entire life with some positive karmic energy in four stages, one's complete focus is on obtaining Moksha to the exclusion of all else. Every doctrine of ancient India, carved out by the ancient sages, is based on scientific and rational reasoning. However, to put them to use they needed to be socially embedded. Hence, methods like the Ashram (Sanskrit word, means 'stage of life') system were included in the Vedic society.

Each stage has its own duties that help the spiritual evolution of a human. Together the four Ashram systems take man to perfection by successive stages, e.g., 'Brahmacharya' (the period of studentship), 'Grihastha' (the stage of the householder), 'Vanaprastha' (the stage of a forest-dweller, hermit), and 'Sanyasa' (the life of renunciation or asceticism). The entire earthly existence of the Atman is thus very systematically and orderly arranged.

The first stage 'Brahmacharya' represents the bachelor student life and focuses on education and included the practice of celibacy. The student goes to a 'Gurukul' (house of the Guru) and lives with the 'Guru' (mentor) where he acquires knowledge of science, philosophy, logic, and practice strict self-discipline. He also learns to live the life of Dharma with righteousness, morals, and duties. The students did not pay any fees in cash. In the ancient Vedic Culture, the Guru and his disciple were inseparable in a way. The Guru cannot exist without being a part of a true disciple's personality or character. The Gurukul education system was not commercial during those days, and the respect with which the society looked upon the teachers was itself a great reward. In simple words, the Guru is the teacher after the parents.

Physical exercises and manly games of all kinds had formed a definite part of their education. In the Ramayan and Mahabharat we read of the ways in which the youths had practiced horse-riding, chariot-driving and the use of weapons. After this stage, the youth was to present his teacher with a gift (Guru Dakshina – an ancient tradition of acknowledgment, respect and thanks) according to his ability, and return home to enter the household life.

> "*vedānadhītya vedau vā vedaṃ vā'pi yathākramam*
> *aviplutabrahmacaryo gṛhasthāśramamāvaset*" (Manusmriti: 3.2).
> [Having learnt, in due course, three Vedas, or two Vedas, or one Veda, he should enter upon the state of the householder, having never deviated from the vows of studentship.]

The second stage, 'Grihastha' refers to the individual's married life with the duties of maintaining a household, raising a family, educating children, and leading a family-centred meaningful social life. The Mantras chanted during the marriage ceremony were handed down to posterity thousands of years ago by the ancient sages who got them in their state of super-consciousness or communion with the Divine. The Mantras express perfect ideas and have great spiritual potency. The vibrations set in motion by chanting the Mantras purify the marriage hall as well as all those present there. Certainly, great sacredness is attached to the marriage.

"*yatra nāryastu pūjyante ramante tatra devatāḥ*
yatraitāstu na pūjyante sarvāstatrāphalāḥ kriyāḥ" (Manusmriti: 3.56).
[Where women are honoured, there the Gods rejoice; where they are not honoured, there all rites are fruitless.]

"*santuṣṭo bhāryayā bhartā bhartrā bhāryā tathaiva ca*
yasminneva kule nityaṃ kalyāṇaṃ tatra vai dhruvam"
(Manusmriti: 3.60).
[In that family where the husband is pleased with his wife and the wife with her husband, happiness will assuredly be lasting.]

It is Dharma that had united them. For this reason, matrimony is considered too sacred to break up. In the Grihastha stage most intense physical, sexual, emotional, occupational, social and material attachments exist in a human being's life. This is the most important stage in sociological context because they produce food and wealth for sustaining people in other stages of life, and also the offspring that continued mankind.

"*brahmacārī gṛhasthaśca vānaprastho yatistathā*
ete gṛhasthaprabhavāścatvāraḥ pṛthagāśramāḥ" (Manusmriti: 6.87).
[The Student, the Householder, the Forest dweller, the Ascetic these, the four separate orders, spring from the Householder.]

"*arveṣāmapi caiteṣāṃ vedasmṛtividhānataḥ*
gṛhastha ucyate śreṣṭhaḥ sa trīnetān bibharti hi
yathā nadīnadāḥ sarve sāgare yānti saṃsthitim
tathaivāśramiṇaḥ sarve gṛhasthe yānti saṃsthitim"
(Manusmriti: 3.89-90).
[Of all these, by the precepts of the Veda-Shruti, the householder is called the best; he actually supports the other three.
As all streams and rivers flow to rest in the ocean, so all the Ashrams flow to rest in the householder.]

The third stage, 'Vanaprastha' is the retirement stage where a person hands over household responsibilities to the next generation, takes an advisory role, and gradually withdraws himself from the social life. This is a transition phase from a householder's life to one with greater emphasis on spiritual liberation.

> "*gṛhasthastu yathā paśyed valīpalitamātmanaḥ apatyasyaiva cāpatyaṃ tadā'raṇyaṃ samāśrayet*" (Manusmriti: 6.2).
> [When the householder notices his wrinkles and greyness, and sees his child's child, then he should retire to the forest.]

The last stage 'Sanyasa' is marked by renunciation of material desires and prejudices, represented by a state of disinterest and detachment from material life, generally without any meaningful property or home (ascetic), and focused on Moksha, peace and simple spiritual life.

> "*vaneṣu ca vihṛtyaivaṃ tṛtīyaṃ bhāgamāyuṣaḥ caturthamāyuṣo bhāgaṃ tyakvā saṅgān parivrajet*" (Manusmriti: 6.33).
> [Having passed the third portion of life in the forests, let him, having abandoned attachments, wander (as an ascetic) the fourth portion of life.]

Therefore, the first half was a preparation for life, and the second a preparation for death. While Brahmacharya and Grihastha show the 'Pravritti Marga' (towards the world), Vanaprastha and Sanyasa indicate the 'Nivritti Marga' (away from the world) through introspection and renunciation. These stages are facets of Dharma concept; something essential to complete the full development of a human being and fulfilling all the needs of the individual and society.

The activities in every stage also reduce attachment for the great illusion (Maya), and help us to consider others as a part of one's family and to diminish the ego. We not only learn the golden rule but also put it into practice – what is contrary to the welfare of one's own self should not be discharged or done in regard to others. A very famous conclusive sentence of Mahabharat is supposed to be the essence of the principle of Dharma.

> "*atmanah pratikulani paresham na samaoharet*" (Mahabharat: 5.15.17).
> [Don't do what you do not want to be done unto you.]

A sixty-two-year-old businessman who had an NDE during a cardiac arrest had the same wisdom.

> "*One thing I learned was that we are all part of one big, living universe.* ***If we think we can hurt another person or another living thing without hurting ourselves we are sadly mistaken****.... We are*

connected with all things and if we send love along those connections, then we are happy." (Moody and Perry, 1988, p. 34).

This is the remedy for most of the problems and evils of life born of the separation of society into selfish individualities. It is the process of integration not only of the individual but of the family, community, nation and the world at large, through the expression of the great preservative force tending to universal solidarity – Dharma. Arnold J. Toynbee commented,

"*It is already becoming clear that a chapter which had a Western beginning will have to have an Indian ending if it is not to end in self-destruction of the human race. At this supremely dangerous moment in human history, the only way of salvation is the ancient Hindu [Dharmic] way.* ***Here we have the attitude and spirit that can make it possible for the human race to grow together into a single family.***" (Knapp, 2006, p. 8).

The development of the Atman is a gradual process over many thousand years on earth realm where the four-ashram system helps to speed up the process. There is no compulsion that everyone should strictly pass through all the stages. Sage Sukadeva (main narrator of the scripture Bhagavad Purana) took Sanyasa from birth and Adi Shankaracharya took Sanyasa without entering Grihastha. This happens for highly developed souls whose karmic debts to the world had been fully paid in a previous birth. They can renounce worldly ambitions and take up Sanyasa even at a young age. In general, a 'Brahmin' (priest class) is expected to pass through all four stages, a 'Kshatriya' (king, warrior class) pass through the first three, a 'Vaishya' (trader, agriculturist) have the first two and a 'Shudra' (unskilled manual labourer with no formal education) has only one stage – that of marriage, i.e., Grihastha. These are only guidelines because Sanatan Dharma is never authoritative. The duties during the periods are progressive stages of self-sublimation and self-transcendence which reach their fulfilment in Sanyasa.

Sanatan Dharma advocates four legitimate goals in life, called 'Purushartha' (Sanskrit word, literally means an 'object of human pursuit') for achieving fulfilment. The four Purusharthas are Dharma (moral values), Artha (economic values), Kama (sexual pleasure, love, psychological values) and Moksha (spiritual values). All four goals are important, but in cases of conflict, Dharma is considered more important than Artha or Kama. If Dharma is ignored, Artha and Kama, i.e., profit and pleasure lead to social chaos. Spiritual emancipation is the main goal of life, and other goals are necessary stepping stones towards it.

"*kāmasya nendriya-prītir lābho jīveta yāvatā*
jīvasya tattva-jijñāsā nārtho yaś ceha karmabhiḥ"
(Bhagavad Purana: 1.2.10).
[Life's desires should never be directed toward sense gratification. One should desire only a healthy life, or self-preservation, since a human being is meant for inquiry about the Absolute Truth. Nothing else should be the goal.]

"*aśeṣeṇa parityāgo vāsanānāṃ ya uttamaḥ*
mokṣaṃ ityucyate brahmansa eva vimalakramaḥ"
(Yoga-Vasistha: 1.3.8).
[Complete abandonment of desires, styled as the best state of liberation, is the only pure step towards blessedness.]

"*ayaṃ vāsanayā deho dhriyate bhūtapañjaraḥ*
tanunāntarniviṣṭena muktaughastantunā yathā"
(Yoga-Vasistha: 1.3.10).
[Our desires which uphold our living bodies (and minds) bind us fast as by strings to our bodily prison. These being loosened, the inward Atman is liberated.]

"*nanvarthā vitatānarthāḥ saṁpadaḥ santatāpadaḥ*
bhogā bhavamahārogā viparītena bhāvitāḥ"
(Yoga-Vasistha: 6.2.47.39).
[Wealth is the source of endless misfortune, prosperity is perpetual adversity, enjoyment of pleasure is enduring disease – all these are misunderstood by the perverse intellect.]

There is a point. Accumulating wealth by honest means and spending it are not considered as obstacles to the spiritual aspirant. Similarly, sex is never branded as immorality. What matters is the attitude with which the wealth or sex is used. How can that without which the creation is impossible be called immoral?

Saffron and white are very important colours in Sanatan Dharma. Saffron is the colour of fire. Fire has a very prominent place in ritualistic tradition of Sanatan Dharma because fire burns anything it touches; same way saffron colour denotes relief from material world. White represents purity, cleanliness, peace and knowledge. The Goddess of knowledge, Devi Saraswati is always shown as wearing a white dress, sitting on a white lotus. The ancient sages wear saffron and white colour cloths because they have burnt all their material pleasures with the help of fire of spiritual knowledge and 'Atma-gyan' (self-realisation).

The Vedic seers discouraged meat-eating. For them the 'world' did not mean only the human beings, but the animal kingdom, vegetation and other aspects of nature also. Each aspect and power of nature is controlled by a 'Devata' (deity). These deities are real. During NDE more frequently persons encounter with the deities in the soul realm. Each 'Devata' is so massive, so powerful, so encompassing that it is often described that they exist as a 'Presence' without needs of name, identity, or definition. The Vedic 'Yajna' and 'Yaga' (sacrifice and fire ritual) with chanting of appropriate Mantras in front of sacrificial fire are the rituals to satisfy these deities to grant us rain, food, health, wealth and children. Immolation of animals in the sacrifices is not encouraged. In this way the whole world feels satisfied. This is the basic idea behind the system of Vedic sacrifices. Lord Krishna has expended the concept of Yajna to such dimensions that there is almost unlimited scope to practice it in our daily lives. Gifts of money by the wealthy, knowledge by the wise, or protection by the influential are no way inferior to the sacrifices done in the fire.

The teachings of Sanatan Dharma extend beyond the earth realm. In the celestial realms where the Atman resides in the period between two successive earthly lives, development continues, and many sections in the Dharmic scriptures confirm this.

The NDE cases give us enough evidence that a mysterious and highly organised spirit world exists which is beyond our earthly comprehensions. Other evidence comes from deathbed phenomena, after-death contacts, séances and obviously soul memories recovered under hypnosis. After spending decades on research many world-famous spiritual regressionists have constructed a working model of the spirit world where the Atman continues search for truth. Despite widely disparaging religious and cultural backgrounds, all of them give approximately the same description of the spirit world.

There are many planes in the afterlife. According to Bruce Goldberg (1982, pp. 34-35) there are five lower planes. Our karmic cycle is worked out in these five planes. The lowest of these planes is the Earth plane (physical plane) where we function with a physical body. The greatest amount of Karma is erased or added at this level. This is the most difficult level. After death the Atman first enters the astral plane, and from here a series of rising dimensions starts which blends into the spiritual. The ghosts, earthbound spirits and those souls that need to take an early rebirth to progress their karmic cycle lingers in this plane. The astral plane exists here on Earth but we are unaware of this plane.

An Atman can be a ghost or earthbound for various reasons, such as, sudden death (confused or bewildered by an unexpected change), unfinished business (money matters, to help out children), guilt (suicide victims), revenge (a murder victim), resentful (others enjoying their old homes and possessions) etc. Their spiritual progress is greatly hindered and Lord Krishna pinpoints lust, anger, and greed as the three causes for it. Greed is a transformation of lust which later transforms into anger.

> "*tri-vidhaṁ narakasyedaṁ dvāraṁ nāśhanam ātmanaḥ*
> ***kāmaḥ krodhas tathā lobhas*** *tasmād etat trayaṁ tyajet*
> *etair vimuktaḥ kaunteya tamo-dvārais tribhir naraḥ*
> *ācharaty ātmanaḥ śhreyas tato yāti parāṁ gatim*"
> (Bhagavad Gita: 16.21-22).
> [**Lust, anger and greed** are the three gates that lead to hell, and they cause the destruction of the soul. Therefore, one should completely renounce them.
> Those who are freed from the three gates to darkness endeavour for the welfare of their Atman, and thereby attain the supreme goal.]

After the astral plane, there are four higher planes, such as the causal plane, mental plane, etheric plane, and soul plane. At the soul plane, the earthliness of the soul changes completely and the process of reincarnation starts. The Atman is asked to study, analyse and understand various events from many past lives and how they fit into the Atman's karmic patterns. This is how the Atman is prepared for its next life on Earth.

Above the soul plane there are many planes that ultimately lead to God or nameless plane. In Patanjali's Yoga Sutras, there are seven levels of 'prajñā' (in Sanskrit, prajñā means wisdom).

> "*tasya saptadha pranta bhumih prajñā*" (Yoga Sutras: 2.27).
> [The one having surpassed the seven stages (saptadha pranta) with ultimate wisdom (prajñā) reaches final stage.]

> "*ritambhara tatra prajñā*" (Yoga Sutras: 1.48).
> [There, the consciousness is truth and right-bearing (ritambhara)]

Through the seven stages of wisdom the Atman develops. The word 'ritambhara' is a very meaningful word that is made up of two words, 'ritam' (right, truth) and 'bhara' (bearing) or right/truth-bearing. Ritam refers to the cosmic order and the eternal laws – natural, moral and spiritual.

Many Dharmic scriptures use the word 'Loka' to mean plane or soul realm. The seven lokas consist of Bhuloka, Bhuvar loka, Swarg loka (Indraloka, heaven), Maharloka, Janaloka, Taparloka, and Satyaloka. The lokas are usually described as places of eternal light and goodness. Concepts of heaven and hell are complicated aspects in Sanatan Dharma. The Upanishads and the six philosophies mention very little about heaven (Swarg) and hell (Narak), but they are mentioned in all eighteen Puranas. The heaven is inhabited by devas, sages, and many great and noble souls who performed good deeds upon earth and earned merit to qualify for their stay there.

The early Vedic Seers had a clear understanding of various planes of wisdom, and they knew it in their own philosophical way. All these planes of wisdom have only one purpose, i.e., for the Atman to realise its true nature – indistinguishable from the Absolute Godhead, the Brahmam. This realisation leads to liberation (Moksha). The spiritual regressionists are revealing the same truths today that had been recorded by the Dharmic Sages several thousand years ago.

Neither life nor afterlife are permanent as they are both part of the grand illusion, i.e., Maya. That's why a true Dharmic never lures for the paradise.

CHAPTER - 6

MOKSHA – The doctrine of liberation

"Our true and only purpose is to perfect our soul and ascend to the higher planes to reunite with God, or whatever you term the perfect energy that created our Universe."

Bruce Goldberg

"We grow, we live, we love, to return in endless cycles until at last we slough off the imperfection which we picked up along the way and are fit to become a part of God Himself."

Ruth Montgomery

Moksha refers to the liberation of the Atman from Maya's illusion, the freedom of the cycle of Samsara and the unification with Brahmam. Moksha is known as Nirvana in the other heterodox Indian philosophies such as Buddhism and Jainism. For the adherents of Dharma, the successes of the material world, great as they are, are not considered sufficient. Through sacrifices and offerings, we might reach the joys of heaven, but the question (framed by Adi Shankaracharya) remains – 'tatah kim, tatah kim', means, What else? What next? – and from here the ideal of Moksha comes in.

"dharmasya hy āpavargyasya nārtho 'rthāyopakalpate
nārthasya dharmaikāntasya kāmo lābhāya hi smṛtaḥ"
(Bhagavad Purana: 1.2.9).
[All performance of Dharma is meant for ultimate liberation (Moksha). It should not be performed for material gain. Furthermore, one who is engaged in the ultimate occupational service (Dharma) should not use material gain (Artha) simply for sense gratification.]

"ahamkaaram balam darpam kaamam krodham parigraham
vimuchya nirmamah shaanto brahmabhooyaaya kalpate"
(Bhagavad Gita: 18.53).

[Having abandoned egoism, strength, arrogance, desire, anger and greed, free from the notion of 'mine' ness and tranquil in mind, he becomes worthy of becoming one with Brahmam.]

As we grow spiritually through many reincarnations and work out Karma, then fears, prejudices, and judgments will start disappearing from our awareness, and our eventual ascension will be faster. The resulting expansion of this awareness will allow God to reveal the ultimate truth once and for all to us.

"*When we learn all the lessons necessary to show kindness and unselfish love to all those with whom we come into contact, our cycles will end. When they end, we will go beyond the soul plane to the higher planes and, eventually, to God.* ***Karma is merely a process of evolution, of achieving greater levels of enlightenment.***" (Goldberg, 2004, p. 267).

"*We not only were created in God's image but of the very stuff of God, so that in order to complete our cycle and return to Him, we must absorb the philosophy of the Universe and come to understand its laws, so that* ***we never again will be out of harmony with the creation.***" (Montgomery, 1972, p. 57).

To work out our Karma faster, we must fully understand and accept the universal oneness of all mankind – "*The truth is that there is no such thing as race or colour, but simply different souls which spring from the same source, God.*" (Montgomery, 1972, p. 166). This is exactly what Shankaracharya said in the Atma Bodha and Manisha Panchakam, and Lord Krishna said in Bhagavad Gita.

"*nanopadhivacœadeva jativarṇa ramadayaḥ*
atmanyaropitastoye rasavarṇadi bhedavat"
(Atma Bodha: Mantra no. 11).
[Because of its association with different conditionings (Upadhis) such ideas as caste, colour and position are super-imposed upon the Atman, as flavour, colour, etc., are superimposed on water.]

"*brāhmaṇa-kṣatriya-viśāṃ śūdrāṇāṃ ca parantapa*
karmāṇi pravibhaktāni svabhāva-prabhavair guṇaiḥ"
(Bhagavad Gita: 18.41).
[Of Brahmanas, Kshatriyas and Vaishyas, as also the Shudras, O Arjun, the activities are distinguished in accordance with the qualities born of their own nature.]

"*vidyā-vinaya-sampanne brāhmaṇe gavi hastini*
śuni caiva śva-pāke ca paṇḍitāḥ sama-darśinaḥ"
(Bhagavad Gita: 5.18).

[Enlightened persons perceive with equal vision a gentle and learned Brahmin, a cow, an elephant, a dog and an outcaste.]

The wise people see divinities everywhere, and find no distinction in the world of names and forms because social position is determined by conduct, not by birth.

Once a person is liberated, enjoying the glory of enlightenment, he seeks to help others also to unify with the self – "*You do have the option of remaining on these lower planes as a guide, but free of the discomforts you currently experience.*" (Goldberg, 2004, p. 268). Thus, liberated from reincarnation but still living in the body, the sage is untouched by merits and de-merits and free from Karma.

Trailanga Swami (pre-monastic name Shivaram) was a near mythical figure in India, as there were many evidences about his spiritual powers. This highly developed Yogi stated that if someone attains the desirelessness state, this world is then altered into the heaven. And he can be liberated from the cycle of birth and death. Just like, this world is a chronic disease and the medicine is the way to detachment from disease.

> "*Obviously we here are yet to experience that bliss, but there is a teaching here that* ***when souls near that final perfection they once again review not only their past lives but every thought and concept and idea which has touched them, or they it, since the beginning of the life of all of us****. This is during the sixth plane. They finally decide that no stone remains unturned that they have not repaid in some manner or thought or way, and that they therefore have atoned for misdeeds and are ready to join God. There is no conceit in this decision but a totally accurate assessment of life since the beginning.* ***They then are drawn into the oneness of God in perfect peace****. This is hearsay, of course, as those souls will never return or resume the wheel of destiny when the perfect moment comes.*" (Montgomery, 1972, pp. 161-62).

One consequence of attaining Moksha is the sudden expansion of consciousness into the realm of infinite knowledge.

> "*tada sarva avarana mala apetasya jnanasya anantyat jneyam alpam*" (Patanjali's Yoga Sutra: 4.31).
> [Then, by the removal of those veils of imperfection, there comes the experience of the infinite, and the realisation that there is almost nothing to be known.]

When the last veil of illusions is disappeared, Karma and 'Klesha' (sufferings) are completely removed. The recurrence of these two instruments of bondage is impossible because the Atman cannot fall again into 'Avidya' (ignorance) and start generating Karma which binds. There is no 'Samskara' to keep the Atman bound to the world of manifestation. With this ultimate perfection, the Atman enters the realm of Infinity. When we are in the realm of 'Infinity' we are not in the realm of magnitudes at all. As example, one divided by Infinity and one trillion divided by Infinity is zero. In this condition, even the highest kind of knowledge cannot be compared with the enlightenment and the Atman passes into the realm of pure consciousness. The last Sutra of Patanjali's Yoga Sutra says,

> "*... kaivalyam svarupa pratistha va chiti shaktih iti*"
> (Yoga Sutra: 4.34).
> [...there comes liberation, wherein the power of pure consciousness becomes established in its true nature. 'Iti' (the end to denote the end of the teachings)]

The Vedas prescribe varieties of social and ritualistic duties for individuals. But those who grasp their underlying motive, and fulfill their duty toward God by rejecting all intermediate instruction wholeheartedly, they are the highest devotees. Thus, one who is attaching the mind to God is automatically fulfilling the purpose of all the Veda-Mantras.

> "*OM asato mā sad gamaya*
> *tamaso mā jyotir gamaya*
> *mṛtyor mā amṛtaṁ gamaya*
> ***OM śānti śānti śāntiḥ OM***" (Brihadaranyaka Upanishad: 1.3.28).
> [Lead us from unreality (of transitory existence) to the reality (of the Eternal Self), Lead us from the darkness (of ignorance) to the light (of spiritual knowledge), Lead us from death to immortality. **Let There Be Peace Peace Peace.**]

The 'Shanti Mantra' or the peace incantation "***OM śānti śānti śāntiḥ OM***" is said to be the ultimate teaching of Vedic literature.

All the pleasures of the whole world are a mere drop when compared to the infinite bliss of Moksha. Moksha is 'Sarva-Duhkha Nivritti' (freedom from all sorts of pains) and the attainment of 'Paramananda Prapti' (supreme bliss). 'Duhkha' means pain or suffering. Births and deaths generate the greatest pain. Freedom from births and deaths is freedom from all sorts of pain. The Absolute, according to the Yoga-Vasistha, is 'Satchidananda Para Brahmam', who is non-dual, partless, infinite, self-luminous, changeless and eternal.

> "*taraṅgādimahāmbhodhau bhūtavṛndaṃ tathātmani*
> *idaṃ nāstīdamastīti bhrāntirnāmātmanātmani*"
> (Yoga-Vasistha: 6.11.36).

[All beings are situated in the Universal Atman, as the waves in the vast expanse of the ocean, therefore it is erroneous to say the one resides in the spirit, and another to be beside it.]

Moksha is the necessary opposite to Maya, for without the delusion, there is nothing for one to realise. This knowledge is the first step that leads to Moksha. To avoid rebirth and to attain Moksha, the Bhagavad Gita suggests a divine centered life in which life becomes a sacrifice and every action an offering to overcome the problem of Karma and its consequences.

"*tad-buddhayas tad-ātmānas tan-niṣhṭhās tat-parāyaṇāḥ*
gachchhantyapunar-āvṛittiṁ jñāna-nirdhūta-kalmaṣhāḥ"
(Bhagavad Gita: 5.17).
[Those whose intellect is fixed in God, who are wholly absorbed in God, with firm faith in Him as the supreme goal, such persons quickly reach the state from which there is no return, their sins having been dispelled by the light of knowledge.]

"*ananya-chetāḥ satataṁ yo māṁ smarati nityaśhaḥ*
tasyāhaṁ sulabhaḥ pārtha nitya-yuktasya yoginaḥ"
(Bhagavad Gita: 8.14).
[for those Yogis who always think of Me with exclusive devotion, I am easily attainable because of their constant absorption in Me.]

"*mām upetya punar janma duḥkhālayam aśhāśhvatam*
nāpnuvanti mahātmānaḥ sansiddhiṁ paramāṁ gatāḥ"
(Bhagavad Gita: 8.15).
[Having attained Me, the great souls are no more subject to rebirth in this world, which is transient and full of misery, because they have attained the highest perfection.]

In sum, Moksha is for all. The best among us will attain Moksha with a few lives while the worst will take several hundred lives on earth. We are not required to have supernatural power to attain Moksha. All we have to do is to develop our natural abilities to the highest degree. Excessive materialistic attitude towards life and the world makes the minds of people restless, unstable, diverted and imbalanced. As a result, people cannot realise the value of morality, spirituality and the life itself. The concept of Moksha is significant in demolishing or eradicating moral crisis, instability and survival crisis from the present society.

Does Moksha mean complete annihilation of the individuality of the consciousness as implied by the well-known sentence 'the Dewdrop slips into the Shining Sea'? If the individuality is merged and lost completely it cannot separate and manifest again. The Dharmic scriptures give the technique for achieving the final goal as far as human beings are concerned, but what lies beyond is totally beyond our comprehension and therefore cannot be the subject of study.

Most probably the Quantum Souls still maintain their individuality even after merging with the Divine Reality. The discarnate spiritual teacher Seth revealed that initially the Universe existed in a state of potentiality within the dreams of the God where the self-aware individual souls also resided. All the souls had lived even before big bang and will continue to live even after big crunch. After another big bang the Universe will come into existence again and the souls will continue their journey till big crunch. If the individuality is completely dissolved, how do we then account for its reappearance in the new Universe? We are forbidden to know the answer. The deeper secrets will reveal themselves in due course when we are ready for them. At present these are utterly beyond human imagination.

CHAPTER - 7

What attracts people to Sanatan Dharma?

"*So now we turn to India. This spiritual gift, that makes a man human, is still alive in Indian souls. Go on giving the world Indian examples of it. Nothing else can do so much to help mankind to save itself from destruction.*"

Arnold J. Toynbee

"*The vastest knowledge of today cannot transcend the 'buddhi' [intelligence] of the Rishis in ancient India; and science in its most advanced stage now is closer to Vedanta than ever before.*"

Alfred North Whitehead

"*The Veda was the most precious gift for which the West had ever been indebted to the East.*"

Francois Voltaire

Sanatan Dharma is man's relentless search after truth, where total freedom of thoughts and actions are of utmost importance. No Dharmic scripture ever forbid anyone to question its fundamentals. Even an atheist has the absolute right to condemn Sanatan Dharma openly. Voltaire, in his review on tolerance, wrote, "*I may disagree with what you say, but I will defend to the death your right to say it*". Sanatan Dharma is the embodiment of what Voltaire wrote. There is absolutely no intolerance. Thus, in one part of the world we may come across an ascetic who had abandoned all claims to social or family standing and renounced the world by performing his own 'Śrāddha' (Sanskrit word, means funeral), and in another part we may come across concepts that parallel quantum physics, and nuclear structure and reactions.

The first time the American public formally learned about Sanatan Dharma was through the World's Parliament of Religions, a gathering of practitioners of different faith traditions at Chicago on September 11, 1893. On this auspicious day an obscure young monk with an inspiring personality from Calcutta (India) stood up and famously began his speech with the immortal words "Sisters and Brothers of America". To these words, he got a standing ovation from a crowd of seven thousand that lasted for two minutes. It was most unusual for an Indian monk to embrace the audience as a single family at a time when societies were segregated, and racial superiority was an accepted part of life. When silence was restored, the monk began his speech in fluent educated English, "*It fills my heart with joy unspeakable to rise in response....*" that heralded a new era in inter-religious understanding and propagation of Indian spiritual thoughts in the West. The monk spoke in a powerful voice,

> "*By the Vedas no books are meant; they mean the accumulated treasury of spiritual laws discovered by different persons in different times. Just as the law of gravitation existed before its discovery, and would exist if all humanity forgot it, so is it with the laws that govern the spiritual world. The moral, ethical, and spiritual relations between two souls, and between individual spirits and the Father of all spirits, were there before their discovery, and would remain even if we forgot them.*" (Paranjape, 2015, p. 6).

This remarkable monk in a splendid robe, yellow turban, handsome bronze face and great dark burning eyes was none other than Swami Vivekananda (pre-monastic name Narendra Nath Datta) – the chief disciple of the nineteenth-century Indian mystic Sri Ramakrishna Paramhansa Dev. It was at that time when the American public first saw and heard people from "Eastern" spiritualism on their own soil – "*Asian teachers presented their faiths directly to Western Audiences... [inaugurating a] new stage in the history of Eastern spirituality in the United States.*" (Jackson, 1994, p. 15). Newspapers like the New York Herald wrote of him saying "*Vivekananda is undoubtedly the greatest figure in the Parliament of Religions. After hearing him we feel how foolish it is to send missionaries to this learned nation*". (Chattopadhyaya, 1999, p. 150). Prof. J. A Wright of Harvard University wrote that to ask Vivekananda for credentials is like asking the sun if it can shine. The appreciation continued as he journeyed through America, France and England after the talk for next two years. Vivekananda spoke extensively about Vedanta Philosophy and the spiritual benefits of Yoga and meditation, explaining how they were common resources for all human beings, and not just for the Indians.

Swami Vivekananda established the New York Vedanta Society in 1894. Soon Ramakrishna Centers were gradually established in New York, Boston, St. Louis, Chicago, Los Angeles and San Francisco. In 1895, he conducted the first Vedanta retreat (live discussion on Vedanta and applying ancient principles to modern issues) for the more dedicated seekers in Thousand Island Park in New York and initiated the first 'Sanyasi' (Sanskrit word, means someone who has reached the life stage of Sanyasa, or 'renouncement of material possession') in America – Leon Landsberg (renamed, Swami Kripananda), Dr. J. B. Street (renamed, Swami Yogananda) and Marie Louise (renamed, Abhayananda). Later, an Irish woman, Margaret Noble, followed him and devoted the rest of her life to the education of Indian woman and to the cause of India's independence. In India she took the name Sister Nivedita.

Vivekananda's mission was spiritual, neither political nor even social, in the last analysis. Vedanta movement was successful because of its practical, experiential methodology and direct mystical approach. Vedanta's greatest appeal was its universality versus Western Christianity's dogmatism, an appeal that remains popular today. His mission opened the way for later Indian spiritual teachers traveling West, such as Swami Rama Tirtha and Paramahansa Yogananda in the early half of the twentieth century.

Rama Tirtha was a great ascetic and an enlightened mystic. He went to America and Japan to spread the message of Vedanta with his inspiring and soul-elevating speeches. He had gained a large number of disciples and started many societies. One of the societies was Hermetic Brotherhood which was dedicated to the study of Vedanta.

From 1965 onwards scores of spiritual teachers from the East have come to America and established ashrams giving seminars on the Upanishads, the Bhagavad Gita, Yoga Sutras and the Vedanta Philosophy of Adi Shankaracharya without any personal expectations. Their mission was not just limited to spirituality but they also did substantial work for the defence of the nation whenever it was in difficulties.

Abhayananda (former Marie Louise) took a mission to spread Vaishnavism in the world. To help her in her mission Baba Premananda Bharati (pre-monastic name Surendra Nath Mukherjee) arrived in New York on October 15, 1902 and soon became a popular spokesman of Dharma in the West. Bharati greatly benefited from Vivekananda's success in the West, and a number of devotees aided him in his mission. Till his return to India during 1907, Baba Bharati attracted a great deal of public attention with his outspoken teachings that criticised Western materialism and colonialism, along with a missionary critique of Dharma. During his stay Baba Bharati inspired William Walker Atkinson (1862 - 1932) a highly successful author and one of the most influential writers associated with the 'New Thought' to write on Indian subjects. When Atkinson published under the pen name of Yogi Ramacharaka, he helped to popularise Dharmic concepts in America, with Yoga Philosophy being his primary interest along with the Bhagavad Gita and the Upanishads. The thirteen works of Yogi Ramacharaka have been widely translated throughout the world, and after a century are still being reprinted.

In 1896, Vivekananda asked Swami Abhedananda (pre-monastic name Kali Prasad Chandra) to join him, and propagate the message of Vedanta in the West. Abhedananda went to the USA in 1897, when Vivekananda asked him to take charge of the Vedanta Society in New York. Here he preached messages of Vedanta and teachings of Sri Ramakrishna Paramhansa Dev for about twenty-five years, travelling far and wide to the United States, Canada, Mexico, Japan and Hong Kong. Finally, he returned to India in 1921. His great wisdom, in-depth intellect and oratorical power caused widespread admiration, and people crowded to listen to him. He was also a prolific writer and his books on life after death, etc. are still famous. An American disciple of Abhedananda, Mrs. Mary LePage (also known as Sister Shivani) wrote an account of his visit to America.

During September 1965, a sixty-nine-years-old Eastern Philosopher and scholar, by the name A. C. Bhaktivedanta Swami (pre-monastic name Abhay Charan De) travelled to New York alone as a passenger on a small cargo ship, named 'Jaladuta' (Scindia Steam Navigation Company). In his possession were a suitcase, an umbrella, a supply of dry cereal, about seven dollars' worth of Indian currency and several boxes of books. He knew no one, with absolutely no visible means of support, no friends, no followers, not his youth, and in fragile health (during the passage he survived a massive heart attack). But he had a big dream – to present the spiritual knowledge of the Vedas and to spread the teachings of Lord Krishna to the entire English-speaking Western world as his spiritual master Srila Bhaktisiddhanta Saraswati Thakura had instructed him. For one year he struggled hard, and gradually began to attract some small interest in his teachings. In July 1966, while still working alone from an obscure storefront on New York City's Lower East Side, he founded a spiritual society intended for worldwide participation – the International Society for Krishna Consciousness (ISKCON). By 1977, A. C. Bhaktivedanta Swami, or Srila Prabhupada (as his followers affectionately called him) had spread the teachings of Krishna Consciousness to every major city in the world, and had formed an international society comprising thousands of dedicated members. He had established 108 temples with magnificent estates spread across six continents, and had circled the globe twelve times to personally guide the membership of his broadening mission.

In these twelve years, Srila Prabhupada had also translated, written, and published fifty-one volumes of books in twenty-eight different languages, tens of millions of which had been distributed throughout the world. He had delivered thousands of lectures, written thousands of letters, and taken part in thousands of conversations with followers, admirers, and critics alike. His words expressed exactly what he is. He had also won the esteem of hundreds of prominent scholars and social figures who had genuine appreciation for his contributions to spirituality, philosophy and culture. In 1970, Srila Prabhupada founded the Bhaktivedanta Book Trust, now the world's largest publisher of Vedic literature. Srila Prabhupada was a man of enlightenment. He knew that the truth is never contained in the arrangements of written words; it is within the speaker himself. Lord Krishna said in Bhagavad Gita,

> "*bahoonaam janmanaamante jnaanavaanmaam prapadyate*
> *vaasudevah sarvamiti sa mahaatmaa sudurlabhah*"
> (Bhagavad Gita: 7.19).
> [After many births and deaths, he who is actually in knowledge surrenders unto Me, knowing Me to be the cause of all causes and all that is. Such a great soul is very rare.]

The success of ISKCON is outstanding and beyond comparison with any other spiritual organisations. Westerners are attracted because when they ask questions, they get answers with proper explanations and proper understandings. There is a lot of depth, richness and substance to the philosophy and the culture of the movement.

This was a historical reversal of the Western missionary movement that swept India for centuries, beginning as early as Vasco da Gama's successful voyage to India in 1498, and continuing to the present.

Many Westerners are turning to Sanatan Dharma because they feel the need of the hour is to imbue the society with higher spiritual knowledge and values. People with high moral values and ethical integrity cannot tolerate the general decline of the value system in a society. Many of them suffer from varieties of spiritual fatigue and mystical deprivation in an environment of wealth, power and pleasure, and at the same time they are over-satisfied with scientific rationalism. They understand that the so-called materialistic solutions of their problems are no solutions at all but merely statements of the same problems in different terms which really push back the problems to a deeper level. They need the strength and insight to convert the chaos of life into a pattern of peace and happiness and general welfare of the declining society.

In such a situation, they turn towards the deeper wisdom of a more ancient culture for a spiritual reawakening and resurrection, such as the profound philosophy of Vedanta, the awe-inspiring wisdom of the ancient Rishis, the spiritual path of Yoga and meditation etc. Schrödinger wished to see, "*some blood transfusion from the East to the West to save Western science from spiritual anaemia*". (Dhar, 2004, p. 66). In general, what attracts Westerners in Sanatan Dharma are summarised below.

Sanatan Dharma formulates itself as 'Manava Dharma' (Dharma for all human beings) where each individual is honoured as Divine and all nature as sacred. Something like 'Holy Jihad' and forced or deceitful conversion to Sanatan Dharma are never heard of. Humanity is never divided into believers and non-believers, rather we are encouraged to discover our inner unity; everyone is accepted with open arms. No one is ever rejected as condemned by God or the Divine because all living beings must eventually return to the highest state of bliss. The following Mantra captures the gist of ideal human conduct.

> "*mātṛdevo bhava*
> *pitṛdevo bhava*
> *ācāryadevo bhava*
> *atithidevo bhava*" (Taittiriya Upanishad: 1.11.2).
> [Treat your mother as a God, treat your father as God, treat your teacher as God, treat your guests as God.]

In other words, a Dharmic must treat every person – from a pauper to the most powerful – with love, respect and reverence. No distinction should be made based on the guests' caste, colour or creed.

One British spiritual aspirant who came to India in the early twentieth century was Ronald Henry Nixon (May 10, 1898 – November 14, 1965). When the First World War broke out, he enlisted in the Royal Flying Corps. As a fighter pilot he was subjected to intense pressure and had several near-escapes from death (for most members of the services the life expectancy was said to be fifteen days). After the war, Nixon enrolled in King's College, Cambridge, where he studied English literature. During this period Nixon also studied philosophy, and became acquainted with Advaita Vedanta. Soon he developed an interest in going to India to learn more about the practical aspects of Sanatan Dharma that will help him to enquire into the meaning of life. In India, he adopted Krishna Prem as his monastic name. His intellectual and inspirational qualities gained him wide fame and many disciples in India. This is reflected in numerous books on his life and teachings. When Krishna Prem died in 1965, he was hailed by Sarvepalli Radhakrishnan, then president of India, as a 'great soul'.

Dharmic system of values is a complex one. It includes knowledge, it embraces active work, it emphasises sacrifice and service to others, and culminates in renunciation. There is no statement in the scriptures starting with "Thou shall not" There is not a single statement that 'You will go to hell if you don't follow me or obey what I say' like what we read in other religious scriptures. Liberation is for everyone. Sanatan Dharma does not claim monopoly on God or the truth. God-realisation is the right of every human being. A Dharmic firmly believes in this Upanishadic statement.

> "***satyameva jayate*** *nānṛtaṃ satyena panthā vitato devayānaḥ yenākramantyṛṣayo hyāptakāmā yatra tat satyasya paramaṃ nidhānam*" (Mundaka Upanishad: 3.1.6).
> [**Truth alone wins**, not falsehood. By truth the Devayanah (the path of the Devas) is widened, that by which the seers travel on, having nothing to wish for to where there is that – the highest treasure attained by truth.]

This wisdom is what Swami Vivekananda expounded in the West in the most powerful voice. The strength of the deeper wisdom works like a time-tested therapy for the salvage of the desire-afflicted Atman by building up the complete immune system.

Paramhansa Yogananda (pre-monastic name Mukunda Lal Ghosh) popularised Yoga in the West. Though Yoga is a philosophical, ethical, spiritual, and physical practice, Westerners mainly know about the physical part. Interestingly, to make Yoga appeal to all such statements like "Yoga has no religion" has been widely proposed in media and by the secularists. But no one can deny that Yoga is a Dharmic tradition firmly rooted in the Vedas and the principal Upanishads. In 1946, Yogananda published the book 'Autobiography of a Yogi' – his spiritual search for enlightenment. It has since been translated into forty-five languages. In 1999, it was designated one of the "100 Most Important Spiritual Books of the twentieth Century" by a panel of spiritual authors and publishers. By 2012, this book sold over four million copies and counting. Yogananda's centers, books, and teachings blend Eastern and Western spirituality.

The Indian Guru, Mahesh Yogi, brought transcendental meditation (a specific form of Mantra Meditation) to the West in 1959 and became a spiritual teacher to The Beatles, comedian Jerry Seinfeld and countless other celebrities. Since then, Eastern movement form of meditation has become increasingly more prevalent in the West. Today there is a lot of scientific research demonstrating the benefits of this practice.

Another precious gift of Sanatan Dharma to the world is Ayurveda (systematic knowledge of the lifespan) – an alternative medicine system originated in ancient India. Ayurveda has been adapted for Western consumption, notably by Baba Hari Dass in the 1970s and 'Maharishi Ayurveda Organization' in the 1980s. Ayurveda is fully recognised by the WHO as a medical science. Today Ayurveda is one of the fastest growing CAM (Complementary and Alternative Medicine) methods in Germany, Austria, and Switzerland. Ayurveda's concept that one's thoughts create health or ill health in the physical body resonates with that of quantum physics which says that our thoughts create the physical reality. Some scholars assert that some of the concepts of Ayurveda have existed from the time of the Indus Valley Civilisation or even earlier. Ayurveda developed significantly during the Vedic era. Therapies are typically based on complex herbal compounds, minerals and metal substances (perhaps under the influence of early Indian alchemy or 'Rasa Shastra'). Ancient Ayurveda texts also taught surgical techniques, including rhinoplasty, kidney stone extractions, and the extraction of foreign objects.

Temples in India are one of the most valuable assets. Tourists across the world come to India to visit these temples and to know more about the culture and traditions of the country. For most of them the idea of India and of Sanatan Dharma had been a search for bliss and the consciousness of the highest degree. Mystical 2,000 years old temples in India are a few of the factors for which India is famous for. As example, the 2,200-year-old Dwarkadhish Temple (dedicated to Lord Krishna) constructed of limestone and sand in the ancient town of Dwarka. The town has its history dated back to the Mahabharat time. The architecture was constructed over the land reclaimed from the sea by Lord Krishna. The Kailash Temple (also known as Kailashanatha Temple) was constructed between 757 and 783 AD in India's Sahyadri Hills. Labourers and craftspeople used nothing more than hammers and chisels to slowly scoop out about 400,000 tons of solid volcanic rock over the course of more than twenty years. The temple was carved out of a mountain (a single rock) by vertical excavations (means, the builders started from the top to the bottom). Konark Sun Temple is a UNESCO World Heritage Site and one of the prime tourist attractions of Odisha. The glorious Jagannath Temple of Puri was built in the eleventh century by King Indradyumna. Jagannath temple is one of the most famous temples in the world due to multiple reasons. Ratha Yatra is a festival that happens around the ancient temple every year to honour Lord Jagannath (a form of Lord Vishnu) and his siblings. The festival is so famous that people from all around the world gather around Puri to witness it.

In India, the Sanskrit language and literature have been almost forgotten but it has influenced the European writers in a big way. There is a misconception that Sanskrit language is only a language for chanting Mantras in temples. Actually, that is less than five percent of the Sanskrit literature, more than ninety-five percent of which has nothing to do with rituals. The word 'Sanskrit' means 'perfected, pure or refined'. Scholars and linguists agree that Sanskrit is the most scientific and systematic language the world has ever known. The ancient sages were wise beyond today's imagination, otherwise how can we explain the existence of an ancient language with grammatical construction far more sophisticated than that in use today. NASA claims that Sanskrit is the most suitable language to develop computer programming for their artificial intelligence program.

Every Sanskrit Mantra that is chanted in Vedic rituals has special potency. When they are pronounced and chanted properly, they exert a salutary effect on the minds of those who hear them. The Veda-Mantras work in two ways – because of the power of sounds (word), and because of the self-discipline it brings to the one chanting them. Also, chanting Sanskrit increases brain cognitive functions and is termed as 'Sanskrit effect'. Germans have realised the value of Sanskrit and the scriptures written in this language. Presently fourteen German Universities and four British Universities are teaching Sanskrit. The Heidelberg University organises Sanskrit speaking courses in Australia, Europe, North America and even in India. Will Germans be the ultimate custodians of Sanskrit, its rich heritage and culture? If the demand for Sanskrit and Indology courses in Germany is any indication, that's what the future looks like.

The Bhagavad Gita has deeply influenced Western philosophers and common people alike. Westerners find this book significant because it requires people to completely change their mindset, rather than merely changing their life styles or outward appearances. It advocates a balanced life. Albert Einstein, American author and philosopher Henry David Thoreau, French-German theologian Albert Schweitzer, Swiss psychiatrist Carl Jung, German-Swiss author Herman Hesse, American author Ralph Waldo Emerson, Austrian philosopher Rudolph Steiner, English author and philosopher Aldous Huxley, American astronaut Sunita Williams, Hollywood actor Will Smith and Norwegian philosopher Arne Naess have acknowledged the influence of Bhagavad Gita as an enlightening guide to spiritual evolution. Former Turkish PM Bulent Ecevit, when asked what had given him the courage to send Turkish troops to Cyprus, replied that he was encouraged by the Bhagavad Gita which taught that **if one were morally right, one need not hesitate to fight injustice**.

The American theoretical physicist, Dr. J. Robert Oppenheimer is known as the father of the atomic bomb and was involved in the atomic bombings of Hiroshima and Nagasaki during the Second World War. He had read the Bhagavad Gita in Sanskrit in 1933 in the original form and remarked that while witnessing the explosion of the Trinity nuclear test, he thought of this Shloka.

> "*divi sūrya-sahasrasya bhaved yugapad utthitā*
> *yadi bhāḥ sadṛśī sā syād bhāsas tasya mahātmanaḥ*"
> (Bhagavad Gita: 11.12).
> [If the radiance of a thousand suns were to burst forth at once in the sky, that would be like the splendor of that Mighty One (The Cosmic or the Universal Form).]

Years later he explained in the television documentary 'The Decision to Drop the Bomb' (1965) that another Shloka had also entered his head at that time where Lord Krishna persuades to do his duty. Then he recited the original text in Sanskrit.

> "*kālo 'smi loka-kṣaya-kṛt pravṛddho lokān samāhartum iha pravṛttaḥ*
> *ṛte 'pi tvāṃ na bhaviṣyanti sarve ye 'vasthitāḥ pratyanīkeṣu yodhāḥ*"
> (Bhagavad Gita: 11.32).
> [The Supreme Personality of Godhead said, I am time, the mighty destroyer of the worlds, and I am here to annihilate all these people. Even without your participation, the soldiers grouped in the opposing army shall cease to exist.]

Hence, Bhagavad Gita is not a religious book because it does not teach any 'religion'. Many English versions of this book are available in the market. Sir Edwin Arnold's translation under the title 'The Song Celestial' is the most popular. This book is translated into almost all of the major languages in the world. There is no missionary zeal behind the publication of this book. Westerners did it out of their sheer love for the non-dogmatic philosophy and depiction of the entire human life. This book offers what Henry David Thoreau described as a "*stupendous and cosmogonal philosophy...in comparison with which our modern world and its literature seem puny and trivial.*" (Krishnadas, 2010, p. vi). This scripture has an answer to every problem an individual may face in his (or her) life. Aldous Huxley wrote,

> "*The Bhagavad Gita is the most systematic statement of spiritual evolution of endowing value to mankind. It is one of the most clear and comprehensive summaries of perennial philosophy ever revealed; hence its enduring value is subject not only to India but to all of humanity.*" (Krishnadas, 2010, p. vi).

Rudolf Steiner commented, "*In order to approach a creation as sublime as the Bhagavad Gita with full understanding it is necessary to attune our soul to it.*" According to Wilhelm von Humboldt, the Bhagavad Gita is "*The most beautiful, perhaps the only true philosophical song existing in any known tongue .... perhaps the deepest and loftiest thing the world has to show.'* (Nehru, 1946, p. 99). Elsewhere he wrote to his friend that after reading the book, "*I felt a sense of overwhelming gratitude to God for having let me live to be acquainted with this work. It must be the most profound and sublime thing to be found in the world.*"

If you read the Bhagavad Gita only for knowledge, you can become a glorified 'Pandit' or a grand philosopher, but if you make this book an integral part of your own Atman by grasping the meaning and experiencing the reality it offers to you by your sincere thoughts, words and actions, you become the living Gita. In fact, this is the whole purpose of the Bhagavad Gita – the path to enlightenment and Moksha.

Dharma has the greatest number of followers regularly engaged in pilgrimage of any religion in the world. The Kumbha Mela is world's largest religious gathering and has been for many centuries, with as many as thirty million participants (Feb. 10, 2013) and fifty million participants (Feb. 04, 2019) on a single day. Foreign devotees come at a massive scale every year to seek holy blessing from the hermits. Thousands of them renounce their religion and turn to Sanatan Dharma with a ceremony and take new names.

It was never the motive of sages and warriors of Vedic era to capture other territory by force or deception. But archaeological studies reveal the existence of relics of Vedic civilisation in many countries. For instance, excavations have brought up the text of a treaty between Rameses II and the Hittites dating back to the fourteenth century BC where the Vedic Deities, such as Mitra, Varuna and Indra are mentioned as witnesses to the pact. There is a connection between the name of Rameses and that of Lord Ram. The Vedic Deity Mitra is the same as the Iranian Mithra during third and fourth centuries CE.

Sanatan Dharma historically had spread throughout Central Asia, Indo-china and Indonesia. Aspects of Dharma came with Buddhism wherever it went as far as Japan, which still has many temples dedicated to the deities. Vedic related traditions of the Zoroastrian, Greek, Roman and Celtic spread to Europe in ancient times. The largest traditional temple complex is Angkor Wat in Cambodia, showing that Dharma is not just an India based but a universal and global tradition.

India shares an ancient and interesting bond with Korea. Korean legend states that the Princess of Ayodhya named Heo Hwang-ok, also known as Suriratna, went all the way to Korea some 2,000 years ago to marry King Suro of Geumgwan Gaya. Together, they both are heralded as the ancestors of more than two-thirds of Koreans today. Every year, hundreds of South Koreans visit Ayodhya (the birth place of Lord Ram), to pay homage to their ancestor. Heo Hwang-ok is worshipped as the most blessed queen ever to have set foot on Korea. In Thailand all kings in the current 200-year-old Chakri Dynasty are considered by the people as descendants of Lord Ram.

There is evidence of Dharma having once flourished in Western Hemisphere. In Mexico, a festival called 'Ram-Sita' is celebrated at the same time of 'Navaratri'. Often the earth is dug up, and the images of Ganapati are discovered. The aborigines of Mexico also shared the Vedic view of the divine in the forces of nature and worshipped them as deities. The Aztecs (the word 'Aztecs' is a distorted form of 'Astikas') had inhabited Mexico before the Spaniards conquered that land. The aborigines of Australia dance in the nude. Photographs have shown that the dancers have a third eye drawn on the forehead. Many anthropologists captioned these pictures as 'Siva Dance'. Greece had an ancient religion and had big temples where various deities were worshipped. They had many Vedic elements in it. The Semitic religions of the pre-Christian era in the region associated with Jesus had shared the Vedic view of the divine in the forces of nature and worshipped them as deities. There was a good deal of ritual in all such religions. Many of these religions, including that of Greece, had once attained to the heights of glory. According to the anthropologists, religions in their original form exist only in areas like the forests of Africa. But even these ancient faiths contain Vedic elements. All these details were discovered by Europeans, the very people who pooh-poohed India as 'the land of snake charmers'.

Chapter - 8

Occult mysticism – supernatural power of the Yogis

In recent years the word 'Yoga' has been heard more in the gyms than in spiritual discussion, but this term in its original sense has little to do with exercise. Yoga is a philosophy-based practice, and the entire purpose of Yoga is spiritual in nature.

The Yoga Sutras of Patanjali are the basic texts of Yoga (one of the six great orthodox schools or systems of Indian philosophy). Sage Patanjali was the first to codify the system/science of Yoga. Though he is often called the 'Father of Yoga', he did not create it. Following three Sutras contain his entire message in a nutshell. The remaining Sutras are an expansion of this introductory statement.

> "*yogash chitta vritti nirodhah*
> *tada drashtuh swarupe avasthanam*
> *vritti sarupyam itaratra*" (Yoga Sutras: 1.2-4).
> [Yoga is restraining the mind-stuff (Chitta) from taking various forms (Vrttis).
> Then the seer abides in itself, resting in its own true nature, which is called self-realisation.
> At other times (other than that of concentration) the seer is identified with the modifications.]

Yoga connects one's consciousness to the Supreme Consciousness by controlling one's body, mind and senses whereas good health is just a by-product of this endeavour. Hence, when Yoga is practiced with a spiritual outlook, the end purpose is transformation and awakening of our true inner self. In simple terms Yoga is a perfect scientific art that unites the mind with the God or the Truth. One who experiences this oneness of existence is said to be a Yogi.

> "*śrī-bhagavān uvāca*
> *jitendriyasya yuktasya jita-śvāsasya yoginaḥ*
> *mayi dhārayataś ceta upatiṣṭhanti siddhayaḥ*"
> (Bhagavad Purana: 11.15.1).
> [The Supreme Personality of Godhead said, the mystic perfections of Yoga are acquired by a Yogi who has conquered his senses, steadied his mind, conquered the breathing process and fixed his mind on Me.]

> "*jitendriyasya dāntasya jita-śvāsātmano muneḥ*
> *mad-dhāraṇāṁ dhārayataḥ kā sā siddhiḥ su-durlabhā*"
> (Bhagavad Purana: 11.15.32).
> [For a Sage who has conquered his senses, breathing and mind, who is self-controlled and always absorbed in meditation on Me, what mystic perfection could possibly be difficult to achieve?]

Vairagya means the detachment from worldly things, a freedom from worldly desires, or calmness. Since all desires produce a kind of bondage, they must all ultimately be released. Each desire is intrinsically linked to the ego, and thus is a veil between our limited being and the Infinite. Therefore, the main challenge in Vairagya lies in the difficulty of discriminating between false values and true values in life.

> "*abhyasa vairagyabhyam tat nirodhah*" (Yoga Sutras: 1.12).
> [These thought patterns are mastered through practice (abhyasa) and non-attachment (Vairagya).]

> "*drista anushravika vishaya vitrishnasya vashikara sanjna vairagyam tat param purusha khyateh guna vaitrshnyam*" (Yoga Sutras: 1.15-16).
> [That effort, which comes to those who have given up their thirst after objects either seen or heard, and which wills to control the objects, is non-attachment (Vairagya).
> That extreme non-attachment, giving up even the qualities, shows (the real nature of) the pure consciousness, Self (Purusha).]

If one asks as to what the Yogis do for the society, the answer is that they are like the trees, the spiritual trees. As the trees standing at their own places purify the atmosphere and help bringing rains, the Yogis purify the minds of people, help them to stay in the right path of Karma and channelise the grace of the God in them.

Yoga is not a religious practice but a complete path by itself. Though Patanjali's Yoga Sutras are integral part of Sanatan Dharma, there is no sovereign claim over it – one can practice Yoga and remain faithful to their personal, chosen religion.

8.1: Introduction

The word 'Yoga' is derived from the Sanskrit root 'Yuj', meaning 'to join' or 'to yoke' or 'to unite'. In only two syllables, this word encompasses the entire body of spiritual experiences and experiments of thousands of enlightened sages. In Vedic vision, Yoga can be any spiritual practice that helps to experience Divinity. Each individual's path to enlightenment will be as unique as the individual themselves. The real purpose of Yoga Sadhana is expressed in these Sutras.

> "*yoganga anusthanad ashuddhi kshaye jnana diptih a viveka khyateh*" (Yoga Sutras: 2.28)
> [Through the practice of different steps to Yoga, impurities are eliminated, and an illumination arises that culminates in discriminative wisdom, or enlightenment.]

> "*tavābhyāsaṃ vinā kāle nākāro brahmatāṃ gataḥ*
> *sthitaḥ kalanarūpātmā tena tannānupaśyasi*" (Yoga-Vasistha: 3.21.42).
> [Without practice of Yoga, you cannot approach God with your mortal frame. The Atman tainted by sense can never see the image of God.]

There are four classical types of Yoga – Bhakti Yoga, Jnana Yoga, Karma Yoga and Raja Yoga.

Bhakti Yoga is the path of devotion. The method of attaining God is through love and the loving recollection of God.

> "*samadhi siddhih ishvarapranidhana*" (Yoga Sutras: 2.45).
> [Accomplishment of Samadhi from self-surrender to God.]

Jnana Yoga is the path of knowledge. This is not the knowledge in the intellectual sense, but the knowledge of Brahmam and Atman and the realisation of their unity. The actual word is 'Atma Jnana' (knowledge or direct experience of the Atman). The Jnana Yogi uses the powers of the mind to discriminate between the real and the unreal, and the permanent and the temporary. One who embarks on this path may go through several stages of enlightenment before achieving Moksha.

Karma Yoga is the path of work – specifically, the path of dedicated work renouncing the results of our actions as a spiritual offering rather than claiming the results for ourselves.

Raja Yoga is the path of meditation. As a king maintains control over his kingdom, we can maintain control over our own 'kingdom' – the vast territory of the mind. Here we use our mental powers to realise the Atman through the process of psychological control. Meditation is an intensely personal matter. Only a genuine spiritual teacher can accurately gauge the student's personal tendencies and direct the student's mind accordingly.

Yoga and Samkhya systems operate on similar philosophies. "*saankhyayogau prithagbaalaah pravadanti na panditaah*..." (Bhagavad Gita: 5.4) means, children, not the wise, speak of Samkhya (knowledge) and Yoga (performance of action) as distinct. The next Shloka says, "... *ekam saankhyam cha yogam cha yah pashyati sa pashyati*", means, he truly 'sees', who 'sees' Samkhya and Yoga as one. Samkhya does not believe in a personal God while God is the supreme belief for a man devoted to Yoga. Samkhya provides a theoretical exposition of human nature and a theoretical way to Moksha, while Yoga deals with the techniques.

Yoga arose at the beginning of human civilisation when man first realised his spiritual potential for it is both the 'Path' and the 'Goal'. The teachings are so ancient that no one knows their exact origin story. Archeological excavations in the Indus Valley had depicted Yoga meditation. Various understandings of Yoga are also presented in the Mahabharat. But Western Indologists have dated Indian spiritual literature as originating in very recent times only. Why is this so? The Christian Church at the time of Charles Darwin (1809-1882) believed that the earth was created by God about 6,000 years ago (about 4,000 BC). This figure was arrived at by counting the generations since Adam and Eve. Darwin figured the earth to be at least 300 million years old. This was one reason why his 1859 work of genius 'Origin of the Species' was so violently opposed by the Church. It is important to note this when trying to 'fix dates' in the history of Yoga. The Christian-funded Indologists certainly could not date any Indian spiritual text earlier than 4,000 BC (the date when God supposedly created the world!). In fact, they had to retain a respectable distance from that 'sacred date' and hence, they fixed the dates of all Indian spiritual texts, including the Vedas, as much later in time.

The Indus Valley Civilisation is commonly accepted in modern times to be more than 9,000 years old. The town of Mehrgarh has been dated back to 6,500 BC by archaeologists. The Rig Veda, which is composed at least about 7,000 years ago, mentions the origins of Yoga as a backdrop to pre-Vedic Indian traditions. The term Yoga had appeared in early sacred writings of India (e.g., in the Taittiriya and Katha Upanishads). It was believed to be revealed to the sages so that humanity could have an opportunity to realise its divine nature. The sages mastered the yogic system and successfully revealed divine knowledge within their minds, and then they were able to guide sincere aspirants on the path of Yoga.

8.2: Who is a Yogi?

A Yogi (noun) is a person who has practiced Yoga with a lifetime of sacrifice and hard work without being attached to the fruits of action, and attained a higher level of consciousness.

After decades of 'Sadhana' (methodical discipline to attain desired knowledge or goal solely dedicated to achieving Moksha) they attain 'Siddhi' (a high degree of physical and spiritual perfection or enlightenment through Sadhana) and 'Vibhuti' (power or manifestation), and become 'Siddha Purush' or 'Sadhak' for males, and as 'Sadhika', 'Sadhvi' and 'Sadhvine' for females. Many of them show astonishing paranormal powers, abilities, and attainments that are the products of yogic advancement through Sadhanas. The yogic path to Moksha has many obstacles but there are solutions too.

The Sadhak (and Sadhika) jumps ahead of the normal evolutionary path of the remainder of mankind, and they achieve in one life what the average man will take another few thousand years to attain.

"*tivra samvega asannah*" (Yoga Sutras: 1.21).
[Success is speeded for the extremely energetic.]

"*tapah svadhyaya ishvara-pranidhana kriya-yogah*
samadhi bhavana arthah klesha tanu karanarthah cha"
(Yoga Sutras: 2.1-2).
[Mortification, study, and surrendering fruits of work to God are called Kriya Yoga (Yoga in the form of action).
That Yoga of action is practiced to bring about Samadhi and to minimise the coloured thought patterns (Kleshas).]

"*samyak vijnanavaan yogee*
swatmanyeva akhilam jagat
ekam cha sarvam atmaana
eeekshyate jnana chakshushaa" (Atma Bodha: Mantra no. 47).
[The Yogi endowed with complete enlightenment sees, through the eye of Knowledge, the entire Universe in his own self, regards everything as the self and nothing else.]

The Yogi attains 'Samadhi' by strict spiritual discipline while fully concentrating on the goal. This is a blissful super consciousness state in which he perceives the identity of the individualised Atman and the Cosmic Spirit. Samadhi is beyond the normal mind and intellect, and it can only be fully appreciated by direct experience. For example, consider three people standing on a platform and seeing a train from a distance. The first person sees the headlight and says, 'Oh! A train is nothing but a light', and he leaves. The second person waits longer and is able to see the steel body of the train. He says, 'A train is a huge moving iron box', and leaves. The third person waits further, boards the train, explores the compartments and fully experiences what a complete train is. In Samadhi the mind is in its most concentrated state and can be compared to normal thought as a laser beam can be compared to normal light.

> "*tad eva artha matra nirbhasam svarupa shunyam iva samadhih*" (Yoga Sutras: 3.3).
> [When only the essence of that object, place, or point shines forth in the mind, as if devoid even of its own form, that state of deep absorption is called deep concentration or Samadhi.]

There are two types of Samadhi – 'Samprajnata' or 'Savikalpa' (the self attains only a partial liberation from the mind), and 'Asamprajnata' or 'Nirvikalpa' (the self achieves complete freedom and regains its original nature as pure spirit). Both the types have several levels of refinement.

> "*vitarka vichara ananda asmita rupa anugamat samprajnatah*
> *virama pratyaya abhyasa purvah samskara shesha anyah*"
> (Yoga Sutras: 1.17-18).
> [The deep absorption of attention on an object is of four kinds, 'Vitarka' (gross), 'Vichara' (subtle), 'Ananda' (bliss accompanied), and 'Asmita' (with I-ness), and is called Samprajnata Samadhi.
> Asamprajnata Samadhi is attained by the constant practice of cessation of all mental activity in which the 'Chitta' (mind) retains only the unmanifested impressions.]

During Samprajnata Samadhi the Yogi loses all human consciousness for a short period of time. In this state, the concepts of time and space are different than in material nature. However, this is not yet a permanent state and everybody has to return to ordinary consciousness.

The second level of Samadhi (i.e., Asamprajnata, Nirvikalpa) is when the Yogi goes deeper into himself away from the world outside and no provocation will affect him. Here, the Yogi attains discriminative wisdom and perfect purity of mind. His mind takes on some of the omniscient and omnipotent Cosmic qualities. He may experience 'Ritambhara Pragya' (thoughts spontaneously manifest into reality). In this state, the Yogi sees without eyes, tastes without tongue, hears without ears, smells without nose, and touches without skin. His mere intention can work miracles. The Yogi simply wills and everything comes into being. The past and future are blended into the eternal present. Time and space have been transcended. Adi Shankaracharya attained Nirvikalpa Samadhi before he was twelve.

8.3: The supernatural power of the Yogis

The ancient Dharmic scriptures, history as well as authentic records from the pens of early and modern foreign visitors to India flourish with stories of the marvellous powers attained by the practice of Yoga. But these powers are incidental results of Yoga, rather than an end in themselves.

Sage Patanjali details the Siddhis or manifested psychic accomplishments in the Sutras 2.35 to 2.45. At the next level Patanjali specifics the concept of Pranayama and its healing physiological benefits. Pranayama enables our mind to attain fitness for the higher aspects of Yoga as it is a bridge between the external and internal worlds. Soon the Yogi learns 'Pratyahara' (withdrawing of the mind from all the sensory engagements).

"*sva vishaya asamprayoge chittasya svarupe anukarah iva*
indriyanam pratyaharah
tatah parama vashyata indriyanam" (Yoga Sutras: 2.54-55).

[When the mental organs of senses and actions cease to be engaged with the corresponding objects in their mental realm, and assimilate or turn back into the mind-field from which they arose, this is called Pratyahara.

Through that turning inward of the organs of senses and actions also comes a supreme ability, controllability, or mastery over those senses inclining to go outward towards their objects.]

At this level the Yogi deals with attainment of much higher supernatural powers. Sage Patanjali then describes the special experiences and powers that result from performing 'Samyama' on various gross and subtle objects. Much of the Patanjali's Yoga system is summed up in one word 'Samyama' – extraordinary focus of the mind.

"*tad jayat prajna lokah*" (Yoga Sutras: 3.5).

[Through the mastery of three-part process of 'Samyama' (concentration, meditation and Samadhi taken together), the light of knowledge, transcendental insight, or higher consciousness (Prajna) dawns, illumines, flashes, or is visible.]

Samyama is a practice by which the Yogi can gain tremendous knowledge and power. It can be applied with a focus on any one object at a time. The main leads of the two great epics Ramayan and Mahabharat had displayed and used enormous ascetic/yogic powers. Such powers existed prominently during the entire Vedic period. They still exist as examples of many Yogis all over the world validate such existences.

"*śrī-bhagavān uvāca*
siddhayo 'ṣṭādaśa proktā dhāraṇā yoga-pāra-gaiḥ
tāsām aṣṭau mat-pradhānā daśaiva guṇa-hetavaḥ"
(Bhagavad Purana: 11.15.3).
[The Supreme Personality of Godhead said, the masters of the Yoga system have declared that there are eighteen types of mystic perfection and meditation, of which eight are primary, having their shelter in Me, and ten are secondary, appearing from the material mode of goodness.]

According to Bhagavad Purana (11.15.4-7, 17, 19, 28) the mystic perfections are *aṇimā* (becoming smaller than the smallest), *mahimā* (becoming greater than the greatest), *laghimā* (becoming lighter than the lightest), *prāpti* (one acquires whatever one desires), *śakti-preraṇam* (manipulating Maya), *vaśitā* (the power to bring others under control), *kāmāvasāyitā-siddhi* (obtaining anything from anywhere), *anūrmi-mattvam* (being undisturbed by hunger, thirst and other bodily disturbances), *dūra śravaṇa darśanam* (hearing and seeing things far away), *para-kāya praveśanam* (entering the bodies of others), *sva-chanda mṛtyuḥ* (dying when one desires), *anudarśanam yathā saṅkalpa saṁsiddhiḥ ājñā apratihatā gatiḥ* (executing one's determination and giving orders whose fulfilment is unimpeded), *parama-ānandam āpnoti yatra kāmaḥ avasīyate* (obtains the greatest happiness as all his desires are completely fulfilled), *tatropalabdhā bhūtānāṁ haṁso vācaḥ śṛṇoty asau* (able to perceive within the sky the speaking of all living entities), *viśvaṁ paśyati dūrataḥ* (remote viewing), *trai-kālikī* (knowledge of past, present and future) etc.

These powers are genuine, and not something created by the Yogi's imagination. But how these powers develop we don't know. We will simply assume that after thousands of years of exploration, discussion and improvement about the Yoga techniques, advanced Yogis have developed far beyond the capacity of modern science, and we'll leave it at that.

*** *** ***

A Yogi lives in poverty but attains a state of unexcelled happiness. They withdraw from the society because they see society as a distraction from the yogic journey towards God.

"*same śucau śarkarāvahnivālukā- vivarjite śabdajalāśrayādibhiḥ*
Mano 'nukūle na tu cakṣupīḍane guhānivātāśrayaṇe prayojayet"
(Svetasvatara Upanishad: 2.10).
[Let Yoga be practiced within a cave protected from the high wind, or in a place which is level, pure and free from pebbles, gravel and

fire, undisturbed by the noise of water or of market stalls and which is delightful to the mind and not offensive to the eye.]

They have no bonds or attachments to anyone or anything. When Swami Bhaskarananda Saraswati was eighteen years old, his parents forced him to marry. The following year when his wife was blessed with a child all his relatives were very happy. But the father of the child was swimming in the sea of suffering. He realised that it was the beginning of his attachment-life, and on that very day he left home for good. Only after he became a great spiritual Master with abundant occult powers did he return home, but by then his child was with God.

The Yogis live on earth as if they do not exist. But actually they are the embodiment of God's Vision-Height and God's Reality-Depth. A small cave is the most convenient location for him. A Himalayan Yogi once said,

> "*If you look at a Yogi's cave, in your perception, it is just a little thing – maybe a ten-by-ten small hole to crawl into. But in his experience, it's bigger than the world, because* ***time and space is an illusion created by your mind****. What is small and what is big, what is this much and what is that much, what is now and what is then, is all an illusion of the mind.* ***Once a person has transcended this limitation, he can create a whole Universe in his cave.***" (Sadhguru, 2009, p. 45).

They embrace a life of sacrifice and austerity. Yogi Swami Rama lived in a sealed cave with only a single pinpoint of light. Siddha Krishna Das Babaji lived in a derelict hut in the forest and ate flour mixing with neem leaves. Trailanga Swami talked to others very less or sometime not at all. A crowd of people often attracted to him for hearing of his yogic supremacy in order to get rid of their problems. He had no body perception in him as he could lay very comfortably on the burning sand of the desert which is impossible for the normal man.

For centuries, there are records that these ascetics can sleep on the bed of sharp nails, painlessly pierce their bodies with metal spikes and walk on red-hot coals.

> "*sthula svarupa suksma anvaya arthavattva samyamad bhuta-jayah*" (Yoga Sutras: 3.45)
> [Mastery over the Pancha-Bhutas (the five elements – earth, water, fire, air, space) is attained by performing Samyama on their gross, constant, subtle, all-pervading and functional states.]

> "*grahana svarupa asmita anvaya arthavattva samyamad indriya jayah*" (Yoga Sutras: 3.48)

[Mastery over the sense-organs is attained by performing Samyama on their power of cognition, real nature, egoism, all-pervasiveness and functions.]

The 'Pancha-Bhutas' have a special function in the manifested Universe, that of relating matter with Quantum Consciousness. The external world (Maya) is cognised through our five sense-organs. By gaining mastery over these five elements a Yogi remains unshaken and unaffected.

A Yogi must live in extreme self-control. It is only under such conditions that the grosser energies of the body can be channeled to serve the higher purposes of the Atman. And the earlier in life this self-discipline begins the easier it is to acquire this control.

"*sattva shuddhi saumanasya ekagra indriya-jaya atma darshana yogyatvani cha*" (Yoga Sutras: 2.41).
[From mental purity arises purity of Sattva (purest of subtle essence, internal being), cheerfulness of the mind, concentration, conquest of the organs, and fitness for the realisation of the self.]

A pleasurable feeling is the nature of the Sattva. To the Yogi everything is bliss and every human face that he sees brings cheerfulness to him. Since he has full control over his mind, he is free from all anxieties and lives in real and perfect contentment.

"*kaya indriya siddhih ashuddhi kshayat tapasah*" (Yoga Sutras: 2.43).
[Perfection of the sense-organs and body after destruction of impurity by austerities.]

The essential purpose of 'Tapa' (training the senses) is to purify the body and bring it under the control of the will. It is the presence of impurity in the body and lack of control which stands in the way of its being used as a perfect instrument of consciousness. A Yogi is fully able to read other people's mind like a book.

"*pratyayasya para chitta jnana*" (Yoga Sutras: 3.19).
[By Samyama on the notions or presented ideas comes knowledge of another's mind.]

The Sanskrit word 'pratyayasya' means 'the content of the functioning mind'. The consciousness of an ordinary individual in the waking state functions through his mental body, and therefore a mental image occupies his mind. Anyone who can see this mental image can gain knowledge of that mind.

A highly developed Yogi can acquire the powers of *Duradrishti* (clairvoyance), *Durasruti* (clairaudience), and *Sukshma Drishti* (subtle-sight). Subtlety, obscurity and remoteness are all due to the limitations of the sense-organs. The Yogi relies on the unfoldment of inner organs of perception. These organs are present in a more or less perfect state of development in all evolved human beings and require only to be put to use by proper training through yogic methods. A Yogi can investigate the physical world and manipulate its forces far more simply and effectively than a scientist can do

> "*pravrittyah aloka nyasat suksma vyavahita viprakrista jnanam*" (Yoga Sutras: 3.26).
> [By directing the flash of inner light of higher sensory activity, knowledge of subtle objects, those hidden from view, and those very distant can be attained.]

The Yogi acquires knowledge of our solar system and other heavenly bodies. There are three parts of this knowledge. First, the structure of a solar system which is the fundamental unit in the whole Cosmos. Second, the arrangement of the stars in different kinds of groups such as galaxies, etc. The third is the law which underlies their movements. The yogic knowledge is more interesting and significant than what is obtained by scientific methods.

> "*bhuvana jnanam surya samyamat*
> *chandra tara vyuha jnanam*
> *dhurve tad gati jnanam*" (Yoga Sutras: 3.27-29).
> [By making Samyama on the sun, comes the knowledge of the world.
> By Samyama on the moon, knowledge of the arrangement of the inner stars can be known.
> By Samyama on the pole-star, knowledge of the movement of those stars can be known.]

Investigations based on yogic methods have shown that our known solar system and all lives have a deeper significance which is still unknown to modern science. All solar systems which constitute the Cosmos, though separated from one another by tremendous distances are not really independent of one another. They are rooted in the 'One Ultimate Reality', derive their life from one 'Common Source' and are modeled on one pattern.

Modern science can observe and prove the infinite nature of the Cosmos but cannot explain the Fine Tuning of the Universe and Biocentrism, but a highly advanced Yogi can explain.

In Nirvikalpa Samadhi, all sense of personal identity vanishes, and the real self, the indwelling Godhead is known. A Yogi can induce this superconscious state to another person at will. The nineteenth century mystic Sri Ramakrishna Paramhansa Dev had learnt Advaita Vedanta and Nirvikalpa Samadhi from a wandering Sadhu Tota Puri Swami. One day he induced this superconscious state on his disciple Swami Vivekananda in the temple-garden at Dakshineswar.

Ramakrishna was alone in his room. When Vivekananda entered Ramakrishna asked him to sit down beside him. Then Ramakrishna muttered something to himself with his eyes fixed on Vivekananda and placed his right foot on his body. Vivekananda wrote (Vidyatmananda, 1972, p. xxiii),

> "*At his touch, I had an entirely new experience. With my eyes widely open, I saw that the walls and everything else in the room were whirling around, vanishing into nothingness; the whole Universe, together with my own individuality, was about to be lost in an all-encompassing, mysterious Void! I was terribly frightened and thought I must be facing death – for the loss of my individuality meant nothing less than that to me. I couldn't control myself; I cried out, 'What are you doing to me! I have my parents at home! At this, he laughed aloud. Stroking by chest, he said, 'All right, that's enough for now. Everything will come in time'. The wonderful thing was, as soon as he'd said that, the whole experience came to an end. I was myself again. And everything inside and outside the room was just as it had been before.*"

Most important body parts of a living being are invisible. Research shows that various activities of the body parts have been organised in the most scientific manner (biological fine-tuning) guided by the highest intelligence. A Yogi obtains full knowledge of the machinery of the physical body by performing Samyama on the navel Chakra (Chakras are various focal points used in a variety of ancient meditation practices) because this Chakra controls the sympathetic nervous system working in the body.

> "***nabhi chakra*** *kaya vyuha jnanam*" (Yoga Sutras: 3.30).
> [By Samyama on the **navel center**, knowledge of the arrangement of the systems of the body can be known.]

Swami Rama was the first Yogi from India who was tested by western scientists. The results were published in many science journals. Swami Rama also appeared in some TV shows in USA. He had demonstrated that he can create a big temperature difference on the two edges of the same palm of his one hand. The colours at the two edges were different also. On another experiment he reduced his heart beat from seventy-four to fifty-two beats per minute. He could create a tumour at any place in his body and eventually make it disappear also.

Swami Rama made a very powerful statement for the western scientists, "All of the body is in the mind, but not all of the mind is in the body". That means anything inside the body, even at the cell level, can be completely controlled by the mind. The experiments demonstrated this assertion.

Shyama Charan Lahiri (Sept. 30, 1828 – Sept. 26, 1895), best known as Lahiri Mahasaya ('Mahasaya' is a Sanskrit title means 'large-minded'), was a Yogi and a disciple of the Yogi Mahavatar Babaji. Chandramohan De, a disciple of Yogi Lahiri Mahasaya had just received his medical degree. Full of joy and pride, he came to Lahiri Mahasaya for blessings. Seeing his pride Lahiri Mahasaya asked him a few questions about medical science.

Then he asked Chandramohan, "Can you tell me if I am alive?" Immediately he laid down and stopped his heartbeat. The young man who had just received his degree could not feel his pulse or heartbeat. He was astonished. There were other disciples present and they also could not discern any signs of life in him. He was absolutely like a dead body.

This went on for ten or fifteen minutes. Then suddenly Lahiri Mahasaya opened his eyes and said, "You should always remember that far beyond medical science is spiritual science. The medical world will never be able to fathom the spiritual mysteries. But these spiritual mysteries are not mysteries as such. They are the realities of normal people, and normal people are those who believe in God implicitly". Chandramohan understood his mistake and soon humility took the place of pride.

'Ahamkara' (pride) separates but humility unites because this is the true nature of the Atman. Ahamkara is the vision of a blind man while humility is the vision of an enlightened man. Once a person came to Swami Bhaskarananda Saraswati at a gathering and asked him a few questions. The Guru had answered everybody else's questions, but he would not answer this person. Instead, he insulted him and told him to go away. Everybody was shocked at the Guru's behaviour, and the disciple went home very sad. But that night he had a dream where Bhaskarananda appeared and answered his questions with utmost affection.

The next day the person told other disciples why the Guru had not answered his questions in front of others. Others had asked their questions with utmost sincerity and humility, but he had tremendous pride when he had asked his questions. That is why Swami Bhaskarananda had insulted him instead of answering his questions. But at night Bhaskarananda forgave him and answered in his dream. The person was extremely grateful that Bhaskarananda had punished him for his pride.

There are many 'enlightened beings' in the afterlife realm who do not need to reincarnate anymore on earth because they have completely worked out their Karma. Though sometimes they voluntarily reincarnate on earth to help civilisation growing spiritually, their consciousness remains really centred in the higher planes. To come in contact with these Beings one has to rise to the plane on which their consciousness normally functions. A Yogi is capable to contact them.

> ***"murdha jyotisi siddha darshanam"*** (Yoga Sutras: 3.33).
> [By Samyama on the **'Murdha Jyotish' (coronal light of the head)**, visions of the **'Siddhas' (enlightened beings)**, the masters can come.]

The coronal light of the head indicates the pineal gland which is a small rudimentary organ that lies deep inside the center of the brain. In addition to its functions known to medical science, mystic and esoteric spiritual traditions suggest it serves as a metaphysical connection between the physical and spiritual planes on which the consciousness of the 'Siddha' functions. It is associated with the idea of the 'third eye' (a spiritual symbol of all-knowing), and often perceived as a gateway for the liberation of the Atman. When 'Murdha Jyotish' is activated, it serves as a bridge between the higher and the lower consciousness, and enables the light of the higher worlds to penetrate into the brain. It is only then the 'Siddha' really becomes accessible to the Yogi.

> "*bahih akalpita vrittih maha-videha tatah prakasha avarana ksayah*" (Yoga Sutras: 3.44).
> ['Maha-videha' (disincarnate) is the formless thought patterns of mind that are projected outside of the body. By Samyama on that outward projection, the veil over the spiritual light is removed.]

With this power the Yogi can summon a 'Maha-videha' (departed Atman) on earth plane. There is a well-documented case of Bholananda Giri Maharaj.

The famous Mathematician Somesh Chandra Bose and his wife had shared a unique relationship; they deeply loved each other. But the wife died too early, and in her absence Somesh slowly cultivated the sense of abandonment towards everything. He approached many spiritual Gurus seeking for 'Diksha' (Sanskrit word – a Mantra or an initiation given for preparation and blessing for a religious ceremony), but found no one. Somesh had put forward a condition that he would choose a Guru who can give Diksha to him and his deceased wife. He continued his journey to several places in search of a Guru, and finally arrived at the hermitage of Bholananda Giri Maharaj and narrated his story.

Bholananda smiled and said, "Don't worry, everything will work the way you want. I will give Diksha to both of you." Somesh could not believe his words; he was in a state of bliss. However, he had a doubt "How did I know my wife received Diksha or not? Is it possible for her to appear as an ordinary human being?" Bholananda said, "Definitely, she will appear before you and sit with you to receive Diksha. You can see her before your eyes, but you have to promise me that you will not touch her". He readily agreed for the conditions of Bholananda. Accordingly, on an auspicious day, three seats were arranged – one for Bholananda and another two for Somesh and his deceased wife. He took his seat, and Bholananda next to him, and Diksha rituals began.

Somesh looked at his left and astonishingly saw his wife seated next to him with the same appearance, usual attire, and smile. They looked at each other with intense love and both of them smiled (it means, the apparition was self-conscious, not a replica). But he controlled his desire to touch her. Bholananda whispered blessed Mantra (the sacred utterings of Diksha) in his ears and later to his wife (Maha-videha). They both prostrated before Bholananda, and soon his wife disappeared from the sight. Somesh was so thrilled and happy to see his wife that he shed tears of joy.

Sometimes, the 'Maha-videha' (departed Atman) appears naturally. In scientific terms, this is called 'Crisis Apparition'. Nalinikanta Bhattacharya served as the supervisor of the Narayanpur estate. Once while working late in the night, he suddenly saw the shadowy image of his wife, Sudhansubala Devi, standing silently beside the table. But her wife was supposed to be far away at the native village at that time and certainly not at Narayanpur. The apparition remained there for a few moments only. Nalinikanta felt disturbed and rushed to his village. He came to know that his wife had expired just an hour before he saw her apparition at Narayanapur. Later he happened to see the same apparition several times in quick succession. Previously Nalinikanta did not believe in afterlife, but after his experience he became desperate to know all about the subtle phenomena of life and death.

During a nightdream Nalinikanta saw one Sadhu with a brilliant aura around him. He woke up to find the Sadhu standing beside his bed in a physical body. The Sadhu handed out to him a leaf bearing a Mantra on it and then disappeared. Nalinikanta was spellbound by the incident, and soon got deeply attracted towards asceticism. Later he took to a life of intense 'Vairagya' (renunciation), and became a highly developed Yogi, known as Nigamananda Saraswati Deva.

Reports of materialisation of discarnate entities should take definite rank as a science fact. Scientists do not accept it because they do not understand the system. But it does not make the truth absurd. All they have to do is to study Patanjali's Yoga Sutras and understand. The spiritual Guru Sri Yukteswar had appeared to his disciple Paramahansa Yogananda in physical form after his death. On asking him if he was truly in a physical body, Sri Yukteswar explained,

"*Yes, my child, I am the same. This is a flesh and blood body. Though I see it as ethereal, to your sight it is physical. From cosmic atoms I created an entirely new body, exactly like that cosmic-dream physical body which you laid beneath the dream-sands at Puri [a world-famous pilgrimage city of India] in your dream-world. I am in truth resurrected – not on earth but on an astral planet. Its inhabitants are better able than earthly humanity to meet my lofty standards. There you and your exalted loved ones shall someday come to be with me.*

... my new body is a perfect copy of the old one. ***I materialise or dematerialise this form any time at will, much more frequently than I did while on earth. By quick dematerialisation, I now travel instantly from planet to planet or, indeed, from astral to causal or to physical Cosmos.***" (Yogananda, 2021, pp. 419, 435).

Sri Yukteswar said that his materialised body was ethereal but to people in the earthly dream it appeared physical. This confirms the idea of the dreamlike physical world as a display of Maya. In the afterlife realm the souls move from one place to another by mere thinking, and no solid object is a barrier to them. This is fully consistent with quantum physics.

"*It's the thought that transports us, and since* ***all solid objects on the earth's surface are merely thought forms****, we move through them.*" (Montgomery, 1972, p. 61).

A Yogi can control his hunger and thirst by making Samyama on the pit of the throat and then hunger ceases but the body is not disturbed. In this way he can live for decades.

"*kantha kupe ksut pipasa nivrittih*
kurma nadyam sthairyam" (Yoga Sutras: 3.31-32).
[On the hollow of the throat (comes) cessation of hunger.
On the tortoise channel, below the throat steadiness is attained.]

Sensations of hunger, thirst and similar other phenomena depend upon the secretions of glands situated in various parts of the body. A Yogi has power to control the sensations by regulating the secretions of glands. He can control all the physical actions in the body including movements of the heart and lungs. What a doctor tries to bring about by the action of drugs, the Yogi can bring about by his yogic power.

Sadhu Haridas, a nineteenth-century Indian Yogi, was famous for his miraculous power to control his body completely using his mind power. His most notable feat, carried out in 1837, was to survive burial underground without food or water for forty days. The whole ritual took place in the presence of Ranjit Singh, the 'Maharaja' (a great king) of the Punjab, his whole court and few French and British doctors.

Before the burial Sadhu Haridas purified his system according to the yogic practices, following which he seated himself in the well-known 'Padmasana' (lotus posture). His ears, nostrils, eyes and mouth were closed with cotton and wax. Sadhu laid his tongue far back in his throat. He was then covered in linen on which king's seal was stamped and placed in a wooden box in lotus posture and lowered into the vault which immediately afterwards was covered with earth. Corn was sown in the ground, and the space enclosed with four walls and surrounded by royal guards.

Forty days later, the time specified for the Sadhu's release the corn had reached the height of a man. There was no sign of deception and the seal on the door remained unbroken. Upon unearthing him the medical team conducting the demonstration found his body cold and rigid, and announced they could find no sign of life, saying that it resembled a corpse except that the top of his head was warm. They as well as the king believed him to be dead.

On his being brought back to life the first operation was to draw the tongue away from the back of the throat by means of the fingers. Then his apparently lifeless body was washed with hot water, massaged, and 'ghee' (a form of clarified butter) placed on his eyelids and tongue. In a short time blood circulation started and he opened his eyes. Within thirty minutes he was speaking freely though feebly like a sick person. According to Claude Wade, the British Resident at the Maharaja's court, everyone was convinced that there had been no fraud in the exhibition they had witnessed.

Previous to this demonstration, Sadhu Haridas was buried alive for four months at Jammu by a Minister, Raja Dhyan Singh. On the day of his burial, he was clean-shaven, and four months later upon his release his face was still as smooth as the day of his entombment. This proved that he controlled the vital force and suspended every function within the body while in Samadhi.

How Sadhu Haridas did it? The human body is a mirror of our minds and our human physiology can go without food for days. Yogis in the course of Samadhi, start to slow down their breathing to get into a deep relaxing state. In this process the mind starts to lose awareness of the body and time. Sometimes twenty-four hours spent in Samadhi might seem to be one minute only. With the mind cutting itself off from the body and with decreased activity and metabolism, no energy is spent, thus resulting in low exhalation and pulse rate. At this particular state of the body there will not be any requirement of physical nourishment.

The case of Yogi Satyamurti, a sixty-year-old weak-built man, was a medical mystery. Under the supervision of a medical team Yogi Satyamurti was confined to a small underground pit in an open lawn for eight days. To ensure complete isolation, the pit was perfectly sealed from the top by bricks and cement mortar. To keep track of the physical activities, an ECG was continuously monitored during these eight days and numerous laboratory investigations were carried out before and after the time period.

The ECG record before closing the pit was within normal limits. After twenty-nine hours the ECG tracing was replaced by a straight line, which persisted till the eighth morning. The electrical activity returned about half an hour before the pit was scheduled to be opened. After some initial disturbance a normal configuration appeared. Finally, when the pit was opened on the eighth day as per instructions of the Yogi, the ECG was again found within normal limits. The doctors were amazed as the Yogi had completely stopped his heart or decreased its electrical activity below a recordable level. There is no satisfactory explanation for this super-medical state.

In India, there are hundreds of Yogis possessing perfect health who survive on milk alone. And there are still hundreds of other Yogis who have sustained life for years continuously without food and water. Actually these people have a different perspective altogether. Science is there for them too. But they understand science (modern science) as having a limited knowledge. Hence it is not established, fixed or permanent. But the power of the mind is limitless. Effectively, this power can be converted into different forms of energy.

Bibi Gulab Kaur, a young Sikh woman, survived without food and water for over twelve years. She has been under official observation in Calcutta several times and always under constant guard during scientific tests. The medical team concluded that she had risen above the requirement of food and water, and it not being a matter of days and months, but years.

A woman, Papamma from Gangupudi village (Visakhapatnam), had been living for over thirteen years without taking a drop of water or a piece of food. In the village of Krishnachandrapus there was a young woman, named Provati Dasi who had been living without food or liquids for about twenty years.

In the village of Patrasayar in Bankura lived Giri Bala Devi, aged sixty-eight, who had been fasting for past fifty-six years. At the age of twelve, Giri Bala Devi prayed to God to send her a Guru to teach her how to live without food. She immediately felt a trance-like state, and set out to travel to the Holy River Ganga. At the riverbank her Guru materialised right in front of her and said, "Dear little one, I am the Guru sent here by

God to fulfill your urgent prayer. From today you shall live by the astral light, your bodily atoms shall be recharged by the infinite current". This mysterious teacher taught her a Yoga technique. Since then, this woman Yogi has neither eaten nor taken fluids and has no bodily excretions. She has never been sick in her entire life. She was an adept of Pranayama and Yoga, and said that she gets her energy from air, sunlight and the cosmic power. When one journalist asked, "Mother, why don't you teach others the method of living without food?" Her reply was that she does not want to tamper with **"God's drama of creation"**.

A serious thinker will always ponder – what is "God's drama of creation"? The illiterate woman is actually talking about Maya. When asked why she had been singled out to live without eating, her face lit with wisdom – **"To prove that man is Spirit. To demonstrate that by divine advancement he can gradually learn to live by the Eternal Light and not by food"**.

Shri Prahlad Jani (August 13, 1929 – May 26, 2020) survived without food and water for more than seven decades. An investigation was carried out for fifteen days from April 22, 2010 to May 06, 2010 at Sterling Hospital, Ahmedabad to understand the paradoxical phenomenon. A team of thirty-five researchers confirmed that Jani was taken out of the sealed room for tests and exposure to sun under continuous video recording for the entire period during which he did not eat, drink or go to the toilet. The only contact with any form of fluid was during gargling and bathing periodically. All medical tests on Jani were reported as normal and researchers described him as being in better health than someone half his age.

Shri Prahlad Jani had lived without food and water since 1940 till his death at the age of ninety-one. He remained a mystery for scientists, doctors and common people alike – how did he defy the laws of nature?

> "*svadhyayat* ***Ishta-devata*** *samprayogah*" (Yoga Sutras: 2.44).
> [From self-study and reflection on sacred words (Svadhyaya), one attains contact and communion with the **Ishta-Devata (a worshipper's personal preferred deity)**]

Sanatan Dharma is composed of many traditions and paths to liberation. Hence a wide range of deities are worshipped. A Dharmic may choose one beloved deity as his focus for devotion. The concept of Ishta-Devata or Ishta-Devi (Devi is Female Divinity; Devata is masculine, and the related feminine equivalent is Devi) emphasises the tolerance that the Sanatan Dharma has for religious pluralism. But these deities are all manifestations of the formless absolute reality called Brahmam.

Yoga opens up a channel between the Sadhak and the object of his search. The nature of this communion will differ according to the devotional ability of the Sadhak and the nature of his Ishta-Devata. In such a communion there is free flow of knowledge; power and guidance from the higher to the lower consciousness.

The Ishta-Devi of Shri Prahlad Jani was Goddess Amba. Jani had left his home at the age of seven, and went to live in the jungle. At the age of twelve, he had a spiritual experience and became a follower of the Goddess Amba. From that time, he chose to dress as a female devotee of Goddess Amba, wearing a red sari-like garment, 'bindi' and 'sindoor' as used by married women, jewellery and crimson flowers in his shoulder-length hair. Therefore, he was commonly known as Mataji (means, a manifestation of The Great Mother). Jani believed that the Goddess provided him with water which dropped down through a hole in his palate, which allowed him to live without food or drink. Since the 1970s, Jani had lived as a hermit in a cave in the deep forest in Gujarat (India). He claimed that he could walk 100 or 200 kilometres in the jungle without sweating, or feeling tired or sleepy. His mysterious life was a subject of wide discussion.

The Ishta-Devata protects the Sadhak from hindrances and ill-fated incidents in everyday life, and leads him towards liberation.

Sadhak Kamalakanta Bhattacharya was a great devotee of Maa Kali. One day, Kamalakanta was offering his prayers to Maa Kali's idol, while the general public, King Tejash Chandra Bahadur himself and some of his courtiers were attending the same. Just then the king uttered in a moment of devotion, "Maa, how fierce, yet how compassionate you are. You are so alive!" A courtier who had envied Kamalakanta's goodwill, countered the king, "This idol of Maa Kali you are talking about…hmm… You say it is alive. Ask Kamalakanta to prove it."

On hearing this, Kamalakanta asked the king "Come near the idol of Maa Kali, Maharaj! Touch Her feet with utmost devotion and She shall be alive". The king went ahead and touched Maa Kali's feet with closed eyes and filled with devotion. He could feel the Divine Mother's presence; her feet felt so alive. He was moved to tears. But the courtier was still not convinced. He also touched the idol's feet but he could not feel anything. The king then asked Kamalakanta to prove that Maa is alive to everyone present there.

Kamalakanta could not bear the thought of hurting his Ishta-Devi, yet he took a thorn of 'Bel' (Wood Apple) and pricked the idol's feet and then held a Bel leaf under the wound. Slowly blood started to drip down the idol's feet. To him Maa Kali was not an idol but a living presence of Mother Goddess herself. He cried deeply, as it was painful to see his Mother bleed. While the crowd hailed the Divine Mother and sang, he quietly walked out of the shrine. Such was the strength of his faith and devotion to his

Maa Kali. Even today, that idol is still worshipped and grand festivals are arranged every year in the temple.

The Ishta-Devata of Vishuddhananda Paramahansa (March 14, 1853 – July 14, 1937; pre-monastic name Bholanath Chattopadhaya) was Lord Shiva from his childhood days. Once, his uncle severely scolded him for no fault of his own. This unfair treatment touched his sensitivity to the core. He thought that since a man is only an instrument in the hands of God, the real doer being God himself. It means, the scolding that his uncle had given him must really be the doing of his Ishta-Devata. So, he took hold the idol of Lord Shiva, grasped it to his chest and jumped into the house-pond with an intension to commit suicide for the insult Lord Shiva gave him through his uncle. But a wonder happened. Though pond was full of deep water, whichever way Bholanath moved the water became shallow and never reached above his knees. Bholanath was surprised. Soon others discovered that the idol of Lord Shiva was missing. When a search party came to the pond, they were wonderstruck to witness the scene. This incident strengthened his belief that God alone is the doer of everything.

From his very childhood days Vishuddhananda gave enough evidence of his yogic powers. Some people are born with certain yogic powers. The appearance of such powers is not quite accidental but is generally the result of having practiced Yoga, in some form or another, in a previous life.

Goswami Tulsidas (August, 13, 1532 – 1623) was a great devotee of Lord Ram, and the author of 'Ramcharit Manas' – the life story of Lord Ram with slight modifications. Many international scholars consider this book as one of the greatest pieces of literature ever written in the world. Though Tulsidas was a great scholar in Sanskrit, he wanted the story of Lord Ram to be accessible to general public. Hence, he chose to write in 'Awadhi' (a very sweet language of the common folk) instead of Sanskrit.

Orthodox forces were outraged by Tulsidas' attempts to retell and redefine Lord Ram's tale (originally written in Sanskrit by Sage Valmiki) in Awadhi. They humiliated Tulsidas badly, and also made several attempts to kill him. Some of them sent two thieves to steal the manuscript. But when the thieves tried to break into the hermitage of Tulsidas, they saw a blue-complexioned guard keeping watch at the gate with bow and arrow in his hands. Wherever they moved, the mysterious guard followed them. The thieves were duly frightened and ran away. In the morning however, they asked Tulsidas who the guard was. Tulsidas needed no further explanation. He wept for he understood it was none other than his Lord Ram who had protected him! After this incident, the thieves were reformed and became devotees of Lord Ram.

A. C. Bhaktivedanta Swami (Srila Prabhupada), the founder of ISKCON, had a massive heart attack while travelling by sea to America to preach Krishna Consciousness to the English-speaking people. Srila Prabhupada thought he would pass away, but in his uneasy sleep that night he had a vivid dream (vision) where Lord Krishna appeared in an open boat along with His other incarnations. Lord Krishna was rowing the boat, and the boat was pulling the ship with a rope all the way to America. Lord Krishna was smiling at him. Strangely, for the rest of the voyage the ocean appeared like a placid lake. The Atlantic crossing was so effortless that the ship's captain remarked that he had never seen such calmness of the Atlantic. Initially Srila Prabhupada did not write about this occurrence in his diary but years later he related these events to his followers. During the Atlantic crossing Lord Krishna had taken charge of the ship.

> "*ananyāś cintayanto māṁ ye janāḥ paryupāsate*
> *teṣāṁ nityābhiyuktānāṁ yoga-kṣemaṁ vahāmy aham*"
> (Bhagavad Gita: 9.22).
> [But those who always worship Me (Lord Krishna) with exclusive devotion, meditating on My transcendental form – to them I carry what they lack, and I preserve what they have.]

Trailanga Swami seldom ate though he was over 140 kg with a huge, barrel-like stomach. After weeks without food, he would break his fast with clabbered milk (buttermilk) offered to him by devotees. In spite of this he performed feats of strength which appeared miraculous to an ordinary person.

Many times, others saw Trailanga Swami drinking toxic poisons with no ill effect. A skeptic wanted to expose him as a fraud. So he posed as a devotee and brought him a bucket of calcium-lime mixture used for whitewashing walls instead of clabbered milk when Trailanga Swami was about to break his long fasting. He drank the entire bucket with no ill effect, but the skeptic fell to the ground writhing in pain (pain was not a result of his will but of the operation of the law of Karma). The monk broke his usual silence to explain the law of Karma, its cause and effect.

> "*samana jayat jvalanam*" (Yoga Sutras: 3.41).
> [By mastery over samana (the prana flowing in the navel area), the Yogi is able to cause his gastric fire blaze.]

A Yogi can increase the intensity of the gastric fire to the greatest extent to digest anything that he had consumed. There was a nameless Yogi in the city of Sangrur (Panjab, India) who could consume anything offered to him, food or otherwise, with quantity unlimited. At one sitting he had eaten as much as forty pounds of food and two large baskets of mango fruit. One day he consumed two bottles of black tar offered by a skeptic. Another time he ate the raw meat of an entire goat and then a gallon of whiskey. He refused nothing. None of these items had any aftereffects and his appearance remained unchanged throughout these strange meals. He was unaffected by food – its denial or consumption being the same to him.

Another Yogi by the name Narasingha Swami had the unusual ability to consume anything and everything offered to him. During 1923, many people had witnessed him consuming virulent poisons, crushed glass, nails, acids, etc. – he could eat and digest all things. In one demonstration, he consumed sulfuric acid, nitric acid, hydrochloric acid, mercury and carbolic acid followed by some iron nails, broken glass from a lantern, few stones and pieces of coal. A pharmacist was present there to check the genuineness of the chemicals for the critical audience. An eyewitness wrote,

> "*The Yogi at once drank this (sulfuric acid) and showed his palm and mouth to the audience to disprove any action of the acids on them; they showed no burns.*
>
> *He next placed a piece of glass in his mouth ... we could hear the crunching of the glass between his teeth. Displaying his tongue to the spectators, he showed the broken pieces of glass, almost powdered, lying on his tongue; with a drink of water he swallowed this.... All are as easily consumed by him as luscious fruit with no disastrous after effects.*" (Grewal, 1939, pp. 34-35).

Narasingha Swami had produced several X-ray pictures of his stomach showing the nails and crushed glass. At the end he consumed some cobra poison which justified his name 'Sarba Bhakshak' (eater of all things). He offered to eat a live cobra or any other venomous snake brought to him. On another occasion he consumed enough potassium cyanide to kill any other man within three minutes at most, yet there he stood smiling and unharmed. When questioned if he claimed any supernatural powers, he replied that these powers were attained by following the instructions of the ancient science of Yoga and were attainable by anyone willing to adhere to its practices.

Neem Karoli Baba (1900 – 1973; pre-monastic name Lakshman Narayan Sharma) was known outside India for being the spiritual master of a number of Americans who travelled to India in the 1960s and 70s. He had many high-profile followers, such as Steve Jobs, Mark Zuckerberg, Julia Roberts, Larry Brilliant and his wife Girija. Once a drug addict Richard Alpert wanted to test him. In 1967 when he first came to India, he brought with him a supply of heavy doses of LSD pills (recreational drug). One day he came to Neem Karoli Baba and said, "I have a real material which gives joy to heaven. If you eat it, then all the doors of knowledge are opened, do you know anything about it? Neem Karoli Baba asked, "tell me what is this?". He had a bottle of three pills in his car. Baba took all the pills and swallowed.

The total strength of the three pills was 915 micrograms, whereas a normal dose is about fifty micrograms for a drug addict and fifteen to twenty micrograms for a beginner. Hence, Richard sat there with the hope that this man was about to die. But Neem Karoli Baba did not show any effect of drugs; he kept working. His purpose was just to tell this to Richard that you are wasting your life on a useless thing; this thing is not going to be of any use to you. By seeing this miracle, Richard became a disciple of Neem Karoli Baba and took the new name Ram Dass.

There are many other Yogis living nowadays in India and abroad who demonstrate these wonderful powers; all powers resulting from yogic practices.

An advanced Yogi can make himself the very embodiment of the powers of love, sympathy, courage, patience, etc. and can express them to an extent which seems wonderful to common people.

"*maitri dishu balani*" (Yoga Sutras: 3.24).
[By Samyama on friendliness there comes great strength of that attitude.]

By performing Samyama on the strength of animals a Yogi can acquire strength even that of an elephant. Of course, the elephant does not indicate the limit of the strength which can be acquired, this animal being mentioned merely because it is supposed to be the strongest animal known to us. It is difficult to say what that limit is.

"*baleshu hasti baladini*" (Yoga Sutras: 3.25).
[By Samyama on the strength of elephants comes a similar strength.]

Guru Nanak, the founder of Sikhism, had once shown such superhuman strength. Soon after his enlightenment in 1499, Nanak set out on his journeys to spread his vision of the Divine – on foot, travelling for twenty-four years. Once Nanak along with disciple and lifelong companion Bhai Mardana reached Hasan-Abdal in the summer of 1521. They started reciting Kirtan (Bhakti songs) under a shady tree along with their devotees. This annoyed a local godman, Hazrat Shah Wali Qandhari, who meditated atop a nearby small hill.

Mardana was sent up three times to Qandhari by Nanak so that Mardana could have some water to quench his thirst. Qandhari, the egoist, refused his request, "Why don't you ask your Master?". Nanak pushed aside a big boulder and a fountain of water sprang up and began to flow endlessly and Mardana quenched his thirst. On the other hand, the spring on top of the hill where Qandhari meditated dried up. On witnessing this

Qandhari in rage, rolled a boulder towards Nanak from the top of the hill. Nanak stopped the boulder with his hand leaving its imprint on the boulder. Observing the miracle Qandhari became Nanak's devotee.

Psychic strength is mightier than physical strength because it is founded on the soul's power. Military strength is only bound to the physical world.

Once an English military officer who was very devoted to Swami Bhaskarananda Saraswati was boasting about his latest military achievement. Bhaskarananda said, "That's fine, I admire your bravery. Now, just give me that pencil that is right in front of you. I have to write something." The officer bent down to pick up the pencil but he could not lift it. Again the Guru said, "Please give it to me. I cannot reach it."

The officer tried several times but did not have the strength to lift up the pencil. With utmost affection Bhaskarananda told him, "Look, it is God's strength and capacity that works in and through you on the battlefield. That is why you are victorious. Without God's strength, you don't have the capacity even to lift up a pencil. So don't boast, my child. It is all God's Will."

A Yogi acquires perfect truthfulness. By acquiring this virtue in perfection, the fruit of any action that he may do follows unfailingly. For example, if he says something concerning the future then the event predicted must take place according to his prediction. A Yogi of highest standard will not tell a lie even in his dream.

> "*satya pratisthayam kriya phala ashrayatvam*" (Yoga Sutras: 2.36).
> [As 'Satya' (truthfulness) is achieved, the fruits of actions naturally result according to the will of the Yogi.]

The above Sutra does not mean all the laws of nature are capable of being violated to endorse the whims of such a person. For example, if he says that the sun will not set in the evening then the movement of the earth will stop to make his words effective – this is absurd. Cosmos cannot be upset by the whims and decisions of a perfectly truthful person. One who has developed a very high degree of truthfulness must have acquired previously the capacity to weigh every word that comes out of his mouth.

When an ordinary man says or does anything with a goal in mind it may not materialise. An intelligent person with sufficient knowledge of all the relevant conditions can predict the result to a great extent, but there are many unforeseen circumstances in the future which may affect the course of events. Only he can predict the result with certainty whose 'Buddhi' (Sanskrit word, means intellectual faculty) is developed and purified sufficiently to reflect the Universal Mind in which the past, present and future can be seen to a great extent.

A perfect Yogi becomes like a 'mirror of truth' reflecting the Universal Mind to some extent. A Varanasi Sage, Hari Har Baba, was credited with working a number of amazing miracles. One day while working at the bank of the river his legs were scratched by a species of bramble very common in that spot. In the irritation of the moment, he bursts out, "If only all these brambles would disappear!" And the strange thing was that a few days later those brambles had indeed disappeared completely.

One day when Swami Dhananjoy Das Kathia Baba went for a bath in a well he saw a peacock drinking water. Seeing that a person was coming, the bird flew away and sat on the boundary wall. Dhananjoy thought that the bird and himself were but manifestation of the Supreme. The Brahmam who was omnipresent reside in the peacock and in him as well. Hence the bird should not get afraid of him. Rather the bird would come down to him, open up its beautiful plumage and would begin to dance. The moment this thought arose in his mind, to his great surprise he saw the bird coming down and did exactly what he wanted it to do.

However, Dhananjoy was not satisfied because he took it as a fluke. Next few days he tried and found that the bird was repeating the performance every time. All his doubts were dispelled.

> "*parinimah traya samyama atita anagata jnana*" (Yoga Sutras: 3.16). [By Samyama on the three-fold changes in form, time, and characteristics, there comes knowledge of the past and future.]

A perfect Yogi sees the future continuously glowing and spreading itself in the immediacy of the eternal now, as if the future is at the command of his vision-eye.

Swami Rama came to USA during the early 1970s to visit a research institute. In an informal meeting Swami demonstrated an important feature of the yogic power – the ability to predict immediate future. One woman, Pat Norris, came to see him. When she entered his office, Swami told her to ask seven questions, and one by one she asked them. Then the Swami picked up a paper from his desk, turned it upside down, and gave that to her. In that paper all her questions were already written along with their answers. How can such a thing happen? Pat did not have any chances, choices, or freewill to ask a different set of questions. Swami wrote them down before she came.

There are many such examples to prove that all the past, present, and future events are already written in the memory of the Universe. Any Yogi with the high level power of third eye will be able to describe any event in the Universe at any space time point.

Once a group of seekers was going up to Swami Bhaskarananda Saraswati one by one to bow to him and take blessings. When it was the turn of a certain man. Bhaskarananda told him, "Your father has died. Go home. Soon there will be a telegram for you from your family". The man left for home immediately with a sorrowful heart, and when he arrived at his own home the messenger was waiting with a telegram from his mother containing his father's death news.

A prominent disciple of Bhaskarananda went to stay with him for few days. On the fourth day, he received an express telegram from his home. A serious catastrophe had taken place, and it demanded his immediate attention. His physical presence was also needed. The disciple wanted to leave immediately, but Bhaskarananda said, "No, you can't go. No matter how serious the thing is, you can't go today". The disciple did not want to disobey the Guru, but he was very sad. Finally, Bhaskarananda said, "All right, you can go today. But don't go on the afternoon train at two o'clock. I want you to take the evening train."

When the disciple arrived at the station that evening, he was shocked to hear that the previous train had met with an accident. Many people had died. When he heard this, he was overwhelmed with gratitude to Bhaskarananda. Instead of returning home as he had planned, he went back to the Guru's house and touched his feet with gratitude.

Once Trailanga Swami was absorbed in deep thought sitting near the confluence of the three Rivers – Ganga, Yamuna and Saraswati – near the Triveni Prayag Tirtha Ghat (bathing place for Sadhus). It was raining heavily, but Trailanga Swami remained there unmoved. A devotee, Ramtaran Bhattacharjee asked him to go to a nearby shelter. Trailanga Swami told Ramtaran, "Please don't worry for my sake. I am perfectly at home here, and moreover, I cannot leave this place right now as I know a boat coming near this 'ghat' carrying quite a few people will capsize very soon. I have to rescue the passengers."

Right then in front of Ramtaran's eyes, an approaching boat began to capsize due to the heavy winds, and Trailanga Swami suddenly vanished. After a short while, a confused Ramtaran saw that the boat with its passengers was floating perfectly well and it finally reached the riverbank safely. When the passengers were getting down from the boat, Ramtaran saw that Trailanga Swami was with them. How Trailanga Swami vanished from the riverbank in front of his eyes, and how did he reach the boat? Seeing his wonder-struck eyes Trailanga Swami said, "My son, be easy, it is nothing remarkable to be amazed about. The Almighty God is present everywhere with infinite strength and grace. We too are empowered by that same infinite power, but our addiction to sensory pleasures and material greed negates our entire strength and turns us into slaves of meanness. We never care about spiritual upliftment or try to achieve purity of heart.

Otherwise, man would be immensely powerful, as God Himself is the source of power of his creations. The man who knows this truth and honours this power within can do anything easily without fail. Don't get drenched anymore; go back to your own place."

Now a serious question arises – Swami Bhaskarananda Saraswati saved his disciple's life only by asking him not to take a particular train. He could easily have told the station authorities to pay special attention to the train's journey. But he did not warn them. While Trailanga Swami saved everyone in the boat. Why Bhaskarananda was indifferent or unkind to the ill-fated passengers and the train, but showed his preference to his own little world?

Both Bhaskarananda and Trailanga Swami were highly developed Yogis. Both of them by their actions and inactions just executed the desire of the Supreme Power in the 'Maya' world of multiple realities.

> "*karmaṇy akarma yaḥ paśyed akarmaṇi ca karma yaḥ*
> *sa buddhimān manuṣyeṣu sa yuktaḥ kṛtsna-karma-kṛt*"
> (Bhagavad Gita: 4.18).
> [Those who see action in inaction and inaction in action are truly wise amongst humans. Although performing all kinds of actions, they are Yogis and masters of all their actions.]

Every action or inaction of a Yogi actually helps others. Creation-preservation and destruction-transformation are predetermined in the heavenly abode by the protectors of Karma – the ultimate Cosmic Law.

> "***For things are planned ahead – make no mistake***. *If earthlings realised how much of it is planned ahead, they would not struggle so strongly to avert certain catastrophies, as they view them.*" (Montgomery, 1972, p. 14).

> "*Our Karma of past deeds towards humanity and our mistakes and achievements have* ***all been evaluated with an eye toward the best course of future endeavours***." (Newton, 2016a, p. 202).

Swami Bhaskarananda cannot upset the Cosmic law of Karma. The ill-fated passengers were destined to suffer as per their Karma – ***"For things are planned ahead – make no mistake".*** He got the command from within, from the Supreme Power that he could save only his disciple's life. The Supreme Power wanted him to remain silent about the destiny, and all had been – ***"evaluated with an eye toward the best course of future endeavours".*** A Yogi never curses anyone. Even his anger or indecisions benefit others.

"*ahimsa pratishthayam tat vaira-tyagah*" (Yoga Sutras: 2.35).
[As a Yogi becomes firmly grounded in nonviolence, whoever (human or animal) comes near him will naturally lose any feelings of hostility.]

Love and sympathy are the basis of all the ethics and morality. A Yogi develops 'Ahimsa' (nonviolence) to such a great extent that he carries an invisible aura surcharged with love and compassion even though these may not be expressed emotionally. Trailanga Swami was filled with such love that he was inwardly in harmony with all living creatures and automatically inspired confidence and love in them. Once he came to Nepal's deep forests during pilgrimage – a place infested by venomous snakes and wild animals. A Nepalese King was on a hunting safari in that region, and although a gifted marksman, could not shoot a tiger. Despite repeated misses, the king insisted on getting the tiger and pursued it with all his might. The tiger chase brought the king to Trailanga Swami sitting amiably with the roaring beast. He gently stroked the frightened animal while the king looked on in amazement. He beckoned the king closer to give him this marvellous advice, "Give up your fear, Oh King, for the tiger will not harm you, though you have just been trying to kill it. Just try to understand that nobody can kill anybody. The tiger has become non-violent and so have you. Cast off the lust of violence from your mind for good and see no one as your enemy. God has created everything. Give love, and He will give you love. Always remember this. Be brave and go back now".

Later, the king returned to Kathmandu spreading news of the Yogi and the tiger. Many people aroused with devotion travelled to the jungle for his blessings and Swami's fame began to spread.

That is how the violent and hateful vibrations of those who come near the Yogi are for the time being over-powered by the much stronger vibrations of love and kindness emanating from him and even beasts of prey become harmless and quiet for the time being. Of course, when a creature goes out of the immediate influence of such a Yogi its normal nature is bound to assert itself but even this brief contact is likely to leave a permanent mark on it and uplift it a little.

Sadhu Baba Krishnanad kept a domestic lioness as his pet and travelled throughout India with this pet. The lioness followed her master like a faithful dog, as the animal had forgotten its normal instinct to kill, and although as gentle and submissive as a dog, it fears a camera and upon seeing one will always attempt to run away. Sadhu opened the mouth of the animal and placed his arm inside to demonstrate its harmlessness and gentleness. The animal could certainly have a nice mouthful if it had desired. Evidently the idea has never occurred to the lioness but if it could remember its past, it could easily destroy her master. The food of the animal consisted entirely of vegetables, milk and rice. The people in the cities visited by the Sadhu were not afraid of his strange pet.

> "*aparigraha sthairye janma kathanta sambodhah*"
> (Yoga Sutras: 2.39).
> [Non-possessiveness (Aparigraha) being confirmed there arises the memory of past life.]

This Sutra needs explanation. Our temporary personality is formed anew with every incarnation, but the 'permanent individuality' persists through the succession of incarnations. Rigorous practice of 'Aparigraha' means the Yogi does not remain indebted to others, but becomes independent and free. His mind becomes pure because he receives all the evils of the giver with every gift. These evils lay coating after coating on his mind. By practicing 'Aparigraha' his mind becomes pure, and the first thing he gets is memory of past life.

Trailanga Swami was regarded by devotees as an incarnation of Shiva and referred as the 'The walking Lord Shiva of Varanasi'. Rich visitors liked to decorate Trailanga Swami with gold and gems. Attired like this he would lose consciousness and thieves would remove the jewels. For him, it was as if someone was giving and someone was taking. An incident occurred in which a king offered him beautiful jewels, but the robbers took away everything soon. When the robbers were arrested and brought to Trailanga Swami, he dismissed the whole incident saying, "I am still the same with or without the jewels". Trailanga Swami had renounced everything – even his loincloth. This is the highest level of 'Aparigraha'.

> "*samskara saksat karanat purva jati jnanam*" (Yoga Sutras: 3.18).
> [Through the direct perception of the latent impressions (Samskaras) comes the knowledge of previous incarnations.]

All the experiences which we pass through in life produce impressions upon our minds which can be recovered by diving sufficiently deep into our own consciousness. All highly developed Yogis can come in direct contact with these impressions and thus able to obtain knowledge of previous lives of others and their own.

Shyama Charan Lahiri (Lahiri Mahasaya) worked as an accountant in the Military Engineering Department of the British Indian Government which took him all over India. In the autumn of 1861, Lahiri was posted in Danapur. One morning, the office manager summoned him and said, "Lahiri, a telegram has just come from our main office. You are to be transferred to Ranikhet where an army post is now being established". With one servant, Lahiri set out on the 500-mile trip, and arrived at the Himalayan site of Ranikhet in thirty days.

He used to spend many hours roaming in the magnificent hills as his office duties were not heavy. One day he was astounded to hear a distant voice calling his name. After climbing further on Drongiri mountain, he saw on one of the rocky ledges stood a Sadhu, extending his hands in welcome.

"Lahiri, you have come!" The Sadhu addressed him affectionately, "Rest here in this cave. It was I who called you". In the cave there were several woollen blankets and a few water pots. The Sadhu pointed to a folded blanket in one corner and asked, "Lahiri, do you remember that seat?" Lahiri was dumbfounded. The mysterious Sadhu replied in English, "The office was brought for you, and not you for the office. I see my telegram took effect". Lahiri was in a puzzle. The Sadhu continued,

> "*I refer to the telegram that summoned you to these isolated parts. It was I who silently suggested to the mind of your superior officer that you be transferred to Ranikhet.* ***When one feels his unity with mankind, all minds become transmitting stations through which he can work at will.*** *Lahiri, surely this cave seems familiar to you.*" (Yogananda, 2021, p. 317).

As Lahiri maintained a bewildered silence, the Sadhu approached and struck him gently on the forehead. At this touch, a wondrous current swept through his brain, releasing the sweet seed-memories of his previous life. "I remember!" Lahiri's voice was half-choked with joyous sobs, "You are my guru Mahavatar Babaji! Scenes of the past arise vividly in my mind; here in this cave I spent many years of my last incarnation!" As deep recollections overwhelmed him, he tearfully embraced his master's feet.

"For more than three decades I have waited for you to return to me". Babaji's voice rang with celestial love.

> "*You slipped away and disappeared into the tumultuous waves of the life beyond death. The magic wand of your Karma touched you, and you were gone! Though you lost sight of me, never did I lose sight of you! I pursued you over the luminescent astral sea where the glorious angels sail. Through gloom, storm, upheaval, and light I followed you, like a mother bird guarding her young. As you lived out your human term of womb life, and emerged a babe, my eye was ever on you. When you covered your tiny form in the lotus posture under the Ghurni [name of his native village] sands in childhood, I was invisibly present. Patiently, month after month, year after year, I have watched over you waiting for this perfect day. Now you are with me! Here is your cave, loved of old times; I have kept it ever clean and ready for you. Here is your hallowed asana-blanket, where daily you sat to fill*

your expanding heart with God. My own, do you now understand?" (Yogananda, 2021, p. 318).

This is how Yogi Mahavatar Babaji revived a disciple from death. Babaji told Lahiri that the rest of his life was to be given to spreading the Kriya Yoga message. Soon after, Lahiri Mahasaya returned to Varanasi where he began initiating sincere seekers into the path of Kriya Yoga.

A highly advanced Yogi can teleport himself, can become invisible (Anima – making the body miniature) and can temporarily materialise in another place by manipulating the forces as he likes. Trailanga Swami was always carefree like a child and used to walk on streets in a nonacceptable manner. The British police of Varanasi were outraged by his behaviour and locked him in a jail cell. But he was soon seen on the prison roof. The police put him back into his locked cell, only to see him appear again on the jail roof.

On another occasion, Trailanga Swami was brought to the courtroom of British District Magistrate of Varanasi. While the magistrate was giving him a moral lecture, Trailanga Swami looked around elsewhere, yawning every now and then, totally bored. Then the magistrate said "Throw this man in prison!" Just as soon as these words were uttered Trailanga Swami vanished into thin air in front of the huge crowd in the courtroom. There was shock, there was awe, there were sounds of overjoyed, "Har Har Mahadev!" The magistrate did not believe what he was seeing (I mean, not seeing!).

Just then, an Indian Magistrate spoke up. He explained to the confused English Magistrate that Trailanga Swami was no ordinary man. He is a Yogi of the highest order. He is dissolved in the Oneness of it all. As he was saying this, Trailanga Swami reappeared in the same place and same posture.

The British police soon gave up and let him again walk on the streets of Varanasi.

"*kaya akashayoh sambandha samyamat laghu tula samatatti cha* ***akasha gamanam***" (Yoga Sutras: 3.43).
[By making Samyama on the relation between the Akasa (space) and the body, the Yogi becoming light as cotton wool, goes through the skies (**Akasa-gamanam**)]

"*tatah anima adi pradurbhavah kaya sampad tad Dharma anabhighata cha*" (Yoga Sutras: 3.46).
[Through that mastery over the elements, comes the abilities of making the body atomically small, perfect, and indestructible in its characteristics or components, as well as bringing other such powers.]

This power 'Akasa-gamanam' is not flying through the sky like a bird. It involves resolving the particles of the body into space at one place and then reassembling them at the destination. This is how Trailanga Swami travelled from the locked cell to the jail roof. The physical body is made up of countless particles of matter held together by forces of cohesion. The Yogi acquires knowledge of these forces of cohesion and the power to manipulate them as he likes. He keeps the particles in a resolved state as long as he wants, and when he reassembles the particles the body materialises instantly, apparently from nowhere.

Vishuddhananda Paramahansa had miraculous powers which he manifested from time to time to his disciples when explaining the esoteric significance of Indian Yoga to them. He started his Yoga Sadhana at the age of fourteen. Once Vishuddhananda was teaching his disciple, Upendranath Roy Chowdhury, a police officer, "Look Upendra, the whole creation seems true, but it's just an illusion of mind". The police officer did not believe, and asked, "But I am watching you, is that an illusion?" Vishuddhananda smiled and said, "Where I am?" and then vanished into thin air. After some time, he entered the room from outside and said, "Upendra, one day you will realise everything by yourself."

A Yogi can make himself partly invisible by controlling the rays of the sun and the moon.

> "*kaya rupa samyama tat grahya shakti tat stambhe chaksuh prakasha asamprayoga antardhanam*" (Yoga Sutras: 3.21).
> [By making Samyama on the form of the body, the contact between the eye (of the observer) and light (from the body) is broken and the body becomes invisible.]

Science says that an object becomes visible when the light reflected from it strikes the eye of the perceiver. If the contact between the eye and the light can be prevented, the body will become invisible. This is how a Yogi standing in the midst of a room can suddenly become invisible. Yogi Raj Deo had this miraculous power. Once he sat in an open field at night and claimed that the moon light will not fall upon him. An eyewitness wrote,

> "*Hardly had he uttered these words than we saw his face dimming. In about five minutes we saw that no moonlight was falling on him; he appeared as though in shade. He said that that was controlling the moon's rays.*"

Next day many people went to see him about eight o'clock in the morning. The Yogi was unusually charming, but when they looked at him,

"*We noticed his face become dim. This dimness increased so much that his whole body appeared to be a small spot. In the next two minutes that small spot also disappeared and we saw a headless figure in front of us. We were rather dismayed at the phenomenon but our host who has seen greater things than this encouraged us. Now his body began to get shorter until it totally disappeared. Then his legs began to disappear, similarly to his head and body. Now there was no Sadhu before us.*" (Grewal, 1939, pp. 39-40).

A Yogi can make himself invisible to the eye of the camera. Lahiri Mahasaya had an aversion to being photographed. Over his protest, a group picture was once taken of him with some disciples. The photographer discovered that the plate which had clear images of all the disciples, revealed nothing more than a blank space in the center where the outlines of Lahiri Mahasaya was expected.

When this phenomenon was widely discussed, an expert photographer, Ganga Dhar, boasted that the fugitive figure would not escape him. The next morning, as Lahiri sat in lotus posture on a wooden bench with a screen behind him, Ganga Dhar arrived with his equipment. Taking every precaution for success, he greedily exposed twelve plates. On each one he soon found the imprint of the wooden bench and screen, but once again the figure was missing. When asked, Lahiri replied, "I am Spirit. Can your camera reflect the omnipresent invisible?"

"I see it cannot! But I lovingly desire a picture of the bodily temple where alone, to my narrow vision, that Spirit appears fully to dwell."

"Come, then, tomorrow morning. I will pose for you."

Next morning Gaga Dhar focused his camera. This time the sacred figure, not cloaked with mysterious imperceptibility, was sharp on the plate.

"*etena shabdadi antardhanam uktam*" (Yoga Sutras: 3.22).
[From the above can be understood the disappearance of sound and others (touch, smell and taste).]

The principle referred to in the previous Sutra 3.21 in relation to visual phenomena is also applicable to the other four organs of sensation. Sound is vibration and, if the vibrations which affect any sense-organ and produce the corresponding sensations can be cut off, the Yogi will remain unheard. He can control phenomena connected with touch, smell and taste also.

A Yogi can create many mental images by duplication which are exact copies of his body.

"***nirmana chittani** asmita matrat*" (Yoga Sutras: 4.4).
[**Artificially created minds** proceed from 'egoism' alone.]

The best example of 'Nirmana Chittani' is Lord Krishna's 'Rasa-lila' (in the Krishna Bhakti traditions, the 'Rasa-lila' is considered to be one of the highest and most esoteric of Krishna's pastimes) where every Gopi (cow-herd woman) has a Krishna for herself. The mechanism of creating such vehicles is given in this Sutra. A Yogi does this by 'Asmita' (principle of individuality). An advanced Yogi maintains his 'Asmita' in an integrated condition with all the vehicles of consciousness functioning at different levels. Hence, he has the capability of establishing any number of independent centres of consciousness for himself, and as soon as such a centre is established a replica automatically materialises. The moment he withdraws his will from the 'artificial mind', it disappears instantaneously. This is not teleportation because a materialised body does not form, but only a self-conscious apparition.

Dr. Nishikanta Basu was a doctor by profession practicing in Chicago, USA. He was a follower of Baba Lokenath Brahmachari. One day he was checking an American woman at his clinic who was suffering from severe stomach ulcers. The medicine had no effect on her so she was tired and said, "You are an Indian doctor. Your country is inhabited by Yogis. If you know a miraculous Yogi, heal my disease by knowing from him!"

Nishikanta apologised that he did not have knowledge about that. Suddenly the woman paused for a moment and exclaimed, "Who is that person behind you?" But before Nishikanta looked back, the woman stood up and said, "This Yogi wants to give me something". He walked a little and came forward towards where Nishikanta was sitting and extended his hand. He had in his hand an herb like the roots of a plant. The Yogi gestured and told her to eat, and when the woman ate it, the Yogi simply vanished from the closed room. When Nishikanta asked her about the appearance of the Yogi, the woman gave a detailed description. Nishikanta realised that he was Baba Lokenath. Within few days the woman was completely cured.

The son of a rich widow went to London to study. His mother, however, received no letter from him for four months. Terribly worried, she came to Yogi Gambhirnath, and begged him to tell her something about her son. Gambhirnath took pity on her, and entered into a room for about forty minutes and when he came out he said, "Don't worry. Your son has left England and is now in Bombay. He is coming back to you. In three days he will arrive home". On exactly the third day the son arrived home. When the mother told him the story, the son laughed. "I have been to Europe," he said, "so I know that this is only a kind of superstition you are enjoying."

The mother said, "All right, but at least come and see Gambhirnath." Thus, the son went with his mother. By seeing Gambhirnath, he almost fainted. "Hello, what are you doing here?" he demanded.

On asking the son told them that he had seen Yogi Gambhirnath on his ship a day before the ship was to reach the shore of Bombay. Gambhirnath stood in front of his cabin and that he had talked to him for about five minutes but thereafter he did not see him on the ship nor on getting down at Bombay. On asking about the day and time of his seeing Gambhirnath on the steamer, it was exactly the same when he went to his room for meditation.

A middle-aged disciple of Swami Nigamananda died of an incurable disease. His mother and his wife were thrown into a sea of sorrow. The mother became practically insane with grief. She said to a picture of Nigamananda which was hanging on the wall, "Why do we have to keep you? You have no power; you are useless! I am throwing you into the pond!" She grabbed the picture and started carrying it towards the pond. All of a sudden she heard someone behind her crying, "Mother! Mother!" with a tearful and sorrowful voice. She turned around and saw Nigamananda with tearful eyes saying to her, "Mother, let us go back home. Do not cry for your son any more. I will be your son. Your son is with me, inside me and for me."

The woman was greatly consoled and returned to her house with the picture of her Guru. At the hour that all this occurred Nigamananda was actually four hundred miles away giving spiritual lessons to his disciples at his hermitage.

Another most striking incident took place in the same family. One night a group of robbers came to the house of the old mother and the widow and were about to strike them. They wanted to take away their valuable possessions and money. Both the mother and the wife were terribly frightened and cried for help. Within a few short moments, Swami Nigamananda appeared in the most beautiful and powerful form and threatened the robbers with a Trishul (trident – a traditional weapon with three pointed and sharp ends), saying he would destroy them all. This is how Swami Nigamananda extended his protection-arms to the helpless women by using his spiritual and occult power.

Once the Goddess of plenitude, Maa Annapurna, appeared before Swami Nigamananda and taught him a lesson. That time Nigamananda had been practising severe austerities in Varanasi for quite a few months. One day he was extremely hungry, but he had nothing to eat. In silence he said to the Goddess of plenitude, "Annapurna, how is it that I don't have any food to eat? Just then a very ugly elderly woman with filthy clothes brought him a bag and said to him, "Please hold this bag of food. Let me go and bathe in the pond nearby. Then we shall eat together."

Nigamananda waited two or three hours, but there was still no sign of her returning. Finally, he opened the bag and saw most delicious food and fruits inside. He ate everything himself. That night in a dream Nigamananda saw the Goddess Annapurna. She said to him, "So you see, nobody remains hungry. I feed everyone."

"You feed everyone?" Nigamananda exclaimed. "When did you feed me? I invoked you when I was hungry, but an ugly, dirty, old woman gave me food. You are so beautiful and luminous!"

The Goddess explained, "It was I who came to you in that form."

"Why did you do that?" he asked.

"I wanted to show you that all forms are mine", said the Goddess. "Still you care more for physical beauty than for the soul's beauty. So I wanted to show you that even ugly people can have good hearts. From now on try to feel that physical beauty has nothing to do with a kind, sympathetic heart."

After meeting Mahavatar Babaji, Lahiri Mahasaya continued to work as an accountant in the office at Varanasi. It happened that for a few days his boss, who was an Englishman, was very sad and disturbed. One day Lahiri Mahasaya asked his boss the reason for his sadness. The boss said that his wife was extremely ill in a hospital in England, and that he had not heard any recent news from her or from the family. Lahiri Mahasaya told him, "Let me enter into the adjacent office and meditate for some time. Then I will bring you some news."

The boss smiled at him and inwardly appreciated his good will, but he did not have real faith in him. He felt that to do this kind of thing, one had to be a great spiritual master with tremendous occult power.

After fifteen minutes, Lahiri Mahasaya emerged from the room and said to his boss, "In two- or three-days' time, you will receive a letter from your wife. She is doing well. Please do not worry about her at all." He even told his boss what was inside the letter.

In three days, a letter did arrive from the Englishman's wife, and the contents of the letter were exactly as Lahiri Mahasaya had described them. But the story does not end there. In a few months, the boss's wife sailed for India. Upon arriving in Varanasi, she visited her husband's office. When she saw Lahiri Mahasaya, her eyes opened wide in surprise – "How can this man be here? I saw him near my deathbed in the hospital. He looked at me and smiled, and then I recovered". Her husband and all those who were working in the office were taken aback.

"*pravritti bhede prayojakam chittam ekam anekesam*"
(Yoga Sutras 4.5).
[The one (natural) mind is the director or mover of the many (artificial) minds in their different activities.]

When a Yogi duplicates his 'mind' at many places, the activities of these 'artificial minds' are coordinated and controlled by his 'natural mind'. The 'artificial minds' are merely the instruments of the one 'natural mind' and obey it automatically. They are different existences of the same thing. A business firm may be obliged to open a temporary branch in some locality for a particular purpose. Although business is handled at the short-term branch, the assets and liabilities belong to the head office. The area office is merely an outpost of the head office and has really no independent status. A somewhat similar relationship exists between the 'artificial minds' and the one 'natural mind'. The 'artificial minds' are merely temporary creations which disappear as soon as the purpose is served.

A Yogi can perceive truth directly without any outside help or without the use of the sense-organs. All knowledge comes to him naturally.

> "*tatah mano-javitvam virarana-bhavah pradhana jayah*"
> (Yoga Sutras: 3.49).
> [By that mastery over the senses and acts (Indriyas), there comes quickness of mind, perception with the physical instruments of perception, and mastery over the primal cause out of which manifestation arises.]

The mastery of the 'Indriyas' enables the Yogi to acquire the capacity to perceive anything. This means that the Yogi has to direct his consciousness to any place or thing to become aware of everything instantaneously which he wants to know.

> "*pratibhad va sarvam*
> *hirdaye chitta samvit*" (Yoga Sutras: 3.34-5).
> [Through the intuitive light of higher knowledge, anything might become known.
> By practicing Samyama on the heart, knowledge of the mind is attained.]

Trailanga Swami, Sadhu Deva Puri and Baba Lokenath had this power. Although unschooled and untrained, Sadhu Deva Puri spoke words of great wisdom and understanding that his highly educated disciples had failed to grasp.

One day while sitting with a few devotees in his cottage Baba Lokenath suddenly said, "Vijay is coming. His boat has gotten stuck in the sand of the riverbank near Chamarbari," and asked a few devotees to go receive Vijay and bring him to the cottage. When they reached the riverbank, they found the boat stuck in the sand and asked whether Vijay Krishna Goswami had come. The astonished devotees of Vijay Krishna asked how they knew of his arrival. Baba's devotees told them that Baba had instructed them to go to the riverbank to meet Goswami and escort him back to the ashram.

Rani Rashmoni, the founder of the Dakshineswar Kali Temple, had appointed Sri Ramakrishna as the priest of the temple. Rashmoni, though a very religious person, was nevertheless aware of the material interests of her family. She also managed the assets and prosperity of the house. Once during the time of worship, Sri Ramakrishna paranormally sensed that her mind was engrossed in commercial matters and slapped her on the back. Outraged, the astonished people demanded that she dismiss and punish him. She silenced them by saying that the Divine Mother had illumined her heart through Sri Ramakrishna.

In this level, the Yogi has the power of divine sensation and divine hearing.

> "*tatah pratibha sravana vedana adarsha asvada varta jayanta. shrotra akashayoh sambandha samyamat divyam shrotram*"
> (Yoga Sutras: 3.37, 42).
> [From that arises the knowledge of hearing, touching, seeing, tasting, and smelling, belonging to the knowledge of pure consciousness.
> By Samyama over the relation between space and the power of hearing, the higher, divine power of hearing comes.]

Sounds on the higher planes are certainly different from sounds on the physical plane. A Yogi becomes sensitive to the subtler sound vibrations which are beyond the range of the physical ear. He hears anything spoken or sounded miles away.

The physical body of a Yogi becomes perfect and almost indestructible. For him there is no disease, no pain.

> "*rupa lavanya bala vajra samhanana kaya-sampat*"
> (Yoga Sutras: 3.47).
> [This perfection of the body includes beauty, gracefulness, strength, and adamantine hardness in taking the blows that come.]

The books of India contain many references to the great ages attained by the ancient sages in olden days. In the two great epics Mahabharat and Ramayan, there were few characters (Ashwathama, Hanuman, Kripacharya, Parashuram) who were immortal in their physical body, or would die as per their wish (Vishma, the greatest fighter in the Mahabharat had the boon of will death).

Leaving aside the epics, the Arab historians were astonished to see the unusual longevity of the Indians in earlier days, the average age being one hundred and ten years. The four 'Ashram' system was developed for a life-span of one hundred years. Many Yogis are apparently ageless if judged by their youthful appearance while their ages have exceeded not only the century mark but are near or have surpassed the second one.

Trailanga Swami lived around 270 years and resided in Varanasi approximately 150 years between 1737 and 1887. Robert Arnett wrote that his miracles are well documented that cannot be dismissed as a myth and there were living witnesses to his 'amazing feats'. His life was a revival of ancient Yoga.

Yogi Devraha Baba (also spelled Deoraha baba) was a hermit who lived beside the River Yamuna in Mathura till his death on June 19, 1990. He was considered to be a 'spiritual guide to everyone from a pauper to the most powerful'. The villagers living nearby confirmed that the hermit had lived "*a life longer than our five generations together lived*". Dr. Rajendra Prasad (the first President of India) verified the hermit's old age, and personally attested his age at least 150 years old. He was popularly called as 'ageless Yogi with a secular image'. Some old records strongly suggest his existence for at least about 250 years. Devraha Baba never ate food but only drank water from the River Yamuna.

Baba Lokenath (1730 – June 3, 1890) lived for 160 years. For thirty years, Baba went through the most difficult yogic practices while living in the forests and the valleys, observing the vow of celibacy and fasting. Then he left for the Himalayas, meditated for fifty years, and touched the highest peaks of spiritual illumination, Nirvikalpa Samadhi, at the age of ninety years. After attaining enlightenment, he said, **"I have seen only myself. I am bound by my own Karma".** Then he travelled extensively through Arabia, Israel, Persia, Afghanistan, and various parts of Europe, and finally came down and settled in the Baradi village in Bangladesh for last twenty-six years of his life. According to local legends, Baba Lokenath had denied himself all physical needs, never slept, never closed his eyes or blinked during the twenty-six years.

Baba promised to continue being available to anyone even after his death and forever who prayed and asked for help. One of his famous quotes roughly translates as, **"Whether it is at war, or in the woods, or on the water; if you are ever in danger, remember me, and I shall save you".**

Baba Lokenath had a very ardent follower named Biharilal Mukherjee in Dhaka. Once when Biharilal was travelling by boat and was in the middle of a big river, a furious thunderstorm unexpectedly arose and threatened to overturn the boat. The passengers soon realised that the boat was beyond the control of the boatman and started to say their last prayers. Helpless and fearful Biharilal suddenly remembered the words of Baba, "If you are in danger...". The fervent prayers of the devotee did not fail to reach the ears of Baba. At that time, Anath Bandhu Mallik was sitting near Baba at Baradi ashram. Baba said to him, "O Anath! Biharilal is in danger and is praying to me. I must go and save him". Then he entered into a state of deep trance for some time. Suddenly, in the middle of the river the passengers sensed a Divine Presence on the boat as the capsizing boat slowly recovered its balance miraculously and reached its destination safely.

The miracles of Baba show how much love and compassion he had for each and every living being. There was a very ardent devotee of the Baba. After his death his son invited Baba to their house and pray for the Atman of his dead father and also have dinner with them. Though Baba did not like to attend any social event, but in this case he agreed. The night of dinner came, and all the guests came and left. The next day the man came to meet Baba. He told him that he was waiting for Baba but he had not come. Baba said he did come but he was chased away. The man was shocked who could chase Baba. Baba smiled and replied that he had come to the house in the form of a dog and tried to have some sweets. However, the servants threw him out and also beat him with sticks. He showed him the wounds which were exactly at the same places the servants beat the dog.

This is a common characteristic of all the great Yogis – it is not possible for them to love God without loving God's creatures – one cannot exist without the other. They perceive the majesty of God in each and every part of creation, and become absorbed by it. Just as an ordinary person who is in love will pay great attention and care to his lover and the relationship, great Yogis who deeply love God cannot remain indifferent to the creation of their beloved Master. So, whenever and wherever they see suffering in any of God's creatures, they do everything in their power to provide relief.

Baba Lokenath was considered the mythological wish-fulfilling tree. He believed that each and every creation is itself the very manifestation of Divinity. Once Baba spent months caring for the cubs of a distressed tigress. On another occasion, he stopped a tiger pursuing a gang of young men who had come to the hermitage to do him harm, converting them into devotees by quietly instructing the tiger to never come back to the hermitage. The animal quietly retreated into the forest. He absolutely delighted in personally feeding the ants at the hermitage and called them 'my family'. And when he ate, he would call to the birds to come and sit in his matted hair or on his lap to be fed.

Pavhari Baba was full of love for everything in the world. He would have died for an ant. Wild animals instinctively knew this old Sadhu to be their friend. Snakes and ferocious animals would go into his hold and sleep with him. They all loved him and never fought in his presence.

Yogi Gambhirnath was fond of animals – both ferocious animals and tame household pets. Ferocious animals even roamed among his attendants. These animals were very fond of Gambhirnath, and he gave them much affection and love. One night, a disciple was sleeping beside Gambhirnath's room when some noise from inside the room woke him up.

He quietly opened the door and saw Gambhirnath feeding quite a few mice with small pieces of bread with great affection.

Devraha Baba could understand the language of the animals, heal people by his look or word, give advice and tell the future. In the past he would do predictions of political future for the whole India. For that he was once arrested and only personal involvement of Indira Gandhi (ex. Prime Minister of India) helped to get him out of the jail. This holy man could not protect her but predicted (Indira Gandhi wrote about it) the day she would die.

Hanuman Das Baba of Vrindavan is one of the oldest living Sadhus on earth. Once one journalist asked him how old he was. He replied he could not remember his age, but recalled that he was twelve years old when Lakshmi Bai (the warrior queen of Jhansi) fought the British. His mother was a maid of the queen. This historical event happened in 1857 when the queen dressed as a man, fought a fierce battle and was killed in combat.

Swami Sivananda from Varanasi has a passport that puts his age at 120. The energetic monk puts his longevity down to a disciplined life of Yoga, no sex and an ordinary food habit. Acharya Ramanuja died at the age of 120. Tibbeti Baba lived for 182 years. Swami Ramanand lived for about 148 years, and predicted his death one day before.

A Londoner by the name, Alfred Arnold, was one hundred and six years old but looked about fifty. Questioned regarding his longevity he stated that all credit was due to 'Hatha Yoga' – the science of concentration, and commented, "*There is no reason why anyone using the yogic knowledge should die before he is 150 years old, my teacher told me.*" (Grewal, 1939, p. 106). At the age of seventy he came to Varanasi to experience Dharmic Spirituality and met one 147-years-old Yoga teacher. He learnt rhythmic breathing and rhythmic exercises from his teacher, and became vegetarian.

There are three types of Karma – Sanchita (stored), Prarabdha (matured), and Kriyamana (day to day). A person is destined to work out his Prarabdha Karma in the present lifetime. But a Yogi can separate his active Prarabdha Karma from the dormant Sanchita Karma. When the Yogi makes a Samyama on his Prarabdha Karma, he knows exactly when he will die, even at what hour. He can investigate the karmic potentialities of others and predict their time of death also.

> "*sopakramam nirupakramam cha karma tat samyama aparanta jnanam aristebhyah va*" (Yoga Sutras: 3.23).
> [Karma is either fast or slow to manifest; by Samyama on these Karmas comes foreknowledge of the time of death.]

Raghupati Yogi and Issaki Swamy had predicted certain dates for their deaths. Guru Gorakhnath, Swami Vishuddhananda Saraswati, Madhusudan

Saraswati and Narsinh Mehta predicted their deaths well in advance. Yogananda, few days before his death, began hinting to his disciples that it was time for him to go. Swami Vivekananda, the monk who introduced Indian Philosophy to the West, predicted that he would not live beyond forty years. He died on July 4, 1902 at the age of thirty-nine years. Two hours before his death he strictly asked others to not disturb him.

Another way a highly developed Yogi can foretell death. Future events do sometimes cast their shadows before they actually take place. A doctor, by simply placing his hand on the pulse of a terminal patient, can sometimes say with certainty that the patient is about to die. This prediction is based on certain observations he has made which is within his medical training and experience. Likewise, a real significant sign gives an indication of the coming event. In itself it may be minor and have no rational connection with the thing predicted but to the man who is highly developed spiritually it may provide a definite indication of what is to come in the future.

On September 26, 1895 Lahiri Mahasaya began gathering his disciples, letting some of them know that he would soon be leaving the body. Moments before his passing, he said simply, "I am going home. Be comforted. I shall rise again". He then turned his body to face north, and consciously left his body.

One day Trailanga Swami announced to his disciples that he would like to leave this world. He advised his devotees to make a sandalwood coffin and to put his body within, and then to throw it into the River Ganga. He entered in to Samadhi and consciously exited from the body on December 26, 1887 evening hours.

Following his directions, they placed his body in the sandalwood coffin, and after rituals lowered the coffin into the River Ganga beside which he had resided for so many years. The coffin sank to the bottom, but after some time floated to the surface. When the disciples opened the lid, they found that the box was filled with flowers, and there was no sign of the body.

Levitation is said to have occurred in numerous instances in the lives of Christian Saints, but in these cases the levitating always appeared to be involuntary. The Indian Yogi can levitate himself at will. Thousands of people have reportedly seen Trailanga Swami levitating in a sitting position on the surface of the River Ganga for days at a time, and when the water was clear he would sink to the bottom and sit in meditation for days. He could also apparently disappear under the waves for long periods, and reappear unharmed. He was reportedly seen swimming against the flow of water without moving his limbs, or remaining stationary even through the river was flowing very swiftly.

> "*udana jayat jala panka kantaka adisu asangah utkrantih cha*" (Yoga Sutras: 3.40).
> [By conquering the current called 'Udana' the Yogi does not sink in water, or in swamps, and he can levitate and walk on thorns.]

Lahiri Mahasaya could levitate at will. His wife commented that in one night she had a vivid dream. She saw that the glorious angels floated in unimaginable grace above her. So realistic was the sight that she awoke at once and the room was strangely enveloped in dazzling light. She saw Lahiri in lotus posture, was levitated in the center of the room, and surrounded by angels who were worshipping him with the supplicating dignity of palm-folded hands. Astonished beyond measure, she was convinced of still dreaming. Seeing her perplexed, Lahiri slowly descended to the floor and said, "You are not dreaming. Forsake your sleep forever and forever."

An Indian Yogi, Subbayah Pullavar, levitated for five minutes in front of about 150 witnesses on June 6, 1936 around noon on a cloudless, sunny day in South India. The Illustrated London News carried the story and photos taken from various angles by the reporters.

A person can counter the force of gravity and levitate because the physical Universe is not physical at all. It is just a play of our own conscious thinking, limited by our own consciousness. A Yogi can exceed the limitations by shifting the conscious awareness to the subtle more powerful regions of the mind. Levitation is a very common phenomenon in Pranayama practice.

During a visit to remote monasteries in the 1980s, Harvard Professor of medicine Herbert Benson and his research team studied monks living in the loving lap of the mother Himalayas who could raise the temperatures of their fingers and toes by as much as seventeen degrees by Yoga technique. It is still unknown how the monks are able to generate such heat. The researchers also studied advanced meditators in Sikkim (India) where they were astonished to find that these monks could lower their metabolism by sixty-four percent. There are reports that monks are drying cold, wet sheets with body heat alone. Some monks are spending winter nights 15,000 feet high in the Himalayas, and Tibetan Yogis can generate such body heat that they survive sitting for days on ice without any clothing needed. Sadly, such research does not get funds easily and getting it published is very difficult.

Modern-day Yogi Wim Hof astonished many scientists after he was able to use meditation to stay submerged in ice for almost two hours without his core body temperature changing one bit. He swam under the ice at the Arctic Circle for longer than anyone else. He went to climb Mount Everest in his shorts, resisted altitude sickness, completed a marathon in the Namib Desert (Southern Africa; one of the oldest and driest places on Earth) without drinking a sip of water, and proved under a laboratory setting that he was able to influence his autonomic nervous system and immune system at will. His feats of physiological control and endurance have all been verified by the scientific community. Doctors in Netherlands had injected him 'endotoxin' under laboratory conditions, but he controlled his auto-immune system to avoid any ill effects. He is the holder of twenty-six Guinness World Records. He did it basically through Pranayama.

The Atman of a Yogi can enter a fresh corpse, thus bring it back to life and make it get up and move even while his own physical body is still living. This is called 'Parakaya Pravesa' (Para – another, Kaya – body, Pravesa – entering). A Yogi of high order does this not for any personal gain but for the purpose of doing some important and necessary work for helping the humanity.

> "*bandha karana shaithilyat prachara samvedanat cha chittasya para sharira aveshah*" (Yoga Sutras: 3.39).
> [When the cause of bondage has become loosened, the Yogi by his knowledge of manifestation through the organs enters another's body.]

> "*para-kāyaṁ viśan siddha ātmānaṁ tatra bhāvayet*
> *piṇḍaṁ hitvā viśet prāṇo vāyu-bhūtaḥ ṣaḍaṅghri-vat*"
> (Bhagavad Purana: 11.15.23).
> [When a perfect Yogi desires to enter another's body, he should meditate upon himself within the other body, and then giving up his own gross body he should enter the other body through the pathways of air, as easily as a bee leaves one flower and flies into another]

Adi Shankaracharya during his victorious philosophical travels through India met Mandana Misra and had a debate with him on 'Medha Shakti' (intellectual ability) on Karma Kanda part of the Vedas. Mandana Misra resided in the town of Mahishamati (Madhya Pradesh, India). Both of them agreed on Ubhaya Bharati, a high-souled scholar, pure-hearted and utterly selfless, as one most competent to decide who was the victor in the debate. Ubhaya Bharati was the wife of Mandana Misra. The unique choice that Shankaracharya was willing to have his opponent's wife as judge in the debate was remarkable. It was the greatest testimony to his faith in the utter impartiality of Ubhaya Bharati. The debate between them continued for few months nonstop. Thousands of scholars gathered every day to watch and learn. Mandana Misra, though at a ripe old age, still remained a man with very sharp intellect and a very solid grasp of logic, but he was slowly losing because he lacked some understanding of higher spiritual truths that Shankaracharya had experienced already.

Also, Shankaracharya's realisation of the ultimate Brahmam and his knowledge of Maya enabled him to win over Misra's arguments easily.

At last Mandana Misra was almost ready to accept defeat but Ubhaya Bharati declared that in order to defeat a man in debate, the opponent should also defeat his wife – "You do know that the sacred texts enjoin that a wife forms one-half of a husband's body (the exact Sanskrit word is 'Ardhāṅgī' – 'Ardha' means half, and 'Angi' means body). Therefore, by defeating my husband, you have but won over only half of him. Your victory can be complete only when you engage in debate with me also, and manage to prove yourself better". She asked difficult questions about marital relationships and obligations, sex and family life. She knew that Shankaracharya couldn't answer such questions because of his astute Brahmacharya (celibacy). Shankaracharya asked for some time to give her the answers.

One day, through his yogic powers Shankaracharya came to know of a certain king who was about to die. His name was Amaruka. He told his disciples that he is going to enter into the body of the King Amaruka and asked his disciples to preserve his body in a cave till he returns. So, Shankaracharya became King Amaruka and went back to the king's palace. During his life as a king, he learnt all about the sexual pleasures and family life. Then he returned to his own body, went to Mandana Misra's house and answered all the questions raised by Ubhaya Bharati. This is the oldest Parakaya Pravesa story.

Tibbeti Baba (pre-monastic name Nabin Chandra Chattopadhyaya) made his Atman to permanently enter into another human body. When after wandering for many years he found that his body had grown weak, he decided to enter into the body of a Tibetan Buddhist monk who had just died. After getting the new body he did not look back to his old discarded body but walked out and resumed his wanderings and began making disciples.

Almost identical to the above, there is a case (Sobha Ram/Jasbir Lal Jat) of 'switching body' investigated by Ian Stevenson and recorded in his book, 'Twenty Cases Suggestive of Reincarnation'. Sobha Ram died while returning home from a wedding after falling from a wooden ox cart. He had eaten poisoned sweets. When Sobha Ram died, Jasbir was three and a half years old. He contracted smallpox and appeared to die. As it was night-time his burial was postponed until morning. While waiting, the father noticed Jasbir's body stirring, and eventually the child regained consciousness and strongly identified himself as Sobha Ram. In 1961, Stevenson asked Jasbir whether he had any intermission memories from between his death as Sobha Ram and the moment he entered his current body. He answered that after dying, he met a Sadhu who advised him to 'take cover' in the body of Jasbir. It means, the Atman of Sobha Ram had 'switched body' after physical death and took over the body of Jasbir to continue life on Earth. Jasbir said that in his dreams he still saw the discarnate Sadhu who had advised him to enter his current body, and claimed that he had received from this Sadhu accurate predictions of the future.

Many other Yogis had shown this power, as example, Yogi Tirumular became a cowherd. Once while travelling Tirumular saw a flock of cows grieving over the death of their herdsman, by the name Mulan. Pitying the cows, he used his yogic power and entered into Mulan's body. But his behaviour was strange. When Mulan's wife touched him, he got a shock and sat under a tree in meditation. After some time, he came in search of his original body which he hid in the hollow of a tree trunk. When he couldn't find it, he remained in Mulan's body for the rest of his life.

We have several transmigration incidents in Dharmic scriptures. Tamil Yogi Arunagirinathar became a parrot. The legendary King Yayati of Mahabharat had the power of keeping a youth-like appearance for any length of time. One person occupying the body of another is not a deterred idea since a physical body is an instrument for the work of the Atman on the physical plane.

The word 'Asteya' literally means abstaining from stealing. Here we have to take the word in a very comprehensive sense and not in terms of the penal code. Asteya is abstaining from misappropriation of all kinds, i.e., abandoning the very intent or desire to possess anything that does not belong to us. The thought of acquiring something arises out of greed, a sense of lack, powerlessness, and comparing ourselves to others. When these are eliminated, the virtue of Asteya becomes established in us.

> "*asteya pratisthayam* ***sarva ratna upasthanam***" (Yoga Sutras: 2.37). [On being firmly established in honesty **all treasure presents themselves to the Yogi.**]

We run after wealth, and sometimes we get what we want but more often we do not. This struggle fails to give us real satisfaction. But a Yogi, who had denounced everything in life, all treasures in the world appears at his beck and call. This is what the Sutra says "*sarva ratna upasthanam*". We live in the dream world of Maya, and in a dream the crown of a king and the empty bowl of a beggar have equal value.

Once Vishuddhananda Paramahansa was travelling with his friends on a high mountain. There was no food and few of them were very hungry. Vishuddhananda displayed his miraculous powers and produced food from the air. On other occasions he had produced clothing and many other articles for common use. A poor disciple asked him to produce money. But Vishuddhananda refused by saying, "No, the rupee is made by Government mint. If you want one piece of silver, I can give you that, but I am not starting a new mint here". Then he produced a bar of silver weighing approximately a pound for the poor man. The man later showed it to a silversmith who upon minute examination assured him of its genuineness and purchased it.

Numerous of his disciples had seen his numberless miracles related to subjects like travel through space in the subtle body, healing the sick and deformed and bringing back the terminally ill to life in a second, converting one form of matter into another (a copper coin into a flower, a flower into a crystal, lumps of cotton into pieces of diamond), producing scents, sweets and fruits, seeing things far distant, multiplying small amounts of food etc., into large quantities, appearing simultaneously in several distant places at the same instant, telepathy, clairvoyance, precognition, power to read minds, to see through walls and go across them without hindrance, to foretell future events and even to mentally cause or change the motion of physical objects. Yogi Vishuddhananda died in 1937 in his 'ashram' in Calcutta where many of his fine disciples are still living today.

King Pratap Narayan of Ayodhya was a devotee of Swami Bhaskarananda Saraswati. One day Bhaskarananda took him to a pond and casually asked the king to give him his diamond ring. Bhaskarananda looked at it and appreciated it deeply, and then threw it into the pond. The king was not disturbed at all. He thought, "Perhaps I was too attached to it; therefore, the Guru has thrown it into the water. Anyway, whatever his reason, it is for my good that he has done it."

Bhaskarananda and the king had a long conversation about spirituality, and then he asked the king, "Don't you want to have your ring back?" The king said, "It is all up to you. If you want to, you can give it back. Otherwise, you can let the ring remain on the bottom of the pond". Bhaskarananda said, "All right, I want to give it back to you. Now, just touch the water with your hand."

The Guru had thrown the ring from the spot where they were standing, but the king decided to go to the other side of the pond in order to see if the ring would come back to that side. As he touched the water with his hand, sixteen rings of the same type appeared. The king could not tell which one was his.

"Since you are not attached to your ring", said Bhaskarananda, "I am giving it back". Then he threw fifteen of the rings back into the pond and gave the king the one that was his own.

There is an almost similar type of incident with the King of Ujjain and Trailanga Swami. Once the king visited Varanasi, and when leaving by boat, he noticed a naked man floating on the top of the water. The man floated towards the boat and was brought on board. He was none other than Trailanga Swami.

The king had an elegant sword in his hand, given to him by the British government to honour his courage. Trailanga Swami indicated that he wished to take a closer look at the sword and the king handed it over to him. But after inspecting the sword, he tossed it into the River Ganga.

The king lost his patience and did not hide his anger at this act. Smiling sweetly at the king, Trailanga Swami plunged his hands into the river and drew out two identical swords. He asked the king to identify his own sword from the two, but the king could not, and he lowered his head in shame. In a voice as deep as the rumbling of the clouds, Trailanga Swami told the king, "Foolish man, you are unable to identify your own possessions. I see you as a man who likes to exhibit his wealth, and full of ignorance. You cannot take this sword with you to the afterworld. How can you possess a thing that you cannot take with you during your final journey? Why have you become angry over a thing that isn't yours?" Trailanga Swami gave the king his sword and threw the other one back into the water. The upset king asked for forgiveness, and without a second's hesitation Trailanga Swami granted it and then he again jumped into the river.

But how Bhaskarananda Saraswati and Trailanga Swami did the miracle?

A Yogi can collect existing atomic or molecular components which spontaneously assemble themselves into the desired object from apparent nothingness (as long as the components are not visible when suspended in air currents or on the ground) – all carefully tailored for the desired effect. When a friend of Vishuddhananda Paramahansa asked him how he produces silver from the air his reply was, "*simply out of the finer elements contained in the atmosphere which are in the silver also.* ***I can concentrate the elements*** *and produce silver*". (Grewal, 1939, p. 28). Yogi Bhola Nathji often would produce unlimited quantities of food to feed the many attending thousands though he preferred to live in his small hut. The Sanskrit word is *Prāptisiddhi* – mystic perfection of acquisition by which the Yogi can reach his hand anywhere and obtain whatever he likes.

In the year 1726 AD, Trailanga Swami came to Markandeya Ashram (on the bank of the River Narmada), and lived there with some other pious Sadhus for eight years, spending his nights completely absorbed in meditation. Khakee Baba was another Sadhu who lived there at that time. One day Khakee Baba saw a beautiful scene. All the river's water was milk, and the newly arrived Yogi was drinking it. Khakee Baba understood the vision meant that Trailanga Swami had the power to drink the milk of the river, and that Mother Narmada provided this milk for Trailanga Swami. Also wishing to drink milk from the river, Khakee Baba went to the riverbank but the moment he touched it, it was plain water once again.

No one should think that it is possible for the Yogi to do anything he likes because he can bring about many results which appear miraculous to our limited vision. Even in the exalted conditions of consciousness which the Yogi might reach in the higher stages of Yoga, he is still bound by the laws of nature. As long as his consciousness functions in the realms of nature, it is subject to the laws which govern these realms.

8.4: The danger of yogic power

"*Talk not to me of miracle, for I have left miracles behind!*"

The wisdom of a highly developed Yogi

Sage Patanjali warned against the development of supernatural powers by the practice of Samyama on different objects as they are both an attainment as well as an obstacle to spiritual progress.

"*te samadhau upasargah vyutthane siddhayah*" (Yoga Sutras: 3.38). [They are obstacles to Samadhi, but appear to be attainments or powers to the outgoing or worldly mind.]

Some great Sadhaks who have graced this earth have made ample use of those powers and abilities while others have walked right through them as if they did not exist at all though they were celebrated for severe austerity and corresponding magical powers. Hence, we must realise that there is nothing "must-have" about the acquiring or displaying of these supernatural powers.

When an ordinary person gets interested in Yoga he is still under the domination of ordinary desires, such as power and fame. He may not be conscious of this desire but deep down in his subconscious mind it lurks ready to come up when favourable conditions are present. Now, in the practice of Yoga his lower self sees an opening for acquiring extraordinary powers of all kinds. However, if he makes a deeper study of the subject, he realises that the occult powers which interested him so much are also part of that illusory side of life (Maya) which is the object of Yoga to exceed. In other words, quite often miracles only feed curiosity, and there is a big difference between curiosity and aspiration.

The occult powers cannot bring him enlightenment and peace. It is only when he has completely conquered his lower nature, he can safely exercise these powers for the helping of others, if necessary. Till then his interest in them should be merely to unravel the mystery of life which surrounds him.

To some critics these powers are not really miracles, but the hidden revelations of the forces of nature through which the Yogi passes when one rises from one realm to another realm. In each realm a particular law operates, just as different laws operate in different countries. When one gains entry into a higher realm, he operates with the law of that realm. To a lower realm that upper law looks like a miracle. Thus, what may appear supernatural to a scientist or a layperson may seem perfectly natural to an advanced Yogi.

Power displayed without moral purpose is a poor reason to do Sadhana. Hence, the real Yogis maintain an attitude of utter indifference towards them, and show no interest to the gazer or to the tourist photographer. For instance, Sri Ramakrishna had discarded his attained paranormal powers as futile, vain, and heaps of rubbish. Ramana Maharshi explained that the supernatural powers are not natural to the Self. That which is not natural but acquired cannot be permanent, and thus is not worth striving for.

> "*yunjannevam sadaa'tmaanam yogee niyatamaanasah*
> *shaantim nirvaanaparamaam matsamsthaam adhigacchati*"
> (Bhagavad Gita: 6.15).
> [Thus, always keeping the mind balanced, with his mind controlled, the Yogi attains to the peace abiding in Me – the peace that culminates in total liberation – Nirvana or Moksha.]

Here a logical question arises. Why do the Yogis perform miracles that are witnessed by others if demonstrating their supernatural powers are not their intent? The answer is that such magical powers are merely an incidental by-product rather than an end in themselves. Modern science does not have the last word with regard to God's creation. The infinite wealth of the inner world can easily silence all the achievements of mankind in the outer world.

An ordinary person cannot understand how anyone can possess supernatural powers and yet not even let other people know that he is different from others. Therefore, he naturally concludes that because such powers have never been exhibited in the public, they either do not exist or those who can exercise them are no longer living in the world. There is an interesting story of Mughal Emperor Akbar and Goswami Tulsidas – the creator of 'Ramcharit Manas', most respected by the devotees of Lord Ram. When Akbar heard that Tulsidas had great powers, that he was a 'Siddha Purush' he sent officers to fetch him to court. The emperor spoke of his fame and asked him to perform a miracle. When Tulsidas refused, claiming any and all power rests with Lord Ram, the emperor threw him in the prison. Soon a miracle took place. The City of Delhi was immediately besieged by an army of marauding huge, giant-like monkeys. These monkeys, hundreds and thousands in number, started demolishing the entire city. They threatened everybody, and it was a ravaging experience. Nobody could come out of the house. Soon they started attacking the palace of Akbar himself, and the guards ran away. It was all confusion, and they did not know what had happened.

Akbar did not realise what was happening. Then someone told him, "We have made a mistake in imprisoning Tulsidas. Release him. He is a devotee of Lord Ram, and so Lord Ram's army must have come". Then Akbar released him and apologised. This story shows that when we wrongly oppose a man of power, his power is seen, otherwise we cannot see the power. Similarly, often the powers of a Yogi are not known, as they are hidden.

A careful study of history and other relevant literature will prove conclusively that such powers have been exercised by people practically in all ages. There are people living in the present who can exercise these powers even though they may be difficult to find and may refuse to show these powers to anyone except the trusted disciples.

8.5: Conclusion

Quantum physics and Yoga Philosophy lead to the same conclusion that our consciousness shapes the world.

The eleventh century Buddhist mystic, Jetsun Milarepa had performed such a miracle in a remote Tibetan cave that modern scientists say should simply not exist. To show his mastery of the physical world, Milarepa had placed his open hand against the cave's wall at shoulder level, and then continued to push his hand deep into the rock in front of him as if the rock was not solid at all. Soon the rock beneath his palm became soft and malleable as he left the imprint of his hand deeply embedded in the stone for all to see. The solid rock had really been softened by his touch. What did he change within himself that allowed him to defy the 'laws' that two physical things – like human flesh and a rock – can't be in the same place, at the same time? A Tibetan translator explained,

> "*He has belief. The 'geshe' [Tibetan word for great teacher] believes that he and the rock are not separate. The rock cannot contain him. To him, this cave is not a wall, so he can move freely as if the rock does not exist.*" (Braden, 2008, p. 7).

The qualities of a cave's stone wall depend upon the way we think of them. We believe that the rock was a barrier to the human body, but Yogi Milarepa did not. Both views are correct – it's all about what we choose to believe. The father of quantum physics Max Planck had quoted in 'The Observer' on January 25, 1931 that,

*"**I regard consciousness as fundamental. I regard matter as derivative from consciousness.** We cannot get behind consciousness. Everything that we talk about, everything that we regard as existing, postulates consciousness*". (Fredriksson, 2015, p. 5).

Yogi Vishuddhananda Paramahansa could see through solid walls and go across them without hindrance. Once a disciple put a question to him, "Baba, is there any difference between a Yogi's body and that of an ordinary person, seemingly they look so much alike?" Baba just pushed his hand through a wall which was quite a distance away, by just elongating his arm and his hand was visible on the other side of the wall.

The discarnate spiritual teacher Seth spoke the same truth – Consciousness creates matter. We live in a Maya world. The more we understand the Yoga Philosophy and Seth Material, the less far-fetched this suggestion becomes.

The ancient sages had reminded us again and again that the great secret of creation itself lives within each of us – the power to create in the world what we've imagined in our beliefs. Evidence suggests that the Universe works precisely this way, and is just this simple. In recent years quantum physics has come very close to the ancient Dharmic Philosophy of the Samkhya and Yoga. Yoga is not only scientific; it is more scientific than the modern science yet to discover, that the science of raising human consciousness progressively into higher levels of existence. And when this is done, the mind possesses unlimited power that it can control the earth. The ancient sages gave us all this knowledge absolutely free.

Patanjali's Yoga and 'Siddhis' are worthy of serious study because several of these practices are quite relevant to the research in parapsychology. Parapsychology addresses three major types of paranormal phenomena – Direct knowing (one acquires accurate knowledge or information about events or experiences beyond the reach of the conventional senses), Direct mental influence (telekinesis and psychokinesis), and the last one is afterlife evidence. Many of these closely resemble the attainments (Siddhis) described by Patanjali. Hence the study of the 'Siddhis' could help in elaborating the nature of some superpower manifestations already familiar to the researchers and also could help reveal other forms that have not yet been explored in parapsychology. If investigators engage in yogic practices personally, they will be able to plan and conduct their research projects more creatively and interpret their findings more accurately.

India is indeed a land of mysteries to the rest of the world. This is due to the reason that no other country has so thoroughly studied the Atman – the Quantum Consciousness – as India has done. Modern scientific knowledge suffers from the great defect that it is divorced from knowledge of the inner nature of things with which it deals. In comparison, yogic philosophy integrates all aspects of manifestation (matter and consciousness) into one comprehensive whole. In fact, the theory and practice of Yoga is based upon this idea of interdependence. The extraordinary powers which are acquired through yogic practices show that the fundamental basis of the yogic doctrine is correct. Yoga is equally significant for the ancient era as well as the modern era.

Yoga Philosophy is spreading very fast in the western world. In recent years, quantum physicists have started to explore how meditation may influence the surrounding physical world. This research, as typically characteristic of most work in quantum physics, appears to contradict concepts of classic Newtonian Physics.

Yoga and meditation unleash our inherent supernormal mental powers. Some scientists tried to explain these powers by String theory. According to String theory, the point particles of matter may also be thought of as one-dimensional strings. These strings can oscillate in many ways and each oscillation mode gives rise to a different species of particles with mass, charge, and other properties determined by the string's dynamics. These strings can split and recombine, and all possible events exist simultaneously as probability wave patterns that are either becoming real or disintegrating. A field can be deciphered, altered, molded, and analysed outside of the body to alter the energies inside the body and vice versa. Theories suggest that the ancient Eastern methods of Yoga may be able to access control these vibrations, at least within our own physical bodies and brain structures. This way the realities are changed which we call miracle.

The special experiences and powers that result from performing 'Samyama' on various gross and subtle objects can be explained by quantum entanglement that can cross the barrier of space and time. Following experiment supports this view.

Israeli Physicist Dr. Eli Megidish and his colleagues had conducted a path-breaking experiment in 2013. This experiment is a wonderful demonstration of temporal non-locality on quantum entanglement between two photons. An entangled pair of photons was generated that had never coexisted. Using entanglement swapping between two temporally separated photon pairs, one photon was entangled from the first pair with another photon from the second pair. The first photon was detected even before the other was created. The observed two-photon state demonstrates that entanglement can be shared between time-like separated quantum systems.

And, if such entanglement is possible, then it is also possible to influence the past. Montgomery (1969, p. 58) recorded a case that during

1927, Jane Winthrop regressed a woman, Barbara Larson to the age of nine. Barbara spoke as a little boy who lived in New York (around 1860s), but did not know where her parents were. Jane told Barbara to speak to her grandmother (of past-life). In response, Barbara paused as listening, and then replied, "Granny says how many times I told you they aren't here. Now stop asking me". If present cannot influence the past, how Barbara (living in 1927), interacted with her past-life grandmother (living around 1860s) and had a meaningful conversation with her?

Atwater (1999b, pp. 197-98) recorded that in the early 1970s, past-life regression therapist Dolores Cannon developed a unique method for discerning 'lost' information from people she hypnotically regressed into past lives. In so doing, she found that one of her clients was a student of Nostradamus in a past life, and eventually, Nostradamus himself showed up from the 'past' as energy presence and started talking through the client in trance in the 'present'. Dolores had used a mirror in her study for a focal point in her communications. She had an uncanny feeling that Nostradamus was quite alive in his time frame in France when they linked together and he was receiving the material from the present that he used to write his quatrains in the past. Years later she read in one of his biographies that Nostradamus claimed his revelations came from 'spirits of future' who spoke to him through a mirror.

Dolores actually entangled her consciousness with Nostradamus at quantum level though she was not a trained Yogi. In her technique she merged together the chasm of time – past, present and future. Was Dolores the source of the foreknowledge of Nostradamus? When a highly developed Yogi applies Samyama with the objects or people, he actually entangles his consciousness with them at the quantum level. By this way he not only overcomes the barrier of space but also time. Two photons that exist at separate times and space can be entangled. Likewise, the Yogi through this Samyama/entanglement can receive information about the past, present and future of the object of his focus. This might sound like a third-rated science fiction but it isn't. He has achieved this power through spiritual Sadhana.

Yoga techniques transform an ascetic internally, and this internal transformation affects the external world of the ascetic along with people who share his/her world. All of us are capable of miracles if we go through spiritual Sadhana. We are really very powerful beings in disguise, and we are born into this world with capabilities beyond our wildest dreams. Our powerlessness is an illusion. This is what the leading-edge discoveries are showing us today and what the great Yogis had discovered for themselves in the ancient past.

Chapter - 9

Final conclusion

"I am convinced that everything has come down to us from the banks of the Ganges [the most sacred River Ganga] – astronomy, astrology, metempsychosis, etc..."

Voltaire

"The basic elements of the Eastern world-view are also those of the world-view emerging from modern science."

Dr. Fritjof Capra

"India has never exported war, conflict or terror. She is best known for the Gurus, the Vedas, meditation, Yoga and wisdom and when a Westerner is looking to answer the big questions of life, they travel to India. Yet the whole history of India is the West trying to civilize her."

Patrick Brauckmann

The well-known German Philosopher Augustus Schlegel wrote in his book 'Wisdom of the Ancient Indians' in regard to the divine origin of Vedic civilisation,

"It cannot be denied that the early Indians possessed a knowledge of the God. All their writings are replete with sentiments and expressions, noble, clear, severely grand, as deeply conceived in any human language in which men have spoken of their God...". (Knapp, 2000, p. vii).

The Western world has lost its heart and blocked its way to true wisdom by materialistic supremacy. But it does not signify in any way the state of culture in a country. India is behind the West in its material development, but the West is very far behind India in its inward development in knowledge of the Self – the Atman. In this respect, India is the 'Heart of the World'. The knowledge of the Vedas and all other literature, such as Lord Krishna's message in Bhagavad Gita, the teachings of the Upanishads and Puranas are not limited to only Indians but such knowledge is actually meant for the whole world. Everyone should be given the right and privilege to understand this knowledge because everyone is a spiritual being and has the same spiritual essence.

For last several thousand years Sanatan Dharma had undergone many reform movements in which the basic enduring trait of Dharma had been shaped, sustained and straightened like a centre-of-gravity-doll. The ancient sages were the forerunners of all the reform movements. The Dharma specified in Rig Veda is simple and elegant. The sages added meditation and formulated a pious life style for all the adherents.

Lord Krishna heralded the second reform movement. He set at rest all disputes regarding the relative superiority of Jnana, Bhakti, Karma and Raja over one another and brought about a balance and harmony among these various forms of spiritual disciplines. The clear declaration that one must perform one's duty and contribute to the social welfare is Lord Krishna's greatest contribution to Sanatan Dharma. His continuously active life itself was a glorious demonstration of his philosophy.

Soon after the Vedic era, a lowly section of the priest class (Brahmin sect) had deteriorated the very essence of Dharma. As these lowly people became powerful, many superstitions crept in, and the caste system took firm and deep roots in the society. Mutual hatred based on castes and untouchability, and consequent conflicts raised their ugly heads. Caste is another name for control that puts a limit on human rights. During this time Mahavira Jain and the great Buddha initiated the third reform movement. All the dry and useless logic that the lowly priest class had given to control common masses were substituted by simple but life-giving moral and ethical principles to bring peace and joy in the society.

Neither in the Vedas nor in other scriptures there is any sanction for caste system and untouchability. These are the handiwork of ignorant and selfish people with extremely narrow-minded visions. Many sages of immense wisdom born in the lower caste and among the 'untouchables' were honoured by the entire society is proof enough for this controversy. As example, Vidura, the famous wise man of the Mahabharat was the son of Parishrami – a Shudra woman. In Mahabharat, Vidura is described as the incarnation of Dharma (Adi Parva 63, 95), Dharma became Vidura (Asrama Parva 28, 21), and he used to give religious instructions when king wanted it (Udyoga Parva 33-41).

Rishi Kapinjalada was a Chandal and Rishi Madanapala was the son of a low caste boatwoman (Anushasana Parva 53.13-19), Rishi Matanga was the son of a Shudra woman. In fact, Shudras are often addressed as

'Matanga' in passages like Varaha Purana 1.139.91. Rishi Kakshivat was the son of Usij – a Shudra maid servant (Brihaddevata 4.24-25). The great Rishi Vasistha was born of Urvashi – a nymph, and Rishi Parashar was born of Adyashyanti – a Chandal woman. Rishi Veda Vyasa (Krishna Dvaipayana), who had compiled Vedas, Mahabharat and Puranas, setting the foundation for Sanatan Dharma through history and India's first nation builder, was born of Satyavati – a lowly fisher-woman. Rishi Vishvamitra was not a Brahmin by birth but a valiant warrior, but he was the first Rishi of this 'Kalpa' (the present cycle of creation) who could access all powers of Gayatri Mantra. Satyakam Jabali, the composer of the celebrated Jabali Upanishad, was born to an unwed Shudra mother and his father's name was unknown. Mahabharat (Vana Parva 180) mentions that social position is determined by conduct, not by birth. It is the intellectual and spiritual level that differentiates people. If a highborn man argues that another class is 'untouchable' or of 'lower caste' because they had earned their lowly status through misdeeds in past lives, then he overlooks the possibility that by his own heartless disregard for human suffering he may be earning a similar fate in his next incarnation. Just as our deeds of yesterday can forge today's destiny, so our present conduct will determine our future fate.

There is a very interesting incident in the life of Adi Shankaracharya. One day when Shankaracharya was on his way back from the River Ganga at Varanasi after midday ablutions with his disciples, a drunken raggedly-dressed Chandal approached them with a pack of four dogs. Chandal is the one who looks after the crematorium. To avoid any touch, the disciples hurriedly asked him to keep out of their path. The Chandal replied, "Whom do you want to move, my body or my Atman, the form or the formless, the limited or the limitless?" Shankaracharya was struck with the Chandal's 'Atma Jnana' (Spiritual knowledge of the Self).

The Chandal continued, "This body has its source in the same material food, and performs the same functions irrespective of a Brahmin or a Chandal. If the question is addressed to the Atman – the consciousness – the Atman is the same which is unaffected by anything of the body. How do differences such as 'This is a Brahmin, this is a Chandal' arise in the non-dual experience? Is the sun changed in the least whether its reflection in seen in a pot containing liquor or in the holy Ganga? Is the reflection of the sky in a golden pot different from the one in the mud pot? The one Universal Consciousness, is shining alike in all bodies – is this not the truth?"

This incident had a deep impact on Shankaracharya who realised no one should be differentiated, and at the end the Atman is beyond all other things. Earlier he used to follow the principles where purity and pollution mattered, but now he has realised his mistake when the Chandal taught him a lesson of the unity of the Supreme Consciousness with a piercing satire. As a teacher of Advaita propagating the one Brahmam in all, he immediately recognised that the Chandal taught him his own philosophy correctly. Shankaracharya prostrated before the Chandal by accepting him as his Guru, and conveyed his new wisdom through his composition called Manisha Panchakam.

> "*brahma eva aham idam jagat cha sakalam, chit maatra vistaaritam;*
> *Sarvam cha etad avidyayaa trigunayaa ashesham mayaa kalpitam;*
> ***Ittham yasya dridhaa matih sukhatare, nitye pare nirmale***
> ***Chandaalah astu sah tu dvijah astu guruh iti, eshaa maneeshaa mama***"
> (Manisha Panchakam: Stotra no. 2).
> [I am pure Consciousness, and this entire universe, is only an expansion of pure Consciousness. Out of this Maya all this that we see, made of the three gunas, has been conjured by imagination. **He whose intellect is firmly established in the all blissful, eternal, Supreme Reality, be he a Chandal or be he a Brahmin, such a one is indeed worthy of being a Guru. This is my firm conviction.**]

Sanatan Dharma has equal space for everyone. Many revered holy men of India hailed from so-called untouchable sects, such as, Bhakta Namdev (he was a ruthless bandit), Bhakta Chokhamela (he used to peel off skin of dead animals), Acharya Kanchipurna (the Guru of Ramanuja was a Shudra by birth), Guru Raidas (belonged to the family of the cobblers), Poet-saint Thiruvalluvar (a lower caste weaver) and the fourteenth century ascetic Swami Ramdev (belonged to lower caste). Rani Rashmoni, the founder of the Dakshineswar Kali Temple, belonged to a Shudra family. These examples show that the lower-caste communities have long had a crucial role in the formulation of Sanatan Dharma.

But in the course of time, the teachings of Mahavira Jain and Buddha were misunderstood and misapplied. As a result, a large number of people started deserting the Vedic Dharma. This is the time fourth reform movement took place when Adi Shankaracharya appeared on the scene to resuscitate and reestablish Dharma. He preached that Brahmam or Atman is the fundamental and only reality from which everything else has evolved. Hence, untouchability and caste conflicts are not only meaningless, but the height of ignorance leading to self-destruction. In a short span of life Shankaracharya had travelled all over India (undivided) to restore Dharma.

Then came a series of invasions by savage tribes, and the impact was felt both at the social and at the spiritual levels. At this critical period, a series of great spiritual leaders, like Ramanuja, Madhva, Vallabha, Chaitanya, Sankaradeva, Basava, Ramananda, Guru Nanak, Goswami

Tulsidas, Mirabai, Tukaram, Purandaradasa and many others descended on the sacred soil of India, and protected Dharma, culture and society from the onslaughts of these alien hordes. Dharma might have disappeared from its own land if these great spiritual teachers were not there. This was the fifth reform movement.

Sanatan Dharma is central to the soul of India as a nation. India's place in human history is to function as the global spiritual guide rooted in it. Temples, Mathas (monastic seats) and the pilgrimage sites are the backbone of Sanatan Dharma civilisation. While Islamic invaders tried to destroy Sanatan Dharma through violent attacks against Indian natives, the British invaders used Christian missionaries to come to India and convert people. The first Muslim invasion of India was by the Arabs who were led by Mohammad Bin Qasim in 711 AD. During a period from 1001 AD to 1030 AD Muhammad Bin Ghazni invaded India for seventeen times. Mahommad Ghori began invasion in 1173 AD and continued till his death at 1206 AD. A Muslim army led by the Turkish invader Bakhtiyar Khilji destroyed the Nalanda Mahavira (founded in the fourth Century BC) in 1193 AD which was regarded as one of the greatest seats of learning of the ancient world. Chenghiz Khan marched on Lahore and sacked it on 1241 AD. Of his inroads, the most terrible was under Taimur in 1398 AD, Babar in 1526 AD, Nadir Shah 1738 AD and Ahmadshsh Abdalli in 1761 AD. The need to know the history is not to spread hate but in fact to appreciate the sacrifice and learn from it so that today's generation strive to stop making the same mistakes again. Will Durant (1942, p. 459) wrote,

> "***The Mohammedan Conquest of India is probably the bloodiest story in history.*** *It is a discouraging tale, for its evident moral is that civilisation is a precarious thing, whose delicate complex of order and liberty, culture and peace may at any time be overthrown by barbarians invading from without or multiplying within.*"

Islamic invasions were prompted by two factors – to establish Islam by forcefully converting or by destroying the non-Muslims and putting the women and children in slavery, and the urge to loot India's riches. Many pious women committed mass suicide by self-immolation (sometimes along with their children), known as 'Jauhar' (also spelt as Jowhar or Juhar) – jumping into a pit of massive fire to avoid capture, enslavement and rape by the invading Muslim army usually when there was no chance of victory. They valued their chastity, honour and self-respect more highly than their lives. Occasionally, even the dead bodies were not spared by these invaders whose necrophiliac tendencies are well-recorded in history.

The British East India Company, a violent and rapacious enterprise supported by the British Crown, came to India as traders in spices on

August 24, 1608, at the port of Surat. Soon the company started intruding in Indian politics and saw a steady rise in their fortunes. After the Battle of Buxar (fought on October 22/23, 1764) the company started to transform from a trading company to a ruling one. The powers of the East India Company kept growing, but after the revolt of 1857 it was dissolved and the British Crown took direct control of India to begin the British rule. The imperial rule destroyed India's thriving industries of textiles, shipbuilding and steel through violence, heavy taxes, import tariffs and by imposing their exports and products on the back of the Indian customer. British invaders extorted vast sums of money through torture and cruelty that they shifted to Britain.

Much of the Britain's prosperity was built on the drainage of resources from India. In 1700, India was world's richest country, about twenty-seven percent of global GDP. But in 1947 when India achieved independence, the nation had been reduced to one of the world's poorest countries with just over three percent of global GDP. India would have been a much richer, prosperous and educated country without the British. Will Durant (1930, p. 2) put it, "***England has year by year been bleeding India to the point of death… the most sordid and criminal exploitation of one nation by another in all recorded history***".

In addition to demolishing the economy, the British inflicted massive suffering on Indian people. According to some estimates, some thirty-five million Indians died because of British policy in a succession of famines. The Bengal famine, during 1943-44 claimed over four million lives, and is said to have been engineered as part of an unsympathetic and ruthless economic agenda. The British Prime Minister Winston Churchill ignored farmers' pleas for emergency food aid, living millions to starve as their rice paddy fields were forcibly turned over to jute production. The British did not intend to end the misery caused by the famine, but instead devised a strategy to prolong the starvation. According to the 'Crimes of Britain', during the Bihar famine of 1873, the starving people, in what the empire called the 'distance test', were made to walk over ten miles to and from the relief works. In 1843, Governor-General Charles Hardinge said the construction of railways would benefit the empire for commercial profit and military control of India. Several thousand Indians died during the construction of the rail-roads by Indian taxpayers' money. Jallianwala Bagh massacre (also known as the Amritsar massacre) was one of the greatest atrocities of British rule. It took place on April 13, 1919 when Acting Brigadier-General Reginald Dyer ordered troops of the British Indian Army to fire their rifles into a crowd of unarmed Indian civilians in Jallianwala Bagh killing at least 400, including forty-one children, and over 1,000 were injured.

When Thomas Babington Macaulay toured India between 1834 and 1838, he was shocked to see the cultural superiority of India and also the wealth of India. Macaulay wrote,

> "*I have travelled across the length and breadth of India and I have not seen one person who is a beggar, who is a thief. Such wealth I have seen in this country, such high moral values, people of such caliber, that* ***I do not think we would ever conquer this country, unless we break the very backbone of this nation, which is her spiritual and cultural heritage****, and, therefore, I propose that we replace her old and ancient education system, her culture, for* ***if the Indians think that all that is foreign and English is good and greater than their own, they will lose their self-esteem, their native self-culture and they will become what we want them, a truly dominated nation***." (Kumar, 2017, p. 17).

Macaulay and other conspirators soon initiated a 'civilising mission' to convince Indians that anything European is superior and anything Indian is inferior. They preached the English language to be superior to Sanskrit and other vernacular languages and Indian scriptures inferior to anything European.

As a reaction to this, came the sixth reform movement aiming at restoring the Dharma. Raja Ram Mohan Roy, Swami Dayanand Saraswati, Mahadeva Govinda Ranade, Annie Besant, Dr. Ayyathan Gopalan, Baba Amte, Sri Ramakrishna Paramhansa Dev, Swami Vivekananda, and Vinoba Bhave were the important leaders of this movement. Before the advent of these leaders the state of Sanatan Dharma was same as the state of Christianity in the West today. Sanatan Dharma appeared to have lost its ancient influence, and the challenges were pouring over its head from every side, not only from missionaries but from within also. Those who had read two pages of science were questioning the ancient wisdom of Dharma. Christian missionaries took this advantage and converted some Indians to Christianity through deception.

Max Mueller initiated English translation of Vedic scriptures to destroy the spirit of India and to create a class of Indians who would doubt their own scriptures. His attempt was to show Indian Vedic Culture to be inferior to Christianity. He wanted Indians to accept Christianity to a large extent. The third British Colonialist, Herbert Hope Risley (a race scientist) imposed British designed caste system on Indians. This is very well recorded in history. However, their imposition of English as a superior language of sorts worked as a double-edged sword against them. They underestimated the intellect of Indian leaders who intelligently used the English language in a more forcible way to defeat British propaganda and to protect the rich cultural ethos of Indians. All the missionary hopes were scattered in this sixth reform movement.

Many spiritual institutions, such as Brahmo Samaj (founded by Raja Ram Mohan Roy and Dwarkanath Tagore on August 20, 1828), Arya Samaj (founded by Dayanand Saraswati on April 7, 1875) and the Ramakrishna Mission (founded by Swami Vivekananda on May 1, 1897) had also participated in this movement. Although these movements vary individually in their specific philosophies, they generally stress the spiritual, secular, logical and scientific aspects of the Vedic traditions irrespective of caste, creed and culture. As a result of their ceaseless and even aggressive efforts, Sanatan Dharma not only recovered its balance but made inroads into the strongholds of the Western culture and civilisation. In the early twentieth century, the leaders of Arya Samaj openly converted many notable Christians and Muslims to Sanatan Dharma through 'Shuddhi' (purification) ceremony, set up schools and Vedic organisations. Dayanand Saraswati started his Vedic campaign at Kumbh-mela in Haridwar during 1867. Swami Shraddhanand (also known as Mahatma Munshiram) carried on his mission without deviating from this path. On December 23, 1926 Swami Shraddhanand paid the ultimate sacrifice when he was assassinated by a Muslim fanatic Abdul Rashid.

Soon the mission extended its activities outside India, such as Guyana, Trinidad and Tobago, Suriname, the Caribbean, the Netherlands, the United Kingdom, and the United States. For last few decades, the reform movement has gained further strength through the lives and works of Ramana Maharshi, Sri Aurobindo and a series of spirituo-cultural organisations.

For thousands of years, education through Gurukul system was centered around temples. The temples were also a major conduit for social assistance, social reform, research, culture, education, thought leadership, traditions, social justice and social well-being. Islamic invaders and British colonialists recognised this fact early on. While Islamic invaders destroyed the ancient temples, the British initiated policies to control the temples to extract revenues. British claims on development efforts in India have been conclusively defeated by facts already reported by many researchers. British did nothing for India, except looting.

Both Islamic and British invaders actually brought poverty and bloodshed to India. Islamic rule can be compared to cats prowling on a mouse that was the level of violence against the natives of India. Both were eventually defeated by the inherent strength of Sanatan Dharma.

Sanatan Dharma holds people together by providing them a universal and all-encompassing spiritual vision of reality, a new system of humanistic values, and a radically different general strategy of life. The wisdom and path provided by Sanatan Dharma is beyond time, and hence a Dharmic is scientific and spiritual simultaneously. The latest scientific men are coming to ancient sages, and as far as they have done so, there is perfect agreement. Sanatan Dharma, with its passion for truth and human welfare, will always remain as one of the noblest pursuits of man. In this age of science, freedom and equality, all major religions find themselves at the cross-road of history but Sanatan Dharma will survive and prosper by growing new roots in the changed scene.

References

1. Abhedananda, Swami (1905); Vedanta Philosophy: Self-Knowledge (Atman-Jnana), The Vedanta Society, West Cornwall, GB.
2. Ariel, Aurora Juliana (2010); Earth 2012: The Violet Age: A Return to Eden, Aeos, Inc, California.
3. Atwater, P. M. H. (1994); Beyond the Light: What Isn't Being Said About Near-death Experience. Birch Lane Press, NY.
4. Atwater, P. M. H. (1999a); Children of the New Millennium: Children's Near-Death Experiences and the Evolution of Humankind, Three Rivers Press, NY.
5. Atwater, P.M.H (1999b); Future Memory, Hampton Roads Publishing Company Inc. Charlottesville, Virginia.
6. Atwater, P. M. H. (2007); The Big Book of Near-Death Experiences: The Ultimate Guide to What Happens When We Die, Hampton Roads, Charlottesville, Virginia.
7. Bailey, Lee W. and Yates, Jenny (1996); The Near-Death Experience: A Reader, Routledge, Abingdon, UK.
8. Besant, Annie (1973); Thought Power: Its Control and Culture, Theosophical Publishing House, Adyar, Chennai, India.
9. Braden, Gregg (2008); The Spontaneous Healing of Belief: Shattering the Paradigm of false limits, Hay House Inc., USA.
10. Chattopadhyaya, Rajagopal (1999); Swami Vivekananda in India: A Corrective Biography, Motilal Banarsidass Publishers Pvt Ltd, New Delhi, India.
11. Corey, Michael Anthony, (1993); God and the New Cosmology: The Anthropic Design Argument, Rowman & Littlefield Publishers Inc., Maryland, USA.
12. Cunningham, Paul F. (2009); An Experimental Investigation of Past-Life Experiences, A research proposal document, August, 2009.
13. Curtiss, Homer Frank (1949); Reincarnation, Willing Publishing Company, San Gabriel, California.
14. Davies, Paul (1982); The Accidental Universe. Cambridge University Press, Cambridge.
15. Davies, Paul (1984); Superforce: The Search for a Grand Unified Theory of Nature, Simon & Schuster Inc., NY.

16. Dhar, T. N (2004); Exploring the Mysterious, Mittal Publications, New Delhi, India.
17. Dirac, Paul Adrien Maurice (1963); The Evolution of the Physicist's Picture of Nature, Scientific American, Vol. 208, issue no. 5 (May 1963).
18. Durant, Will (1930); The Case for India, Simon & Schuster Inc., NY.
19. Durant, Will (1942); The Story of Civilisation – Our Oriental Heritage, Vol. 1, Simon & Schuster Inc., NY.
20. Flew, Antony (2008); There is a GOD: How the World's Most Notorious Atheist Changed His Mind, HarperOne, NY.
21. Fredriksson, Ingrid (2015); The Mysteries of Consciousness: Essays on Spacetime, Evolution and Well-Being, McFarland & Company, North Carolina, USA.
22. Gibson, Arvin S. (2006); They Saw Beyond Death: New insights on near-death experiences, Horizon Publishers & Distributors, Springville, Utah, USA.
23. Goldberg, Bruce (1982); Past lives, Future lives, Ballantine Books, NY.
24. Goldberg, Bruce (2004); Past lives, future lives revealed, New Page Books, a division of The Career Press Inc., New Jersey.
25. Grewal, Rishi Singh (1939); Lives and teachings of the Yogis of India, (Vol. 2), Mahatma Gandhi Yoga Ashram, Santa Barbara, Calif, USA.
26. Gribbin, John (2000); The Search for Superstrings, Symmetry, and the Theory of Everything, Little, Brown & Company, NY.
27. Grof, Stanislav (1988); The adventure of self-discovery: Dimensions of consciousness and new perspectives in psychotherapy and inner exploration, State University of New York Press, Albany.
28. Grof, Stanislav (2019); Psychology of the Future: Lessons from Modern Consciousness Research, Dev Publishers and Distributors, New Delhi, India.
29. Gustus, Sandie (2011); Less Incomplete: A Guide to Experiencing the Human Condition beyond the Physical Body, O-books, Alresford, UK.
30. Hasurkar, Shrinath Shripad (1958); Vachaspati Misra on Advaita Vedanta, Darbhanga, India.
31. Hawking, Stephen (1998); A brief history of time, Bantam Press, NY.
32. Hawking, Stephen and Mlodinow, Leonard (2010); The Grand Design, Bantam Press, NY.
33. Hogan, Craig (2008); Your eternal self, Greater reality publications.
34. Jackson, Carl (1994); Vedanta for the West: the Ramakrishna Movement in the United States, Indiana University Press, Bloomington, USA.
35. Jacob, T. R (1975); Concept of Self in Indian Thought, Master's thesis, Faculty of the Graduate School, Marquette University, USA.
36. Jahn, Robert George (2001); The challenge of consciousness. The Journal of Scientific Exploration, vol. 15, issue 4.
37. Knapp, Stephen (2000); Proof of Vedic Culture's Global Existence, The World Relief Network, Baltimore, USA.
38. Knapp, Stephen (2006); The Power of the Dharma: An Introduction to Hinduism and Vedic Culture, iUniverse, Inc. Lincoln, USA.

39. Krishnadas, Suril Kristi (2010); Bhagavad Gita – the Spiritual Song, Trafford Publishing, Victoria BC, Canada.
40. Kumar, Ravi (2017); Glimpses of Hindu Genius, Suruchi Prakashan, New Delhi, India.
41. Lal, Rajendra Behari (1978); Religion in the light of reason and science, Bharatiya Vidya Bhavan, Mumbai, India.
42. Lanza, Robert (2009); Biocentrism: How Life and Consciousness are the Keys to Understanding the True Nature of the Universe, BenBella Books, Dallas, Texas.
43. Laughlin, Robert B. (2005); A Different Universe: Reinventing physics from the bottom down, Basic Books, NY.
44. Laureys, Steven and Tononi, Giulio (2009); The Neurology of Consciousness: Cognitive Neuroscience and Neuropathology, Elsevier Ltd, London.
45. Leane, Elizabeth (2007); Reading Popular Physics: Disciplinary Skirmishes and Textual Strategies, Ashgate Publishing Ltd, Aldershot, UK.
46. Leslie, John (1988); How to Draw Conclusions from a Fine-Tuned Cosmos. In Robert Russell, et al., eds., Physics, Philosophy and Theology: A Common Quest for Understanding. Vatican Observatory Press, Vatican City.
47. Leslie, John (1989); Universe, Routledge, NY.
48. Leslie, John (2001); Infinite Minds: A philosophical Cosmology, Clarendon Press, Oxford University Press, NY.
49. Lewis, James R. (2004); The Encyclopedic Sourcebook of New Age Religions, Prometheus Books, Amherst, NY.
50. Montgomery, Ruth (1969); Here and Hereafter, Fawcett Crest, NY.
51. Montgomery, Ruth (1972); A world beyond, Fawcett Crest, NY.
52. Montgomery, Ruth (1976); The world before, Fawcett Crest, NY.
53. Moody, Raymond and Perry, Paul (1988); The Light Beyond, Bantam books, NY.
54. Murray, Michael J. (1999); Reason for the Hope Within, William B. Eerdmans Publishing Company, Cambridge, UK.
55. Nehru, Jawaharlal (1946); Discovery of India, The John Day Company, NY.
56. Newton, Michael (2016a); Journey of Souls: New case studies of life between lives, Lllewellyn Publications, Woodbury, USA.
57. Newton, Michael (2016b); Destiny of Souls: New case studies of life between lives, Lllewellyn Publications, Woodbury, USA.
58. Oakley, Donald G. (2011); In Search of the Self, Eyrie Press, Fens, North Cambridgeshire, UK.
59. Olivelle, Patrick (2008); Upanishads (Oxford World's Classics), Oxford University Press, UK.
60. Papadopoulos, Renos K. (1992); Carl Gustav Jung: Critical Assessments, Vol. IV, Routledge, NY.
61. Paranjape, Makarand R. (2015); Swami Vivekananda: A Contemporary Reader, Routledge, New Delhi, India.
62. Planck, Max (1944); Das Wesen der Materie (The Nature of Matter), speech at Florence, Italy, 1944 (from Archiv zur Geschichte der Max-Planck-Gesellschaft, Abt. Va, Rep. 11 Planck, Nr. 1797).

63. Prothero, Stephen (2010); God Is Not One, HarperCollins Publishers, Melbourne.
64. Radhakrishnan, Sarvepalli (1960); The Concept of Man, Johnson & Raju, P. T. (Eds.) Publishing Company, Nebraska, USA.
65. Ranganathananda, Swami (1997); Science and Religion, Advaita Ashrama, Calcutta, India.
66. Ring, Kenneth (1980); Life at death: A scientific investigation of the near-death experience, Coward, McCann and Geoghegan, NY.
67. Ross, Huge Norman (1995); The Creator and the Cosmos: How the Greatest Scientific Discoveries of the Century Reveal God, NavPress Publishing Group, Colorado, USA.
68. Runsheng, Tu (2018); Quantum Mechanics' Return to Local Realism, Cambridge Scholar Publishing, Newcastle Upon Tyne, UK.
69. Russel, Peter (2003); From Science to God, Thomson press, New Delhi, India.
70. Sabom, Michael (1982); Recollections of death: A medical investigation, Corgi Books, GB.
71. Sadhguru (2009); Himalayan Lust, Jaico Book Distributors, India.
72. Schiller, Ferdinand Canning Scott (1891); Riddles of the Sphinx: a study in the philosophy of evolution, Dr. Schiller kept his authorship anonymous and so the book's cover indicates that it was written by a "Troglodyte" (a hermit).
73. Schrödinger, Erwin (1956); What is life? and other scientific essays, Doubleday, Garden City, NY.
74. Schrödinger, Erwin (1961); Meine Weltansicht, Paul Zsolnay, Vienna.
75. Sen, Kshiti Mohan (1961); Hinduism: The World's Oldest Faith, Penguin Books Ltd, Middlesex, England.
76. Sharp, Kimberly Clark (1995); After the Light: What I Discovered on the Other Side of Life That Can Change Your World, William and Morrow & Co. Inc., NY.
77. Sinha, Ashok Kr. (2013); Glimpses of the Scriptures of Major World Religions, Xlibris LLC, USA.
78. Smart, Ninian (1964); Doctrine and Argument in Indian Philosophy, George Allen and Unwin Ltd, London.
79. Stevenson, Ian, and Pasricha, Satwant (1980); A preliminary report on an unusual case of the reincarnation type with xenoglossy, Journal of the American Society for Psychical Research, Vol. 74.
80. Stevenson, Ian (1960); The Evidence for Survival from Claimed Memories of Former Incarnations, Part 1, Journal of the American Society for Psychical Research, Vol. LIV (April, 1960), no. 2.
81. Stevenson, Ian (1974); Twenty cases suggestive of reincarnation (2nd ed.) University Press of Virginia, Charlottesville, Virginia.
82. Stevenson, Ian (1983); Cases of the reincarnation type. IV: Twelve cases in Thailand and Burma, University Press of Virginia, Charlottesville, Virginia.
83. Stevenson, Ian (1986); Characteristics of cases of the reincarnation type among the Igbo of Nigeria, Journal of Asian and African Studies, issue 21.

84. Tipler, Frank (1994); The Physics of Immortality, Doubleday, NY.
85. Venkatesananda, Swami and Chapple, Christopher Key (2010); The Concise Yoga-Vasistha, State University of New York Press, Albany.
86. Vidyatmananda, Swami (1972); What Religion is: In the words of Swami Vivekananda, Advaita Ashrama, Kolkata, India.
87. Ward, William (1985); History, Literature, and Mythology of the Hindoos: Including a Minute Description of Their Manners and Customs, and Translations from their Principal Works, Volume 2 (original work published 1817-1820), 3rd ed. 4 vols. B. R. Publishing Corp. Delhi, India.
88. Weiss, Brian (1988); Many Lives, Many Masters, Simon & Schuster Inc., NY.
89. Weiss, Brian (2004); Same Soul, Many Bodies, Free Press, Simon & Schuster Inc., NY.
90. Wigner, Eugene Paul (1959); The unreasonable Effectiveness of Mathematics in the Natural Sciences, Richard Courant Lecture delivered at New York University, May 11, 1959.
91. Willis, Judy (2007); Brain-friendly Strategies for the Inclusion Classroom, Association for Supervision & Curriculum Development, Alexandria, Virginia.
92. Yogananda, Paramahansa (2021); Autobiography of a Yogi, Prakesh Books India Pvt. Ltd, New Delhi, India.